Abraham Lincoln Sculpture
Created by Avard T. Fairbanks

Compiled by

Eugene F. Fairbanks

Abraham Lincoln Colossal Portrait in bronze with sculptor Avard T. Fairbanks. This portrait was placed in Lincoln High School, Seattle, Washington.

Abraham Lincoln Sculpture

Created by

Avard T. Fairbanks

Compiled

by

Eugene F. Fairbanks

Abraham Lincoln Sculpture Created by Avard T. Fairbanks
Compiled by Eugene F. Fairbanks

Library of Congress Control Number (LCCN): 2002095491
ISBN: 0-9725841-0-2

Editing and Proofreading Services: Sara Stamey
Typography, Prepress, and Cover Design: Kathleen Weisel

Printed in the U.S.A.

THE COVER

The Lincoln statue for New Salem, Illinois, is significant, for it was at this village that he started his independent life on a course toward honor and responsibility. His first acquaintance with the frontier village occurred when he managed to release a flatboat stuck at the Rutledge mill dam on the Sangamon river on a trip to New Orleans. On his return, Denton Offutt hired him as a clerk in a store, but before it was stocked and open for business, Lincoln split rails for a living. He had cleared land and split rails since early youth. It was in New Salem that he entered into politics, practiced debate, and became interested in law. In spite of less than six months of school attendance in childhood, he read extensively and studied books arduously. Lincoln sought instructions from Mentor Graham, the schoolmaster, borrowing the only grammar text in the district and studying it intently. He read many borrowed law books and bought a copy of *Blackstone's Commentaries* from a passing westward migrant. This he eagerly studied. As the grocery business waned, he became a postmaster, and later, after studying to become a surveyor, was in demand for road, farm, and city platting.

This statue is an appropriate expression of a vigorous young man about to set aside an ax while holding a large law book, looking forward with anticipation to the future. Dr. Louis Warren described the statue, "The Resolute Lincoln." Thomas Starr called the monument, "At The Cross-roads of Decision." Both are appropriate titles that manifest the important formative years of Abraham Lincoln's early life.

Dedication

This book is dedicated to the memory of my mother, Maude F. Fairbanks, and to Avard T. Fairbanks, my father. Let it serve as a documentary of his sincere efforts to portray Abraham Lincoln as an inspiration to the nation.

An expression of gratitude is not complete without recognizing the encouragement and influence of two skilled artists, John B. Fairbanks, his father, and J. Leo Fairbanks, his oldest brother. They have bestowed upon Avard and other members of their family a reverence and love for art. A few words of J. Leo Fairbanks deserve inclusion.

Creed

Art is for service, for making things beautiful as well as useful;

For lifting men above the sordid things that grind and depress;

To give a joyous optimism in one's work;

To realize, during one's leisure, the ideals that have been contemplated
    in one's most precious moments;

To take pleasure in seeing beauty as it exists in what man has made;
    as well as in one's immediate environment;

To see all the ideal in the real; and

To realize transitory hopes in enduring tangible material.

To me, the purpose of art is to visualize ideals, to realize ideals,
    and to idealize realities.

~ J. Leo Fairbanks

Foreword

The original inspiration for compiling a book of the Abraham Lincoln sculptures created by Dr. Avard T. Fairbanks came many years ago, during the completion of *Lincoln The Frontiersman*. Text and illustrations document the motivation and circumstances to create masterpieces, for public interest and appreciation. Recording the modeling of the heroic statue, the casting, and the background events seems appropriate. Details of the essential research efforts might be helpful to aspiring sculptors.

An artist must study history and the personality to be portrayed in order to be able to render a likeness and express a message; therefore resource facilities and a bibliography are included. Other heroic monuments are discussed, as many aspects differ with each statue. The political process is important for funding and location. Without the numerous committee meetings and the efforts by collaborating individuals, monuments are unlikely to come to fruition.

As the author visited monument sites and studied history, renewed inspirations supported the writing. It became apparent that there had already been many articles in periodicals about these monuments created by Avard Fairbanks. Generally these articles have been of such excellent composition that they deserve inclusion. Therefore, whenever articles by distinguished authors were acquired, approval for their inclusion was solicited and they were included in the text. Articles and quotations by the sculptor were also included wherever they apply. The author has arranged these articles by Lincoln scholars with appropriate illustrations of sculpture. Introductory and connecting paragraphs supply further information. Other commentaries and descriptions have been written by the author after diligent search of history and literature about Abraham Lincoln.

Contents

Acknowledgments

To properly thank everyone who has given assistance in compiling this book is impossible. A few have already journeyed beyond the limits of mortal existence. The help of all is deeply appreciated.

A major portion of the typing was done by Alice Hitz. Other typing was done by Hilda Atkinson and Janice Shepherd. Dr. Arthur Hicks has kindly reviewed and proofread an early text. Most of the members of my immediate family have been of assistance, either working in the darkroom for the development of photographs, or in typing from the manuscript. Sara Stamey has carefully edited the typescript and Kathleen Weisel has skillfully arranged the text and illustration layout. Special thanks go to my wife, Florence, for her patience.

Foremost among those whose writings are included in this book is Thomas I. Starr, a Lincoln historian and president of the Detroit Lincoln Group. His assistance and inspiration to the sculptor were incalculable. Louis A. Warren, Director of the Lincoln National Life Foundation and Museum, has written many articles about Lincoln; one included is "The Resolute Lincoln." Bruce Catton, noted author of novels about Civil War events and editor of *American Heritage,* has permitted the use of his address at the Centennial of the Lincoln-Douglas Debates. The Historian at Knox College at Galesburg, Illinois, has been very helpful in supplying information regarding the Centennial Convocation. Senator Paul Douglas has also kindly consented to the use of his address regarding Stephen A. Douglas, and a dedicatory address for the statue, *Lincoln The Friendly Neighbor.*

The *Hawaiian Educational Review* has permitted articles by Governor Ingram M. Stainback, Mr. Frank Crawford, and Orin E. Long. The Chicago Historical Society has assisted in a search of Archives, sending a copy of the address by Senator Paul Douglas. The *Lincoln Herald* has kindly permitted the reprint of articles in their journal regarding several statues. Other journals granting permission to reprint include the *Michigan Christian Advocate* and the *Michigan Technic.*

Dr. William Wade Haggard, a Lincoln scholar and president emeritus of Western Washington State University at Bellingham, Washington, has given the author encouragement and constructive suggestions toward completion of the manuscript. Earnest Klink, a representative of Lippincott Publishing Company to the medical profession, has encouraged progress towards publication. Broadcast Music, Inc., permitted a reprinting of an article by the sculptor, "The Face Of Abraham Lincoln. "

The greatest source of information and illustrations was the sculptor, Dr. Avard T. Fairbanks. Systematically, over many years of creating sculpture, he took photographs of each piece. The negatives and many prints have been kept on file. With some of the larger statues, he took photographs of representative steps in the process toward completion. No other special acknowledgments accompany these illustrations in the book. A few photographs not specifically designated were taken by the author. Other sources of photographs are acknowledged where illustrated. Photography was also a traditional art in the Fairbanks family. The sculptor's father, John B. Fairbanks, was a pioneer professional photographer as well as a landscape painter. Photography was a second art with the sculptor. He learned much of his ability from his father and his older brother, J. Leo Fairbanks. He also studied technical photography courses in college. The influences of creative imagination and idealism are profoundly manifest in the sculptor's artistic endeavors.

Fig. 1. The heroic statue of *Lincoln The Frontiersman*, modeled in clay, is complete.

LINCOLN THE FRONTIERSMAN

Erected at Ewa Plantation School, Ewa, Hawaii

The heroic bronze monument of Lincoln The Frontiersman at the school in Ewa, Hawaii, is the manifestation of a real human interest story. An article written by Thomas I. Starr, a Lincoln scholar, was published in the *Lincoln Herald,* and it serves to introduce the background events and fulfillment of the dream of Katherine Burke, the monument donor.

Mr. Starr had already been of inestimable help to the sculptor in research and the development of the early, smaller models. His article is quoted ex-cept for the omission of an occasional paragraph that might seem unduly repetitious.

For convenience, the article has been divided into two parts. The first section tells of a school teacher's fond desire for a monument. Between the first and second part of Starr's article, to clarify the chronological sequence, the author and the sculp-tor discuss the modeling and casting of the statue. Illustrations record the progress. The second part of Mr. Starr's article continues after the statue's completion, telling about the dedication in Hawaii.

THE WILL OF KATHERINE BURKE HAS BEEN PROBATED

By Thomas I. Starr, the *Lincoln Herald,* June 1944.

A school teacher dreamed a dream. To assure its fulfillment as best she could, she willed that her small estate—few school teachers have large estates—be devoted in its entirety for the purpose.

On the 12th of February, last, a cord was pulled; and as drapes fell away there was revealed in the bright morning sun a new conception of the form of Abraham Lincoln, cast in bronze in heroic proportions.

It represented the materialization of the dream of Katherine McIntosh Burke, the school teacher; and the artistic creation of the mind and hands of sculptor Avard T. Fairbanks. Fairbanks gained his inspiration for America's newest Lincoln statue from the story of Katherine Burke and her ideals and desires, and from his own personal knowledge and long study of the life and greatness of Abraham Lincoln.

Fairbanks is a Michigan man, Associate Professor of Sculpture on the University of Michigan campus at Ann Arbor. The locale of the dream of Mrs. Burke, and the spot where now stands the nine-foot *Lincoln The Frontiersman* is on another campus, eight thousand miles away—the campus of the Ewa Public School on the Hawaiian Island of Oahu. It is close by to Honolulu and only a few miles from Pearl Harbor. How Professor Fairbanks came to depict Lincoln as the youthful frontiersman will develop later in the story.

Let's first take up the story of Katherine Burke, for she, too, was a frontiersman with pioneering blood in her veins. It led her, in her chosen profession of a country school teacher, to seek new horizons and new frontiers where she could instruct the youth of America. Born in Leavenworth, Kansas, eleven days before the first inauguration of President Lincoln, she grew to young womanhood in the prairie states; she was educated in the State Teacher's College at Emporia and at the University of California. First she taught in the elementary schools of Oskaloosa, Kansas, then in its high school. Later she was employed as teacher and principal in Benson, Arizona, and Pioche, Nevada.

William H. Seward, who had been the Secretary of State in Lincoln's Cabinet, had negotiated with Russia the purchase of Alaska; and "Seward's Folly"

became a new frontier for the United States. As the settlers moved in, the boys and girls of the territory needed education, and to Wrangell went Katherine Burke. For four years she taught in Alaska.

The United States acquired new territory in the mid-Pacific, and a new frontier called to Katherine Burke. There was a teaching job to be done in the Hawaiian Islands. For six years she spent her time and her talents in classrooms on the island of Kauai. Then to the island of Oahu and to the Ewa school she went for eight of the final ten years of her teaching career. Time was catching up with Katherine Burke. Her life had been devoted to the education and training of the younger citizens of American frontiers, and the inspiration and idealism gained from a close study of the life and character of the 16th President of the United States had been an integral part of the course of study which she had been passing on to them. But her time was short, and there were new generations coming who must know the story of Abraham Lincoln and how he stood permanently as a symbol of tolerance and lack of animosity.

It was then that she dreamed her dream, but it was not a vision of the night when the mind is resting; it came from a mind that was awake and alert and came as the result of thoughtful planning and careful saving. She would provide the funds that a statue of Lincoln be placed on the school's campus as an everlasting reminder and inspiration to coming generations of Hawaiian-American youth of the things that Lincoln accomplished and the character of the citizenship he typified "with malice toward none and charity for all."

Katherine Burke was retired on pension by the Territory's Department of Public Instruction in 1929. Nine years later, two days after the Christmas of 1938, and at the age of 76, she passed away at the Mayo Clinic, in Rochester, Minnesota; and to the administrators of her small estate it was left to fulfill the directive of her will. It is doubtful that any heroic bronze statue of Abraham Lincoln, certainly none of the great ones, has ever been created from an amount of money so small as that which this school teacher had saved from her earnings and her pension.

But she had left more than money—she had left a plan to be finished and an ideal which carried with it a challenge. It was these things which caught hold of the Michigan sculptor and led him to accept the commission when it was offered him to create in lasting bronze the material form of the Lincoln of her dreams.

Four times Professor Fairbanks has visited and worked in the Hawaiian Islands. In Honolulu in 1918, he was married to Beatrice M. Fox, who has mothered their eight talented sons, two of whom are now serving in the U. S. Army and one in the Navy.

His last visit to the Islands was in the summer of 1939, when he gave courses in art in the summer sessions of the University of Hawaii. Besides teaching, he delivered there a series of public lectures and did a number of sketches for a monument of Sanford B. Dole, the pineapple "king." In the spring of the following year came the unsolicited invitation from the trustees of the Katherine Burke estate to consider the Lincoln statue and to submit sketches and a proposal for its making and erection.

The conception of *Lincoln The Frontiersman* is best described in Professor Fairbanks' own words as he spoke them over a University of Michigan radio broadcast shortly after the full-sized clay model was completed:

"My first impression was to make a statue of Lincoln with his frock coat as the President of the United States. The long lines of the trousers and the coat seemed rather appealing from just the standpoint of the lines. I pondered over this for some time, but did not make sketches.

"Another thought was Lincoln with a shawl; but this would never do for the semitropical climate of Hawaii. In considering the responsibility before me of doing a work worthy of the trust placed in me, I thought of the hopes of the schoolteacher and her eager desires to inspire the students. I thought of the youthful minds of the students of the school and my responsibility to them to characterize Abraham Lincoln truthfully.

"To make him as a youth seemed to gain the attention of my thoughts. Many times I thought of the things of Lincoln's youth which stood out in my mind. He was strong and he could work well. He worked with a purpose, and he cleared the fields and forests for new growth and new developments. As he developed strong in body, he also was developing in strength of character and mind. He had to cut his way through … he was a *frontiersman!*

"Shortly thereafter I was called West to the funeral of my father. While still at his farm home, and in deep sorrow, for a bit of relaxation, I took an ax and went into a field to clear away some old trees and stumps. As I worked I thought of the Lincoln statue. Lincoln was a man of sorrows, and he was a man of hopes; and as a youth he had worked with an ax. And it was there that the inspiration of Lincoln as a youthful frontiersman, with an ax in hand, came to me. Realizing that I had found something worthwhile, I returned to Ann Arbor and set about making sketches of the idea, first on paper and then in small bits of clay… ."

Other sketches were followed by other models as the inspiration took form, each model a little larger than the rest. Between models there were many hours of concentrated study in the Albert H. Greenly Lincoln collection at the University's William L. Clements Library. Valuable studies were secured also from the Lincoln National Life Foundation, at Fort Wayne, Indiana. Many photos, together with original copies of the Volk mask and hands of Lincoln, were carefully studied and measured.

The final model was completed early in the summer of 1941 and was exhibited to the public for the first time. In the meantime, photographs of the model had been submitted to and passed upon by the trustees of the Burke estate; and one member, Mr. J. D. Bond, chairman of the committee, came to the Ann Arbor studio of Professor Fairbanks to give the final approval.

As one authoritative critic put it, Fairbanks had "put America in Abraham Lincoln as few other artists have ever done. Instead of a listless, gawky, sleepy-eyed Lincoln, as some artists are wont to depict him, Fairbanks made him powerful, alert, aggressive, and gave him eyes through which only Lincoln could visualize far ahead of time itself the great benefits to be enjoyed through a free and united nation… ." (to be continued)

THE CREATION OF A HEROIC STATUE IN CLAY

[This interrupts the article by Mr. Thomas Starr. The remainder will follow information about the creation of the statue.]

When his *Lincoln The Frontiersman* statue for Hawaii was nearing completion, Avard Fairbanks gave a photograph to a visiting news reporter. A few weeks later, much to his surprise and delight, a dozen of the leading journals of the nation featured that portrait on the Lincoln's Birthday edition. *The Detroit News* printed it as a full-page reproduction. This was a spontaneous editorial recognition of a masterpiece. The sculptor had molded into lifeless clay the feelings, the animation, and the character of a great historic figure recreated in the vigor of youth.

Two versions of the creation and casting of the heroic statue follow. The first is the author's remembrance, as a high school-age assistant, of an artistic father. The second is from an article written by the sculptor. To reduce repetition and redundancy, these writings have been merged wherever possible.

Pen and ink sketch of *Lincoln The Frontiersman.*

RECOLLECTIONS OF A YOUNG ASSISTANT

By Eugene F. Fairbanks

Lincoln The Frontiersman, the sculptor's first Lincoln study, was begun in 1939. The smaller models were completed and cast in the fourth-story studio of University Hall, a copper-domed, stately old building of the University of Michigan campus, erected in the 1870s. The front entrance had once been impressive, for it had been the central campus building. There were simulated pillars on the facade, and a broad, sturdy wrought-iron stairs that ascended each side from ground level to the second floor. A broad platform entrance led to the later abandoned auditorium. The stairs had once served well, but had seldom been used during the preceding three decades. A new and larger central building, Angel Hall, had been built immediately in front of the old building. University Hall was scheduled for demolition, but this had been delayed.

There was some concern about the weight of a heroic size statue and the strength of the beams under the fourth floor studio. Therefore permission was obtained to use the main floor of the old, condemned auditorium in the same building. This auditorium itself had an historic atmosphere, for indeed it was contemporary with the Reconstruction Era after the Civil War. The stage curtains and equipment were gone. Balcony seats had been removed to supply a newer amphitheater, leaving beams and trusses of the balcony tiers exposed to view. A few old seats remained in the rear of the main floor with ornate cast-iron uprights bolted to the floor and hinged, unpadded fold up seats.

One could hardly stand on the stage and look out over the quiet emptiness without sensing a spirit of past events, their echoes now still, and of audiences long since departed. Here eminent lecturers and historic personalities such as William Cullen Bryant, Senator Lewis Cass, President Grover Cleveland, and Professor Woodrow Wilson of Princeton University are reported to have spoken. Winston Churchill, a young British Army officer, told about

Fig. 2. Three-dimensional grids are in place on small models.

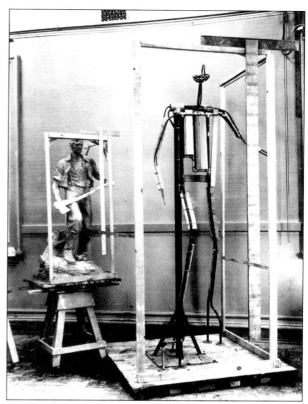

Fig. 3. The armature, right-angle grid and T-square are in place.

the Boer War in 1901. The Ben Greet Company of Shakespearean players from England performed several times. The May Festival of Music was initiated in 1894.[*] Scientific assemblies were held; concerts were given; baccalaureate exercises had been presented; faculty councils had met. One day an old alumnus, curious about the sculpture in progress, told how William Jennings Bryan, famous for his "Cross of Gold" speech, had addressed an assembly. At first he felt flattered by the applause, but was unable to speak as his voice was drowned out by the continuous in-cadence clapping of the students. He walked off the stage, disgruntled when the police were unable to stop the discourteous clatter.

Above the proscenium of the stage was an inscription in ornate gold letters on a blue background, a quotation from the Third Article of the Northwest Ordinance of 1787, *"Religion, Morality, and Knowledge Being Necessary to Good Government and the Happiness of Mankind, Schools and the Means for Education Shall Forever be Encouraged."*

The center arch of the stage, once graced by curtains separating off the backstage area, had been boarded over with odd-width planks; some casual assortment of colors suggested they had come from the scrap pile. More recently, following the condemnation, the stage had been used by the Drama Department for play practice. Two-inch pipe uprights and overhead wires were yet evident where practice curtains had once hung.

Much of the modeling of this statue was done after class schedules, or on weekends, often continuing to very late hours. The temporary lighting over the statue was suspended by cables from the balcony. The business office had also encroached on the old auditorium by placing old filing cabinets along the north wall and occasionally a secretary would open a door to fumble through files. She would appear to retrieve some mysterious document, then disappear again through the north door.

As the work proceeded in evenings, bats would come out of hiding and fly silently about overhead, sweeping up through the balcony, darting between trusses, then back into the stage or up to the dome. High in the cupola of the dome a pair of owls had a nest, having gained entrance through a broken pane

* Reed, David M., University Hall, "Unloved at 76 Saved from Demolition." *The Ann Arbor Daily News,* Aug. 9, 1941.

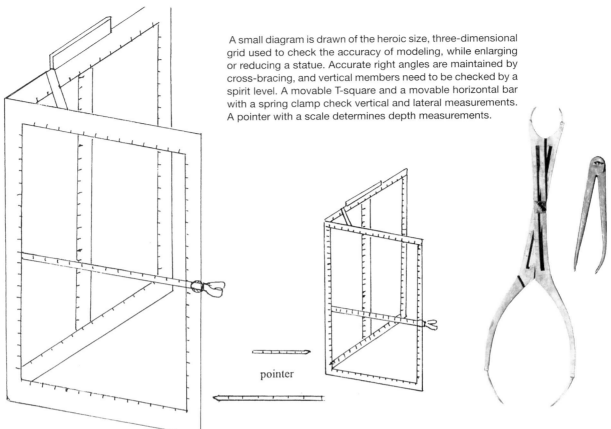

A small diagram is drawn of the heroic size, three-dimensional grid used to check the accuracy of modeling, while enlarging or reducing a statue. Accurate right angles are maintained by cross-bracing, and vertical members need to be checked by a spirit level. A movable T-square and a movable horizontal bar with a spring clamp check vertical and lateral measurements. A pointer with a scale determines depth measurements.

pointer

Fig. 4a. A diagram of the three-dimensional enlarging grid device.

Fig. 4b. Calipers used during enlargment of sculpture.

of glass. Occasionally distant squealing sounds could be heard as they were feeding their owlets.

At the top of the balcony on the fourth floor, statues of previous student exhibits were stored. The dim light of evening through the tall windows often cast weird shadows. The bats, the narrow creaky stairs, the awesome history, and the darkness above the working area gave a hallowed, almost haunted, atmosphere to the makeshift studio. This was punctuated when a door would suddenly rattle open and the night watchman would pass through making his rounds every two hours. Occasionally he would stop to note the progress of the statue.

A two-foot model had been formed in clay before the Detroit Lincoln Club. There the concept of Lincoln as a frontiersman had been enthusiastically endorsed. After approval by the committee in Hawaii, a larger model followed with more detail.

An apparatus is illustrated (Figs. 2, 3) as a guide to assist enlarging or reducing statuary in a three dimensional scale ratio. It consists of two rectangular frames, mutually at right angles, that can be moved around from corner to corner of a square plinth for the statue. The smaller set of frames is ruled in small units and the larger set of frames is ruled in larger units for the intended ratio of planned enlargement, as one-to-two or one-to-three or more.

Movable T-squares, with ruled units in the same manner, are hung from an upper horizontal cross-piece (Fig. 4a). A horizontal ruled movable bar, held in place with a spring clamp, allows checking height and lateral measurements. Depth measurements are facilitated by a ruled pointer that can be advanced against the T-square or the horizontal bar to any part of the statue being modeled.

This three-dimensional grid must have carefully crafted rectangles with square corners and the uprights should be plumb, tested by a spirit level.

Fairbanks sought historical material in libraries, particularly at the William L. Clements Library at the University of Michigan. Cartoons were a helpful source material for costumes. Museums were visited and Lincoln scholars were consulted. One

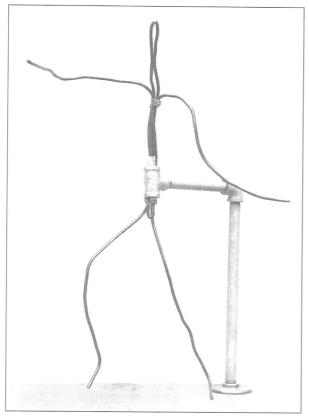

Fig. 5. The armature for a statuette.

Fig. 6. Wire mesh was applied to the armature.

ax-head, owned by a friend of Thomas Starr, was reported to have been used by Abraham Lincoln. The details of this ax were studied and carefully recorded.

Another interesting artifact was a rail-splitter's ax on exhibit at Henry Ford's Greenfield Village Museum, in Dearborn, Michigan. It was carefully examined and measured. This type of ax had a broader blade and was shaped like a wedge. It often functioned as a wedge, as it was driven by a maul to initiate splitting of the log. Tradition also holds that three wedges driven by a wooden maul serve to split the timber for rails. A heroic size (4/3 life size) replica of the ax was crafted in wood for the large statue, on the basis of this information obtained to assure historic accuracy. Abraham Lincoln once recalled that "almost constantly between my eighth and twenty-third year I had that most useful instrument in my hands."

"My, how he would chop!" said Dennis Hanks, his cousin. "His ax would flash and bite into a sugar tree or sycamore and down it would come. If you heard him fellin' trees in a clearin', you would say

there was three men at work by the way the trees fell."

Cast copies of the life mask and hands, made by Leonard Volk, were obtained from Dr. Louis A. Warren at the Lincoln National Life Insurance Company Museum, Indianapolis, Indiana. These were carefully studied so that facial details were accurately portrayed. Thomas Starr was also an invaluable source of information and inspiration as he followed the progress of the monument.

When the 2/3-life-size statue was nearly complete, photographs were sent to the sponsoring committee in Honolulu. Their final approval was given, and work began on the heroic (4/3 life size) statue.

ENGINEERING IN SCULPTURE

By Avard T. Fairbanks

Numerous persons on the campus of the University of Michigan have had an unusual opportunity to watch the progress and development of a heroic size statue of Abraham Lincoln. Of particular interest to those who follow engineering have been the construction processes involved in its set-

Fig. 7. The application of clay, roughed-in modeling of the statue.

Fig. 8. The modeling progresses.

up and the reproduction of this work into a permanent medium. From irons, wood, wire mesh, and clay, it was worked to a high state of completion and was then cast into the harder medium of plaster prior to its being shipped to New York for the final foundry work, where it is now in the process of becoming a bronze statue.

In Hawaii an obscure plantation school teacher (similar to a country school teacher in the States) left her entire savings to be devoted to the concepts she had been implanting in the minds of the many young people of the varied races in the Pacific area. To continue her messages of racial tolerance and opportunities for even the most lowly, she felt that a monument of Abraham Lincoln would most nearly carry out her intentions. He is America's great hero of the frontier, whose ideals and spirit of democracy permeate the souls of all freedom-loving peoples.

Preliminary models of Lincoln were made in a small size about 12 inches tall. After many trials of one study and another, finally the subject as a rail-splitter and as a frontiersman seemed to be the most effective and appropriate.

When the general position was settled, a larger 30-inch size was then developed. As this one was perfected, a half-heroic size (2/3 life, about 48 inches) figure was made. This one became the experimental study for the making of the large model nine-feet tall—of the size known as heroic.

An apparatus is illustrated (Fig. 4a), as a guide to assist enlarging or reducing statuary in a three-dimensional scale ratio. It consists of two rectangular frames at right angles so that it can be moved around from corner to corner of a square plinth for the statue. The smaller set of frames is ruled in small units and the larger set of frames is ruled in larger units, for the intended ratio of planned enlargement, as one-to-two or one-to-three. Movable T-squares, with ruled units in the same manner, are hung from an upper horizontal crosspiece. A horizontal ruled movable bar, held in place with a spring clamp, al-

Fig. 9. Additional modeling in clay.

Fig. 10. The modeling was nearly finished with assistance of the three youngest Fairbanks sons, Jonathan, David, and Grant.

lows the checking of height and lateral measurements. Depth measurements are facilitated by a ruled pointer that can be advanced against the T-square or the horizontal bar to any part of the statue being modeled. This three-dimensional grid must have carefully crafted rectangles with square corners, and the uprights should be plumb, tested by a spirit level.

Four models in all were constructed and carried to completion. Three statues of *Lincoln The Frontiersman*, 1/3 and 2/3 lifesize, both previously cast, and the 4/3 life or heroic size statue in clay ready for casting in plaster, were photographed (Fig. 11).

Throughout the development of all these sizes, the actual size of Lincoln's form and the life mask made of his face and castings of his hands were measured accurately, and the models were made to conform to the real Lincoln measurements and features. Abraham Lincoln was six feet, four inches tall.

The Armatures

The wire, iron pipe, and wooden framework of the models are called armatures. They are very different, of course, from an armature found in an electric motor. However, the technical term in sculpture for the rigid supports of the softer plastic materials is known as the armature.

In the first model only a slight support is required. A 1/4-inch galvanized iron pipe is fitted into a floor flange screwed to the base board. A right-angle joint is fitted onto the upright pipe into which is fitted a short horizontal pipe. A T-joint is fitted onto the horizontal pipe. The armature then resembles the shape of an inverted letter "L" (Fig. 5). The horizontal pipe can go inward towards the central part of the study to be. The vertical part of this supporting member extends from the base board about eight or nine inches. The horizontal pipe of the armature is about six inches long. Together they form the rigid part for the body of the model to be made. Into this T-joint, solder wires are inserted and

9

wedged in place. They stretch from the base board 12 inches upward and back again. These wires form the skeletons for the legs, body, and head. The solder wire is used because of its flexibility.

[Author's Note: One problem with solder, lead, or copper was reaction with sulfur in Plastelina over an extended period. The problem was less with coated wire. Newer modeling Plastelina does not contain sulfur.]

The legs, arms, and head can move about in various positions while the body remains firmly in position. Any type of standing figure can be built upon such a framework. The solder wires are arranged into appropriate position and then rolls of Plastelina are applied until the form of the miniature statue takes shape. The Plastelina model is constructed anatomically to get the human form into the proper shape and proportions. Afterwards the draperies are added. Finally the face and features and other details are made to express the concepts of the sculptor.

There is one difficulty in such an armature, which is the iron framework or supporting member that sticks out from the side of the Plastelina model. This is inevitable, since the legs must be made to be able to change positions and shapes. When the position is finally decided upon, the sketch is worked towards perfection and the cast made; then this is eliminated. In the mold where the protruding structure had been, the remaining space is plugged up with plaster or clay. In the final casting it is retouched away. The reinforcing in the plaster cast is accomplished by irons being cast inside the legs for rigid support.

The second size 30-inch study was made from the first model to gain further details which could not be attained in the 12-inch size. The armature was built in much the same manner, but instead of using 1/4-inch pipe and solder wire, 1/2-inch galvanized pipes and two covered wire cables were employed.

The third model, 2/3-life size or half heroic size (4-foot study), was developed as an experiment in the construction of the larger nine-foot statue. While the smaller models were made in Plastelina, the next two larger ones had to be completed in water clay, it being less costly. Furthermore, instead of using an armature that extended from the outside in towards the body, the armature for the large clay studies had to be built inside.

Accurate measurements had to be made in the enlarging process and, in order to do this, an angle frame was made like two picture frames fastened at right angles to each other. They were carefully ruled on the upright and horizontal members to create a three dimensional grid. All measurements were computed in a ratio scale to each other.

Half-inch galvanized pipes were constructed in the legs of the experimental model, bending at the various joints such as feet, knees, and hips. The pipes extended further on up into the shoulders and head. At the shoulders, T-joints and angle-joints were arranged to fasten the pipes together. Through these were placed 3/8-inch iron reinforcing bars, which extended from the extremity of one arm to the extremity of the other one. This iron reinforcing bar was bent with a wrench in the actual position of the arms according to the smaller model, and its measurements were found by using the angle frames serving as a three-dimensional grid.

Further building of the armature, in addition to building volume around the pipes, was done with 1/4-inch wire mesh. This was constructed to give more nearly the form of the statue. Wire mesh over wooden supports was used to make the shape of the logs and tree trunk. All of these constructions had to be made and measured one inch less than the surface of the clay model to be.

After the final development of the armature, the water clay, which had been mixed and prepared, was put on in rolls, making first the anatomical construction and later the clothing and further details. Finally the character and likeness had to be accomplished.

One of the reasons for a stoutly constructed armature is the fact that clay does not support itself very well. A very difficult problem for the sculptor is to keep the clay from falling, particularly in large studies.

Another problem is to keep the clay wet. Cloths soaked in water may be kept over the study, but they often mar the modeled details of the sculpture by rubbing the surface. A tent of flannel cloth covered with oil cloth was made to cover the study when I was not working on it. This tent had to be kept wet every night to maintain humidity.

Fig. 11. Photo of three sizes of sculpture when the heroic statue modeling is complete.

[Author's Note: At that time Plastelina, an oil and clay mixture, was available but expensive. Avard Fairbanks preferred the texture and ease of modeling with the water clay, in spite of the inconvenience. Presently there are oil-clay mixtures that are relatively less expensive with a favorable texture, and most modern sculptors prefer them to water clay.]

The Heroic Statue Armature

In calculating the larger heroic size from the half-heroic size statue needs, the difference between lineal measure and three-dimensional bulk measure had to be considered. The nine-foot model was just eight times the size in bulk. Thus the armature had to be more rigid, as the amount of clay would be eight times as great. One ton of powdered clay was calculated to be used, and by adding 1/3 more water this would compute the large Lincoln statue to weigh about 3000 pounds. Further adding to this the weight of the armature and also the weight of the plaster when casting it, a possible 5000 or 6000 pounds had to be anticipated.

The problem of weight necessitated the use of a larger two-inch, eight-foot-long supporting pipe, which appeared to come through the tree trunk and on up into the body. This was welded to a piece of 1/4-inch sheet iron, 20-inches square, with braces welded from the pipe to the sheet iron. This was

11

Fig. 12. Initial separation by fences to arms above elbows, forearms and ax, which were to be cast separately, and posterior base section has also been started, anterior view, and left lateral view.

bolted to the boards used for the base. Instead of one pipe in each leg, two were arranged and bent at the joints. In between these pipes were fastened boards of 1 x 2 and 1 x 3 inch widths, and of lengths as needed.

In the construction of the body part, larger boards were used in between pipe construction. Into the T-joints at the shoulders were arranged three 3/8-inch iron reinforcing bars extending from the tip of the right arm to that of the left. Each of these bars could be bent rather easily, but when fastened together by the boards they became very firm and were capable of fully supporting the clay to be put on them (Fig. 6).

Onto the iron and wooden parts of the armature were fastened wire netting and also 1-inch mesh chicken wire. They were constructed to form

the shape of the Lincoln statue less a measure of 1 to 1-1/2-inches for application of clay.

A sculptor must avoid having to conform to an armature. All these measurements were computed by means of angle frames, essentially a three-dimensional grid, calculating depths, heights, and widths from the experimental model. The logs and tree stump armature at the base of the statue were constructed as explained in the experimental model. It is rather interesting to note that the measuring was so well done that the armature construction did not interfere with the clay modeling of the statue in any way.

•

RECOLLECTIONS OF A YOUNG ASSISTANT

… continued

The rigid framework of the armature for the heroic statue *Lincoln The Frontiersman* consisted of an eight-foot section of 2-inch pipe as the main support, and 3/4-inch pipes were bent and attached for additional support of the arms and legs. Three dimensional grids with T-squares were used to assist modeling an enlargement of statuary from the small sculptured sketch to the large heroic statue (Fig. 4). The armature for the heroic statue of *Lincoln The Frontiersman* was made ready for application of clay by chicken wire and wire mesh attached to reinforcing irons and with strips of wood, to create an approximate shape of the sculpture (Fig. 6). Rolls of water clay were rapidly applied until the rough form emerged, shown at an early stage modeling with clay on the armature for the Lincoln statue (Fig. 7).

•

Avard Fairbanks' text in the article
"Engineering in Sculpture" continues.

Clay Modeling

The preparing of a ton of dry clay is a considerable undertaking. When it was mixed with water and made to the right consistency, it was formed into large rolls, 1-1/2-inch diameter. The large rolls were often made into smaller ones by rolling between palms, and then were added to the large armature. The body part was made first, then the legs and arms, and finally the head and the base. All the skill and artistic training comes into play at this part of the work.

Fig. 13. Same, left lateral view.

Fig. 14. The mold was started, right lateral view.

The three-dimensional grids with the large T-squares were used to assist modeling an enlargement of statuary from the 2/3 life size to the heroic size statue. The body was to be made anatomically correct, and the costume has to be made according to the early-1800 period. To gain the true spirit and character of the person to be modeled requires research at libraries, museums, and with historians. Study needs to be pursued so that a true impression of Lincoln and the ideals for which he stood could be adequately and correctly portrayed. The finer details took many more weeks. Each evening at quitting time the clay figure was wet down with a spray and covered with the tent-like canopy to prevent drying and cracking.

One bit of research might be interesting to state here. The ax is the rail-splitter's ax and not the wood-chopper's type (Fig. 9). Material on this ax was obtained at the Lincoln Life Insurance Company museum at Fort Wayne, Indiana. A verification of it was found in ax specimens in the Ford Museum, in Greenfield Village, Dearborn, Michigan.

•

RECOLLECTIONS OF A YOUNG ASSISTANT

… continued

This modeling took nearly a year to complete. The heroic figure, modeled in clay, is shown nearing completion (Fig. 9). The sculptor, assisted by his three youngest sons, performs finish modeling of the Lincoln statue (Fig. 10).

When the sculptor was satisfied that details were complete, and the approval by the executor of the estate was obtained, Ralph Vanni, the dedicated Italian plaster caster, was called to come from Detroit, and the casting began.

At this time Professor Fairbanks had eight sons. The three oldest, Avard Jr., myself (Eugene), and Elliott, were helpful assistants, but Elliott had been called overseas on a mission. Justin and Virgil were beginning to show promise. A friend of Justin, Robert Cooper, voluntarily joined in the work, and his assistance was very welcome.

Mr. Ralph Vanni was an indispensable part of the studio team. He always seemed anxious to come from Detroit to Ann Arbor to help with students' or professors' work. He had learned the trade in Italy as an apprentice while still a boy, and although in his sixties, he was energetic and imaginative as each statue presented new problems. He and the sculptor often discussed the casting in Italian. Speaking in his native tongue seemed to please the older fellow, and it served to renew the sculptor's familiarity with the language he had learned to speak during a year studying in Italy. Mr. Vanni and the sculptor were first busy with the technical details of placing a fence of tin strips to separate parts of the mold. A fence was applied by pressing short strips of two-inch-wide tinned sheet-metal into the clay. In this anterior view photograph the lower posterior sections of the mold have already had plaster applied (Fig. 12). The ax and forearms were cast separately after fences were in place (Figs. 13, 14). The casting progressed when the arms and ax were removed to be cast separately; the fence was applied up and over the head (Fig. 15).

Applying the plaster for the mold was not only fun, but served as a happy climax when the clay no longer needed to be kept moist. Large basins were filled with water to which *bluing* was added. Mr. Vanni sifted the plaster in gradually to avoid bubbles, until only a few islands of powder protruded above the surface. He then vigorously stirred it into a thick, creamy consistency. Each one of the five older boys was given a small bowl from which to spatter a thin layer of blue plaster on the statue.

[Author's Note: Bluing was a preparation of blue or violet dyes used in laundering to counteract yellowing of white fabrics.]

The thin layer of blue plaster was first lightly applied to serve as a warning when later chipping off the mold down to the cast (Fig. 16). The fine detail areas, such as the face and hands, had more careful application by Mr. Vanni, to be sure there were no bubbles in the blue layer. A second lighter blue layer served as a warning that when the waste mold was chipped away, the chisel was near the cast. Gray plaster was then applied to build up the mold. The outer coat of gray plaster was nearly two inches thick. The anterior section was then completely covered with plaster.

The three younger boys—Justin, Virgil and Jonathan—were given smaller jobs to keep their little hands busy. Here the boys were assigned to cutting burlap and angle irons for rigid reinforcement (6 x 12-inch strips of burlap were cut, moist-

Fig. 15. The anterior mold preparation after ax and arm molds are removed.

ened, and made ready to dip in the plaster slurry). They were applied to hold the angle irons in place. As the basins of gray plaster were mixed and applied to the front half, the appearance of a masterpiece changed to resemble a huge roughed-out gray stone (Fig. 17). The posterior mold was applied in sections (Fig. 18). Reinforcing boards and irons were then applied to the anterior (Fig. 19), and to posterior sections. When the reinforcing irons and pipes were added, it became somewhat grotesque.

The front section of the mold must be rigid, therefore it has numerous reinforcing irons and boards to avoid any change of shape when laid horizontally. The posterior of the statue mold had been divided into many sections by fences created by strips of tinned sheet metal with reinforcement, shown prior to their removal (Fig. 20). Each section had plaster applied, in the same manner, first with a blue layer, then the thick gray layer.

A whole day for the crew was thus well spent from early morning to nearly 8 PM. When the last

Fig. 16. The application of blue plaster coat was begun, anterior view.

Fig. 17. The anterior gray coat of plaster was applied.

reinforcing was added, the tools and basins cleaned, Father said, "Let's get changed and go home."

The next day was for well-earned relaxation while the plaster hardened. Michigan has many fine lakes. Boating, fishing, and swimming were favorite family pastimes. A big picnic lunch was packed, and the best part of the day was enjoyed at Pleasant Lake, about 10 miles from the city.

•

Avard Fairbanks' text about casting from "Engineering in Sculpture" continues.

Casting in Plaster
by a Waste Mold Process

After the model was fully developed and after a member of the committee from Honolulu visited the sculptor's studio and approved of its execution, it was ready to be cast into plaster, to change it into a hard medium, so that it could be sent to the bronze foundry.

There are several processes for plaster castings: the piece mold, the glue mold, and the waste mold. The glue mold was used for the smaller sizes, but for the 2/3-life-size, experimental model, and the heroic one, the waste mold process was used. This means that the mold is *wasted* in making the casting; or, in other words, it is chiseled away. The molds need to be made in sections, then taken apart, cleaned, shellacked, greased, and put back together. Then the plaster is poured into the mold.

[Author's Note: During the last three decades of the 1900s, considerable progress has been made for producing better mold material. Flexible molds have nearly replaced the use of waste molds. Polyurethane and silicone molds are flexible and render good detail, but they must be supported by a rigid *master mold*. Considerable time and effort are saved, and multiple casts may be made from a mold. Large statues are, nevertheless, still cast in sections.]

It is impossible to handle a large two-section nine-foot mold so that it can be poured. Therefore, it must be cast section by section. In making the

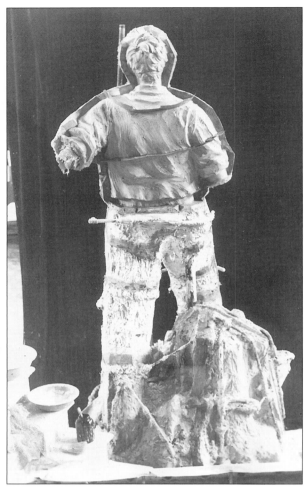

Fig. 18. The lower, posterior mold sections were applied.

Fig. 19. Plaster and iron reinforcements were secured to a sturdy anterior wooden frame.

mold of the heroic Lincoln statue, a large anterior section, the master section, was arranged so as to cast a mold of the entire front of the statue. Strips of tin sheet metal were cut two inches wide and of various short lengths to be pressed into the clay for a fence. These were placed up one side, over the head, and down the other side.

The clay arms and wooden ax were cut off and cast separately (Figs. 12, 13). Strips of tin were then arranged for fences around the back in a horizontal manner, to make sections every 12 to 15 inches.

When the section forming was accomplished, then the entire front portion was made into a mold. Molding plaster was mixed into a large basin about half full of water, with household bluing added to give it color. Powdered casting plaster was added and stirred until about the consistency of cream. Then it was thrown and spattered onto the figure by hand until it gave about 1/8-inch coating all over

one section (Fig. 16). This was repeated with another coat of blue plaster, then a further coat of white plaster, and then later, less expensive gray plaster reinforced with strips of burlap. Finally, reinforcing with iron bars and pipes was added. On this particular piece, two 10-foot long 2 x 4 boards were arranged parallel, with the consideration that the mold would be laid down forward for cleaning, preparation and refilling of the mold with plaster for the casting (Fig. 19).

After the front section of the mold was made, the back was sectioned into about two-foot segments in the same manner, starting at the base. Each section had to be well reinforced (Fig. 21). Upon completion of all the sections, the mold was taken apart and the clay and armature were removed (Figs. 21, 22).

The cleaning was begun by clearing away the clay from the mold, by digging bits from indentations and undercuts with a tool. The remaining clay

Fig. 20. Posterior reinforcements were applied joining sections of mold.

Fig. 21. Posterior sections were removed and some clay was extracted.

that stuck to the surface of the molds was removed by washing with a wet sponge. After retouching, all surfaces were then prepared with two or three coats of orange shellac to seal the plaster. Following this, greasing was done with stearic acid and kerosene mixed to a paste-like consistency. It was brushed generously over the surface to be cast, and then wiped evenly and clean with a grease brush.

Instead of pouring plaster into the mold, the large front section, which was lying face down, was cast by first throwing the liquid white plaster by small handfuls into it to give a coating about 1/2-inch thick (Fig. 25). It was then reinforced with plaster and burlap to about one inch thick. Then large pipes and irons were arranged up and down through the legs and about the base and every portion that required strengthening. They were fastened to the cast with plaster-saturated burlap. The irons were shellacked to keep them from rusting

and to help plaster adhere. Then plaster slurry was thrown by small handfuls into the sections of the base, and after a 1/2-inch coating was accumulated, they were reinforced by plaster slurry-saturated burlap and irons.

The side portions and borders were trimmed flush so as not to affect the fitting, which was done as soon as the plaster was applied to the proper thickness with adequate reinforcing.

After the base sections were added to the front section, plaster ties were added to the sides on the outside (Fig. 26). On the inside, large gaps occurred where the plaster was not fully brought to the edge, or where the trimming was done. These gaps were filled with liquid plaster slurry, and further irons added to securely fasten the sections together to make the casting whole. The large front section, then, with the base sections added, was lifted into an upright position (Fig. 27). Then the various sec-

Fig. 22. Most of the clay and armature was removed.

ter positive was ready for crating and shipping to the bronze foundry.

[Author's Note: A discussion of the casting in bronze included in the journal article was omitted to avoid repetition. A more complete description of this process is included with the description of *A Statue of Lincoln for New Salem*.]

The Lincoln statue was the last of the large monuments to be cast in bronze before the government restricted the uses of copper because of World War II. It is now (date 1942) completed and will be sent to Hawaii as soon as possible.

As Lincoln was the great spirit which maintained a unity of the North and South in a crisis, it is to be hoped that his spirit in bronze may be a factor in the unity of the East and the West, the cultures of the Orient and the Occident.

Fairbanks, Avard T., "Engineering in Sculpture." *The Michigan Technic*, February, 1942.

•

RECOLLECTIONS OF A YOUNG ASSISTANT

… continued

Back at work on the following day, there were molds to be lifted free and clay to be separated. The multiple sections of the back of the mold for *Lincoln The Frontiersman* statue were lifted off to facilitate the removal of most of the clay and armature by working from the rear of the master section of the mold (Fig. 21). As work continued, most of the clay and the and the internal armature was removed (Fig. 22).

Avard Jr., the oldest son, studying engineering, rigged up a double A frame about 15 feet high, which could straddle the statue. A pulley was attached, and this greatly aided lifting off the smaller sections of mold from the back. It was indispensable for raising and gently lowering the massive front section of the mold.

The adhering clay was quickly stripped from the plaster and from the armature. Whereas the creation of the statue had taken months, nearly a year, the salvage of clay took only a few hours. Large chunks and crumbled bits were thrown back into the wet clay bin. The mold sections were lifted off and laid out in sections, after clay was removed. Small residues of clay were sponged out of recesses.

The master section rested on the sturdy 2 x 4

tions were cast and added to the lower portion, previously cast, until the very top section was finally finished. Mold and cast were both firmly fastened together.

The next procedure was to remove the mold. This was first done by cutting away the irons and iron reinforcing by means of hatchets. The second process was to remove the burlap reinforcing and gray plaster (Fig. 28). Then came the white plaster coating; and as one cut to the blue plaster, it was a warning that the surface of the statue was near. Careful chiseling and cutting away of the blue plaster revealed the white statue exactly as it was in clay, save for the fins of plaster that occurred between the sections (Fig. 30). After cutting away the fins and the retouching of some bubble holes and occasional places where the chisel inadvertently chipped through the blue plaster into the white, the plaster statue was finished. With this work done, the plas-

Fig. 23. Mold sections were cleaned and laid out to dry. Note the one-piece anterior section with the wooden frame. The plaster mold after drying was shellacked and lubricated

boards while it was horizontal. The 2/3-life size statue was seen in the background and a tent-like object was the canopy used to cover the heroic statue to maintain moisture and avoid drying of the clay.

Mr. Vanni carefully cleaned the last trace of clay from the mold, washing it with a soft sponge sopped with water. The studio floor was littered with pieces of the mold as they lay there to dry (Fig. 23).

The next step after retouching bubbles and voids, and 24 hours of drying time, was three applications of shellac. The surface of the blue inner layer of the mold changed to brown. When the third coat of the shellac was dry, it was treated with a lubricant, so that the cast might easily separate from the mold. This was a combination of stearic acid (a fatty acid) and kerosene.

The casting was again done in sections. The ax, the hands with forearms, were cast separately. White plaster for the cast was carefully applied to the inside of the mold sections. Internal reinforcing was then applied. The upper part of the body was another section. Although four parts were cast separately, they were made to fit perfectly.

Several lower posterior sections of mold were prepared with cast prior to the main anterior mas-

ter mold. Internal reinforcing was formed, laid in place and attached by burlap strips saturated with the plaster slurry.

Fig. 24. Internal iron reinforcements were shaped then removed prior to application of plaster.

19

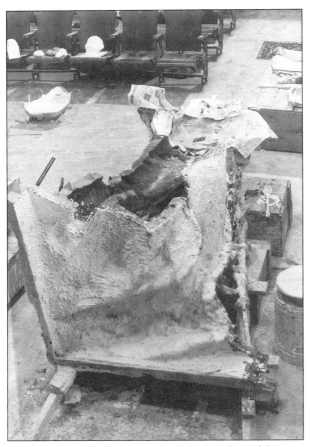

Fig. 25. White plaster was applied to inner surface of the lower mold section.

Fig. 26. Lower posterior mold sections with applied plaster were placed on the anterior sections prior to lifting to upright position.

Internal reinforcing irons were formed prior to the application of the anterior sections and removed until about a one inch layer of plaster and burlap reinforcing was in place (Fig. 24). Special care was taken to avoid bubbles or voids.

The finer, more expensive white plaster was applied in the thin liquid state with a soft brush or by spattering a handful at a time. After the meticulously applied first coat, plaster was added to about two-inch thickness, reinforced with impregnated burlap (Fig. 25). The massive front section was heavily reinforced with irons strapped in place with plaster-saturated burlap. Angle or channel irons and pipes further reinforced the casting to prevent the warping or cracking of plaster.

When each section of mold had its cast applied, they were refitted into place, starting with the base and working up. The reinforcing straps were placed on the inside, easily at first, but with an increased effort as each added piece restricted access. Several lower posterior sections of mold with cast were

applied and internal reinforcing was formed, laid in place and attached by burlap strips, saturated with plaster slurry (Fig. 26). The mold with the applied cast sections was raised to a vertical position, and the remaining cast posterior sections were placed and secured on the anterior or master section (Fig. 27).

When the last piece was fitted in place, the burlap-impregnated strips had to be passed awkwardly through a small opening in the back of the neck and blindly applied to seams and angle irons.

Completion of the cast was another happy climax. The tools were again cleaned, the debris from the floor scraped and swept up. Again there was time out for relaxation while the plaster hardened.

The chipping away of the waste mold could be fun, challenging, and tedious. The tools ranged from hatchets to fine narrow chisels. Mr. Vanni kept his "hatch," a shingle hatchet designed for roofers, honed razor sharp. His strokes were accurate and bold. The sculptor also used a hatchet, but the boys,

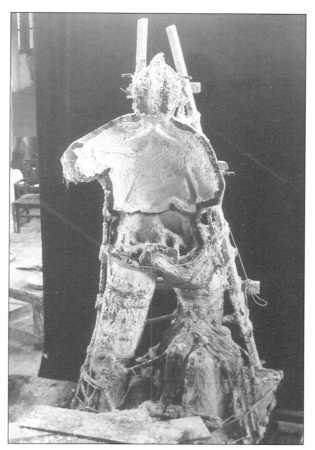

Fig. 27. The mold and cast were lifted to upright position.

Fig. 28. After the wood frame and some metal reinforcements were cut away, the waste mold is viewed being chipped away.

having less experience, were only allowed broad chisels and hammers to cut away the reinforcing rough outer covering (Fig. 28). The floor was soon littered by waste plaster and reinforcing irons (Fig. 29). One boy was constantly shoveling up chips.

Gradually the gray gave way to the thin blue undercoats, warning that underneath, the white plaster cast was close. Smaller chisels and softer hammer blows were then applied. The reinforcing was first chopped away by hatchet strokes down to the belt line, starting at the head, and the waste mold was then carefully chipped away. Often the chips popped off easily; sometimes undercuts made the chipping more difficult. Occasionally chisel nicks were made.

The sculptor alone chipped out the head and hands. The caster chipped and directed the older boys. The irons and plaster were progressively chipped away down to the knees (Fig. 29), then down to the boots. The younger boys were helpful, but sometimes were involved in more play than

work. The arms and the ax were cast separately and were then fastened to their proper position. Virgil and I were photographed helping our father (Fig. 30).

When all the mold was finally chipped away, there were several tubs, nearly half a ton, of waste plaster to be discarded. There was more work to be done—the retouching of bubbles, nicks, and chisel marks, and the replacement of chipped prominences. Efforts to avoid bubbles had been carefully taken, but nevertheless a few occurred and required filling. Half-cup-sized batches of plaster were mixed, and defects were carefully retouched with steel modeling tools as the hand-held plaster slowly solidified. The cast must be retouched to correct chisel marks and to fill voids from bubbles in the plaster. One day, a large crew was assembled; Maude Fairbanks and three sons, Justin, Eugene, and Avard, were busy with the tedious process of retouching (Fig. 31).

The arms, the ax, and the head were carefully

Fig. 29. Further removal of reinforcement and waste mold.

Fig. 30. Sculptor Fairbanks secures fore arm and ax sections to main cast, assisted by sons, Eugene Fairbanks (above) and Virgil Fairbanks (below).

fitted in place. The makeshift studio was cleaned up to a reasonable degree. Drapes were placed about the base. A dark backdrop was hung from a cross wire to give an exhibition-like atmosphere. Photographs were taken and an informal open house was held.

The work was not yet over. The sections had to be separated and lifted off, prior to crating the cast sections. The double A frame was used as a hoist to lift off sections (Fig. 34). This was a carpentry job that the sculptor must direct, for adequate crating was required to avoid damage in shipment to the bronze foundry.

Beside the load of lumber ordered, a large amount of excelsior was required for packing. Numerous odd-angled cross-bracings prevented movement and damage to the delicate plaster. The crates, when loaded, were heavy, and again the crew, about five men and boys, worked arduously to carry the cumbersome crates down the broad stairs to the freight truck. This was the ultimate climax for the studio helpers.

The bronze casting was to be done by the lost wax process at the Roman Bronze Company in Corona, New York. A spell of relaxation would have been in order, but the fall semester of school had already begun; it was autumn of 1941.

The statue was in the process of bronze casting when, on December 7, the attack on Pearl Harbor occurred. It was the last major monument cast before bronze was restricted to war use. Dedication was further delayed by shipping priorities, and it was nearly two years before dedication exercises were held.

The nation at war called upon the boys who had assisted in the production of this statue. Avard, Jr. had become a physicist and contributed his technical skill in engineering research. Eugene served in the Army Medical Corps after completion of medical school and internship. Elliott saw service in the

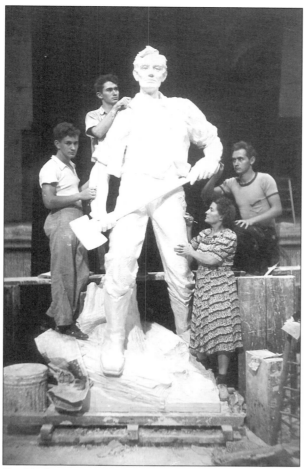

Fig. 31. Retouching proceeds with sons, Justin (left), Eugene (above), Avard (right), and wife, Maude (below on right).

Fig. 32. Statue partly disassembled prior to packing and shipping to foundry.

US Army in England and Germany. Justin served in the Navy. The family was deeply saddened when news came that Justin's friend, Robert Cooper, was a casualty of the battle of Okinawa in 1945.

Elliott and Justin studied sculpture after their military service. Virgil's service in the Navy began after medical school and internship, about the time of the Korean conflict. The three youngest boys had been interested observers, playing around this statue, but they had opportunities to assist on later monuments of Lincoln. Jonathan later served in the Navy and then became an artist, while David and Grant studied medicine. They both served in the National Public Health Service.

When the statue was nearly complete a newspaper reporter from *The Ann Arbor Daily News* interviewed Dr. Fairbanks. He recorded some of the motivations, thoughts, and comments regarding the progress of this heroic monument. Select quotations from Avard Fairbanks, recorded in this news article

at the completion of modeling in clay, are here reprinted:

"Many statues have been made of Lincoln presenting him as a statesman, as a man who has made his attainments in life, but few have shown him as a youthful frontiersman; yet we have so often been told about his life in the early development of our American westward expansion. With these ideas in mind, I have often wanted to make a youthful Lincoln, a typification of our rugged frontiersmen... .

"In contemplation of a statue to be placed at a school, I have thought of the students who will be viewing it, and the impressions it will make in their young lives. So to present Lincoln as a youth, stalwart and capable, when in the work of clearing the woods and of splitting the rails, I have tried to characterize him as a worker; a man capable of performing manual tasks which made him physically strong in accomplishing objectives put before him, no matter how menial they may be... .

"When we consider the complexes of modern civilization, if we are to endure the strains in times of a crisis, we must return to fundamentals. Lincoln's great qualities came forward in the time of a national crisis, and the fundamentals of life which he experienced as a youth fitted him to carry forward the burdens of the nation and unify a mighty people. Great responsibilities he bore through his adherence to simple and elementary principles, particularly those ideals which created and developed our democracy.

"His belief in a charity for all mankind, his lack of any racial animosity, has made Lincoln one of the great figures of world civilization. As the schools in the Hawaiian Islands contain many racial types and classes of people, the appropriateness of a Lincoln statue at the Ewa Plantation school would seem extremely fitting. It should stand forth as a symbol of racial tolerance, an expression of a youthful frontiersman, and a worker. It should inspire hope and courage to the youth of many nationalities of lowly environments, and should make their lives and their aspirations significant. It should also present to them the ideals of a great future for the present civilization in which they live, and government that protects them.

"The artist must study the creation of life and apply that understanding to his interpretation of life. There is a basic correlation between the underlying structural elements of life and a work of art. Art, as in a portrait or a statue of an individual, must reflect more than that which is superficial. An artist must capture the rhythm of life, the flow of muscles, the character of an individual, and make his work dynamic rather than static. He must have an understanding of life itself, of the development of and rhythm of the body, and of the basic underlying patterns.

"But the correlation of anatomy to design is broader than the mechanistic, for idealism too is important. It is through the physical that the latter finds its means of expression.

"One sees in all structure, organic and inorganic, the fundamental law which science now records for us. This bears evidences of design and that which manifests the growth and development of all existence. An interesting correlation is found in the study of human anatomy how tissues build themselves according to the same patterns as have been ascribed to architecture and engineering. These may readily be found in the epithelial tissues and bone development... .

"As for masterpieces, whether in paint or clay, we must see them as portraits of ideals, the spirit of a cause or of a people, not just of persons. In this statue of Lincoln, I have endeavored to present Lincoln not as an individual but as an American, as a dynamic symbol of America, past, present, and future... .

"Art is a truly democratic method of interpretation whereby ideals may be presented and preserved for the understanding of all races, all generations. It is a means of attaining better international understanding and good will.

"As a teacher of sculpture—a profession I had never expected to follow when I began my career as a professional sculptor—my great ambition is to bring the teaching of art into the same public recognition as is accorded to law, medicine, engineering, and the other professions.

"The recognition of the artist through the offering of degrees for serious study and work will bring eventual public confidence in the artist and eventually will discourage many of the fads, and many other 'isms' which have a demoralizing rather than a constructive influence."

Fairbanks, Avard T., excerpts from "Dr. Fairbanks' Statue of Lincoln, Latest Creation By University Man, Will Be Exhibited Here Next Week." *The Ann Arbor News,* Ann Arbor, Michigan, July 4, 1941: p. 3.

•

THE WILL OF KATHERINE BURKE HAS BEEN PROBATED, PART II

The second part of the article now continues and tells of events leading to the statue erection and the dedication.

By Thomas I. Starr, the *Lincoln Herald,* June 1944.

Lincoln The Frontiersman had emerged from a ton of sculptor's clay as the final model stood completed in the center of Professor Fairbanks' studio. To translate it into imperishable bronze was something of a Herculean chore. To create it this far had been the work of an inspired artist; to complete the assignment was the job of an engineer in sculpture.

Many weeks of labor were devoted to the making of the plaster mold during the summer and fall of 1941. The mold was then cut into pieces and prepared for the castings, and finally ready for shipment to an Eastern bronze foundry where the casting was to take place. Had Professor Fairbanks known that he was working against time, the job could have bungled easily. But the world-shaking event of December 7, 1941, came unannounced. The plaster molds were in the hands of the foundry just under the wire, and *Lincoln The Frontiersman* was the last large monument to be made in bronze before the government restricted the use of copper.

The casting proceeded according to schedule, but shipment was delayed due to the prior needs of ship cargo space for war material. The statue arrived in Honolulu early in 1943 after a trip over dangerous waters, to be followed six months later by the block of colorful rainbow granite upon which the statue was to rest.

The selection of the rainbow granite pedestal, made before the Pearl Harbor incident, now seems to have a significant symbolism. The sign of the rainbow was given to Noah after the great flood as a promise from God that there should never again be a deluge of the world.

> "The symbolism may therefore be appropriate in its being so near to Pearl Harbor," Professor Fairbanks believes, "and we may hope that never again will there be a deluge of the world by force of arms."

At 10:30 o'clock on the morning of the 135th anniversary of the birth of the Great Emancipator, the pupils of the Ewa Public School, their families, and friends gathered for the unveiling ceremonies which were marked with simplicity. Hawaiian-born

Fig. 33. *Lincoln the Frontiersman* monument erected in Hawaii.

J. Douglas Bond, a University of Michigan graduate, manager of the Ewa Plantations and one of the trustees of the Katherine Burke estate, was the chairman.

The program opened with music of the Civil War period played by the Royal Hawaiian Band. Frank Crawford of Lihue, Kauai, another of the estate's trustees, told the story of the life of the Kansas-born school teacher who had taken this means to continue her teaching of racial tolerance and of opportunities for even the most lowly. The children of the Ewa school, the beneficiaries of Mrs. Burke, sang Julia Ward Howe's immortal "Battle Hymn of the Republic."

Superintendent of Public Instruction Oren E. Long spoke of "Lincoln—A Heritage of Youth," and the school children sang again. This time theirs was a choral recitation of the words of the "Gettysburg Address." As they spoke to music the final words: "...shall not perish from the earth," *Lincoln The Fron-*

The speakers (left to right): Governor Ingram M. Stainback, Mr. Frank Crawford, Mr. Oren E. Long, and Mr. J. D. Bond.

tiersman was unveiled to look out across the Ewa campus and across new frontiers for all time to come.

Another view of the statue immediately after the unveiling.

The Honorable Ingram M. Stainback, governor of Hawaii, delivered the unveiling address.

"We believe that Mrs. Burke has shown wisdom and understanding in presenting to this school this statue of Abraham Lincoln as a young man," the Governor said, "and that she had the hope that this statue standing here before Ewa school, where the children of so many ancestries—Americans all—work and play and learn together, would serve to remind them of the miracle that character, courage, and work can accomplish.

"We join with her in hoping and believing that Abraham Lincoln, the frontiersman, may inspire the children at this school with a love of country, and a love for their fellow man without which true democracy can not exist."

The playing of the "National Anthem" by the Royal Hawaiian Band was preceded with the singing of "America" by the audience, ending with that verse which is the most appropriate of all patriotic prayer benedictions: "Great God our King."

The estate of Katherine McIntosh Burke—schoolteacher—has been closed. As her dream has been fulfilled.

Starr, Thomas I., "The Will of Katherine Burke Has Been Probated." the *Lincoln Herald,* Harrogate, Tenn. June, 1944, Vol. XLVI, No. 2.

SHE WAS A TEACHER

By Mr. Frank Crawford, Executor, Katherine M. Burke Estate

"Today, through this work of a great artist, the lesson the little girl learned long ago in Kansas, is the last lesson its old principal gives out to Ewa School."

Mr. Chairman, Ewa School, Your Friends and Guests: Mr. Long has asked that I give, as he has told me, "an interpretive statement of the life of Katherine M. Burke." To give such an interpretation I shall try to tell a story. I trust that it may not stray far from the truth. Mrs. Burke named me as executor of her will. One of the bequests in the will gave a certain fund to three trustees—the Superintendent of Public Instruction, the Manager of Ewa Plantation, and the executor—directing that they "purchase and erect a statue of Abraham Lincoln at Ewa School."

To those who did not know Mrs. Burke well, this may seem rather an unusual bequest. But when we come to know more of the history of her long and active life and learn something about her forebears and their background, then this bequest seems to be quite in character with her life work.

She was a teacher

Not all lesson are learned, or taught, in schools. Our modern psychologists go to some pains to tell us that certain incidents in our early days often have a lasting influence in our lives in after years. Quite true—but not so modern.

A certain wise man who built a temple several thousand years ago said something about "…training up a child in the way he should go, and when he is old he will not depart from it."

We have learned that Mrs. Burke's people came from Kentucky to Kansas in early times. No doubt she, as a little girl, listened at the knees of her elders to tales of those stirring times when there was a local civil war in Kansas over the grave question whether that territory should come into the Union as free or as a slave state.

Henry Clay's Missouri compromise law, which had stood for a generation as charter to free soil for Kansas and Nebraska territories, had been repealed.

About this time, a tall lawyer in Illinois made a speech on the subject of this repeal at the first convention of a new political party held in Bloomington. This has become known as "Lincoln's lost speech," for it is told that he so carried away his whole audience by his eloquence that not one reporter remembered to record the speech for his paper. And so the master speech was lost. But there was one ringing sentence recurring in that speech— "Kansas must be free." Those freedom-loving men of Kansas had found a leader. What was more, they felt that he was one of them. He, too, had shared the toil, the hardships and privations of those pioneers who would build homes for free men in a wilderness.

With such a background, from such neighbors, the little girl learned her first lesson in Americanism. Never in a long lifetime did she forget her lesson. She, in time, became a pioneer schoolteacher. We have learned that she taught schools in Kansas, Arizona, California, Alaska, and finally in Hawaii.

She was one of those courageous souls who met life's problems cheerfully and unafraid, with never a complaint. She had good business judgment, a sharp wit, and a keen sense of humor. Like some other pioneers, she did not seek trouble, but —well, she wasted no energy running away from it if it came her way. She was not much given to the preaching of high principles: rather she put them to practice in her daily life.

In settling her estate, I received letters from persons, some in strange lands: evidently she had helped them in their dire need—and none but the one receiving such aid would ever know that it had been given.

One of the last teaching positions she held before reaching the age of retirement was that as Principal of Ewa School. She seemed to have had a great *Aloha* for this school. After retiring she traveled widely in many countries for some nine years. In a letter from one of her friends in Washington, I was told that she left there telling them she was going West on another little trip. She went to the Mayo

Clinic in Rochester on what she no doubt knew would be her last journey. A short note handed her nurse, making disposal of a few personal effects and asking that her ashes be buried in Lihue Cemetery, and she passed on with the same courage she had lived. This, briefly, is the story of an old-fashioned American schoolteacher. The trustees appointed in her will have been very fortunate in finding an artist, Mr. Avard Fairbanks, to carry out her wishes. He did not know Mrs. Burke. But it may be that he too has some of that pioneer background, for in writing to Mr. Long, he tells that in the study of his subject he has chosen "not Lincoln the great statesman who has reached his high attainments, but Lincoln, the young man…" shows him, using his great strength as did other young pioneers of his day who worked, with their hands, to build this country we now call America.

Yet in the lifted face of the young frontiersman, the artist seems to have put the vision of a prophet—a seer into the future, as if he could foretell the great task that lay before him. And so today, through this work of a great artist, the lesson the little girl learned long ago in Kansas is the last lesson its old principal gives out to Ewa School. Aye—she was a teacher.

Crawford, Frank, "She Was a Teacher." *Hawaii Educational Review,* February, 1944: p. 168.

Reference Article

ABRAHAM LINCOLN

By Ingram M. Stainback, Governor, Territory of Hawaii

Standing here in sight of Pearl Harbor—we might well say with Lincoln: "It is for us the living, rather, to be dedicated here to the unfinished work which they who fought here have thus far so nobly advanced."

Mr. Chairman, Honored Guests, Ladies and Gentlemen, and Pupils of Ewa School: Abraham Lincoln is one of our Presidents whose stature has grown both at home and abroad with the passing of the years, until today he is almost a national deity and an international inspiration. Let us hope that in this deification of Lincoln we will not lose sight of his many human qualities.

When the statue of Lincoln was unveiled near Westminster Abbey in London, the British Prime Minister said:

"I doubt whether any statesman who ever lived sank so deeply into the hearts of the people of many lands as Lincoln did. I am not sure that you in America realize the extent to which he is also our possession and our pride. His courage, fortitude, patience, humanity, clemency; his trust in the people; his belief in democracy, and some of the phrases in which he gave expression to those attributes, will stand out forever to guide troubled nations and their perplexed leaders."

There is nothing I can add to what has been said at home time and time again concerning him.

It is, however, a pleasure for me to appear here and take part in the dedication of this statue representing Lincoln the rail splitter, the young man just entering into manhood. It is particularly appropriate to have Lincoln on the school grounds; Lincoln believed in education, he believed in schools even though, as stated by himself, his total attendance at school did not exceed one year. He believed in the opportunity of every child to obtain an education without the handicaps that beset him. This was part of his platform when he first ran for election to the Illinois legislature.

While Lincoln attended school only for a short period, he was an exceedingly well-educated man whose education progressed throughout his life. It should be an inspiration to any child who thinks he is lacking in opportunity, to read and study the life of Lincoln and find out the secret of his success, how this man with barely a year in school became a leading lawyer, a member of the state legislature, a member of Congress, and finally President of the United States in its most critical period; I said secret—I believe it is no secret as Lincoln himself said to a young student of the law that to become proficient he must "work, work, work."

To this I would add Lincoln's foundation stone was character which included courage, though Lincoln himself did not mention that requisite for success. How could a young man with so little schooling become such a master of the English language, such an able logician in his law work, such a forceful and clear thinker on the national problems of his day, and such a courageous and able administrator?

While Lincoln's schooling was meager and his access to books most limited, he thoroughly mastered every book that he used in furthering his education. He would go over the same matter again and again to see that he understood it. After he had thoroughly mastered and understood his subject he taught himself to express this idea in such clear, simple language that it could not be misunderstood. He wrote much and often. In his early life he did not have much to read but thoroughly understood what he read.

As Mr. Long has stated, the very few books that he had occasion to study were *Aesop's Fables*, the *Bible*, *Paradise Lost* and *The Revised Laws of Indiana*, which contained in its preface the Declaration of Independence. The effect of these writings can be seen in all Lincoln's speeches and writings. You will note throughout all his speeches a simplicity of language—adjectives are almost entirely lacking—with clearness, a balancing of words and sentences that gives force to what he says.

While studying law he is said to have found difficulty in satisfying himself as to when he had "proved" something beyond a reasonable doubt; to enable himself to realize when he had "proved" a proposition, Lincoln undertook the study of geometry and mastered it while still struggling with law and, incidentally, he neither graduated from nor attended any law school, yet became one of the ablest lawyers of his day, particularly in jury trials.

To industry Lincoln added great moral courage. Lincoln was one with Jackson, Marshall, and Webster in believing that we were one indivisible nation, not a union of states that might withdraw at will; that to secure the blessings of freedom and democracy this union must be preserved as a single nation; and he showed his real courage and fortitude in facing the disasters and setbacks of the Union armies during the early years of the Civil War… .

To those of use who are familiar with the draft riots in New York, the "copperheads" of Indiana,

and the strong movement of "peace at any price" throughout the northern states after the early military disasters, it is apparent that Lincoln needed all of his courage and determination.

The battle of Gettysburg appeared to be the beginning of the end of the Confederacy, but only the beginning, as the war lasted almost three years after Gettysburg. Probably one of the most appropriate two-minute speeches ever delivered in the English language was Lincoln's Gettysburg Address. The speech fitted the place, the time, the occasion. The place was the battlefield, the occasion the dedication of the National Cemetery.

His words spoken there might well be spoken to us here today as we look upon the victories of 1943, the Gettysburg of the present war, but still face the long struggle ahead. Standing here in sight of Pearl Harbor, on the battlefield, on this Island where our dead of December 7 are buried, we might well say with Lincoln, "It is for us, the living, rather, to be dedicated here to the unfinished work which they who fought here have thus far so nobly advanced. It is rather for us to be here dedicated to the great task remaining before us—that from these honored dead we take increased devotion to that cause for which they gave the last full measure of devotion; that we here highly resolve that these dead shall not have died in vain."

We believe that Mrs. Burke has shown wisdom and understanding in presenting to this school this statue of Abraham Lincoln as a young man; that she had the hope that this statue standing here before Ewa School, where the children of so many diverse ancestries—Americans all—work and play and learn together, would serve to remind them of the miracle that character and courage and work can accomplish; that, however humble the circumstances of birth, however limited the comforts of life, the opportunities for an American child in this land of democracy and freedom are limited only by the ambitions, character and determination of the individual. We join with her in hoping and believing that Abraham Lincoln, the rail splitter, may inspire the children at this school with a love of country and a love for their fellow man without which true democracy cannot exist.

Stainback, Ingram M., "Abraham Lincoln." *Hawaii Educational Review,* February, 1944: p. 167.

LINCOLN: A HERITAGE OF YOUTH

By Oren E. Long, Superintendent, Department of Public Instruction

"No matter how difficult the conditions confronting him, no matter how heavy his burdens, he kept on striving, always facing forward. This is a priceless heritage to the youth of the United States."

On this occasion, it is fitting that so large a part of the audience is made up of children, for the youth of our country revere and love Abraham Lincoln above every other character in our history. No other American passed from a cradle so humble, to a grave so illustrious. We are proud that in our country every individual has an opportunity to contribute in relation to his powers and his personal worth. History says to every boy and girl: "The institutions of the United States exist that its citizens may grow in health, in culture, and in spiritual worth." Lincoln exemplifies this national ideal.

Portrait details, right oblique view.

Lincoln's most striking characteristic was his Americanism. It was the essence of his thought, his utterances, his character. He was the product of its freedom and its challenge to personal effort. He built the ladder up which he climbed from poverty to power out of rails which he had split with his own hands.

This is one reason why he stands as a priceless heritage of youth. His life is a challenge to constant effort in pursuit of noble ideals. His ambition was undaunted by disappointments; his hope undimmed by hardships. His career stands as a warning against a life of ease and as a hope to those who face difficult problems.

Even in his political life, he did not attain success until near the end of his career. Until he became President, he lost more elections than he won. When Stephen A. Douglas defeated him for the United States Senate in 1858, he frankly admitted his disappointment. Asked how he felt about it, he replied he was like the boy who stubbed his toe; he was too big to cry and it hurt too bad to laugh.

When he became President, his leadership was not fully accepted. A considerable number of editors, including the great Horace Greeley, criticized him as few other leaders have ever been criticized.

Sensitive to criticism and craving public approval, he never had the satisfaction of experiencing popularity until near the end of his life. He was re-elected President by a large majority—his first clear-cut victory at the polls. Shortly after this, while he was conferring with a number of leaders at the White House, a large crowd assembled outside to applaud the President. Guards offered to drive them away, but the President asked that they be permitted to continue. Lincoln admitted that he enjoyed it. He said he was like the old farmer back in Illinois who said, as he reached for his sixth piece of ginger bread; "I guess there is no one in Sagamon County who likes ginger bread better than I do and gets less of it."

No matter how difficult the conditions confronting him, no matter how heavy his burdens, he kept on striving, always facing forward. This is a price-less heritage to the youth of the United States.

Another reason why Lincoln lives today was his power to express the most profound principles and ideals in the simplest of words. Lincoln tells us how he developed this ability. He had a desire, an *active* interest to improve his powers of expression.

In discussing this interest, he said:

"I can remember going to my little bedroom after hearing the neighbors talk of an evening with my father, and spending no small part of the night walking up and down and trying to make out what was the exact meaning of their, to me, dark sayings. I could not sleep, though I often tried to, when I got on such a hunt after an idea, until I had caught it; and when I thought I had got it, I was not satisfied until I had repeated it over and over, until I had put it into language plain enough, as I thought, for any boy I knew to comprehend."

To me, this is one of the most remarkable incidents in Lincoln's life. That a young boy should have felt so strongly the burden of being unable to express himself clearly and should have spent sleepless hours in an effort to overcome this burden is an inspiration to all of us.

We may think of him as being unusual, but he was unusual only in the intensity of his desire to *understand* and to *express* himself. This desire for self-expression is common to all men; but with Lincoln the desire became a passion. He worked at it. When he heard long, hard words, he tried to substitute for them short, simple words that a boy could understand. He dropped long Latin words and substituted short Saxon words.

This interest, plus the influence of three great books, the Bible, Aesop's Fables, and Pilgrim's Progress, determined his style and made him one of the greatest spokesmen of all time. He was able to express in words what others were only beginning to feel. He thus became a leader of men—in his age and perhaps in all ages—because he interpreted men to themselves. He used the words a mother uses in talking to a child; the words of the clerk at the crossroads store; the words of the market place. And yet, in these simple words, he expressed the most profound ideas.

Portrait details, left oblique view.

The Gettysburg Address is an example of this. The dedication of a national cemetery was a great occasion. Edward Everett was the orator of the day. He spoke for almost two hours, giving one of the greatest classical addresses of that period. Lincoln spoke only about two minutes. The entire talk contains but 266 words.

The next morning, Mr. Everett wrote to the President: "I should be glad if I could flatter myself that I came as near to the central idea of the occasion in two hours as you did in two minutes."

Lincoln really said all that there was to say. He knew that in the audience before him were people who had lost sons or brothers or husbands or fathers on that battlefield. To them, it was holy ground. They were not interested in a long dissertation on democracy or a tirade on the evils of slavery. They wanted someone to express their emotions—to interpret events almost too sacred for words. This is what Lincoln did—in words "plain enough for any boy… to comprehend."

This same mastery of simple language is found

in his second inaugural address. This ability was not inherited; it did not come from his environment. It was an achievement based on an interest and constant effort. Lincoln's accomplishment is an encouragement to all who desire to express themselves more effectively.

There is another Lincoln quality which makes his life a power in influencing the ideals of youth: *his love of truth*. He was not merely honest in the statements he made; he went beyond this. In his law practice, he invariably faced all the facts in a case, bringing out those unfavorable to his side as well as the favorable.

He won from his great political opponent, Stephen A. Douglas, this tribute: "Lincoln is the fairest and most honest man I have ever known." Biographers are agreed that, as man and lawyer, he was absolutely honest. He never tried to confuse a jury or to trap an honest witness into an apparent falsehood. In a civil case where he appeared as attorney, he felt that the opposing counsel, a young lawyer, had not presented two important points in the case. This troubled Lincoln. When he arose to present his case, he pointed out that his opponent had failed to present two points. Much to the surprise of the court and the indignation of his own client, he presented the points as favorably as he could and then proceeded to answer them. A better understanding of the issues involved was obtained. The result was that the case was discontinued and settled out of court. The nickname, "Honest Abe," stands as the perfect tribute to his love of truth.

Every school child knows the story of his mistake in making change and of his walking several miles that evening to correct the error. In a time of sharp practice, of conducting business "within the law," there is need for an emphasis on Lincoln's devotion to truth—his love of what was right. "He knew no fear," says a fellow lawyer, "except the fear of doing wrong."

This is the man whom we cherish as the greatest heritage of American youth. He loved humanity and understood the common people. "The strongest man in the countryside, champion wrestler; the chief magistrate of a great nation in its time of bitter agony; beloved by more human beings than any man in his lifetime; unquestioned master of the strongest men of his day; yet, after a day spent in vast problems of war and of state, he came home rejoicing almost to tears because he had made two mothers happy, and in his own simplicity of style he wrote: "As I have passed through life, I have *plucked a thorn* whenever I could and *planted a rose* wherever I thought a rose would grow."

"Lincoln… does not belong to the past, not even to the present, but to our noblest future." He exemplifies our country's highest ideals; his virtues are the hope of our nation and of all mankind. This statue, which is to be unveiled today, stands as a symbol of his virtues and political ideals. When we invite the youth of this community to look at Lincoln, we invite them to view their own best future, and to accept as their own, the responsibility for self-improvement and for becoming the best possible citizens in this land of freedom and opportunity.

Long, Oren E., "Lincoln—A Heritage of Youth." *Hawaii Educational Review*, February, 1944: pg. 169.

Young Lincoln Reading *The Life of George Washington*. Statuette, photo by Rolf Kay.

YOUNG LINCOLN READING
The Life of George Washington

Although the young Abraham Lincoln had very little school education, he was an avid reader. His mother often read to him when he was a child and helped him learn to read. In his youth he borrowed whatever books were available in the neighborhood. Later, he told a friend that he read every book he could borrow within a fifty mile radius. Besides the *Holy Bible, Aesop's Fables* and *Robinson Crusoe*, he studied *A History of the United States* by Grimshaw. He became especially interested in a book entitled *The Life of George Washington* subtitled *With Curious Anecdotes, Equally Honorable to Himself* and *Exemplary to His Young Countrymen* by Mason Locke Weems. Lincoln borrowed the book from Josiah Crawford, a neighbor, and placed it on a shelf near an unchinked log, where it was damaged by rain. He paid for the book by three days labor pulling fodder. It then belonged to him to read and often re-read.

Modern critics are both mirthful and uncharitable when reviewing *The Life of George Washington* by Mason Locke Weems, published in Philadelphia in 1800. Reverend Weems had served as a minister in the area near Mount Vernon about the time of the Revolutionary War. He later became an itinerant bookseller, and a popular salesman through his talents of comedy, violin playing, and giving sermons. He traveled through the south, selling books for his publisher, including several of his own. The anecdote most often quoted in this book involves the cherry tree and young Washington saying to his father, "I cannot tell a lie." Young Lincoln studied this book as well as other histories. It made a profound impression on the growing youth.

Fortunately he read this curious work very seriously. George Washington became an exalted figure in his imagination. In later life, whenever the real character of General Washington was considered, Lincoln claimed it was wiser to regard him as a superior being, heroic in manner and deeds, as portrayed by Weems, than to contend he was only a man, though wise and good, still subject to error and folly. While addressing the New Jersey Senate in 1861 he stated: "May I be pardoned if, upon this occasion, I mention that away back in my childhood, the earliest days of my being able to read, I got hold of a small book, such a one as few of the younger members have ever seen—Weems' *Life of Washing-ton*. I remember all the accounts there given of the battlefields and struggles for the liberties of the country, and none fixed themselves upon my imagination so deeply as the struggle here at Trenton, New Jersey. The contest with the Hessians, the great hardships endured at that time, all fixed themselves on my memory more than any single Revolutionary event; and you all know, for you have all been boys, how these early impressions last longer than any others. I recollect thinking then, boy as I was, that there must have been something more than common that these men struggled for."

In modeling this composition as a statuette, Avard Fairbanks hoped and planned to create a heroic bronze statue with a young Lincoln reading by the fire. Behind the seated figure would be a heroic figure of George Washington carved in white marble symbolizing a guiding spirit.

Weems' *Life of George Washington* appears then to be an introduction to Lincoln's study and admiration of the accomplishments of the first President. It is very evident in the farewell speech at Springfield, Illinois, to his friends and townspeople. As President-elect, a few minutes before departure, he mounted the platform of the railroad car and made a few remarks. Among these he said: "I now leave, not knowing when or whether ever I may return, with a task before me greater than that which rested upon Washington. Without the assistance of that Divine Being who ever attended him, I cannot succeed. With that assistance I cannot fail. Trusting in Him who can go with me, and remain with you, and be everywhere for good, let us confidently hope that all will yet be well."

Life of George Washington: An Inspiration to Young Lincoln Medallion.

Life of George Washington: An Inspiration to Young Lincoln Medallion

Since there are more than a thousand medals struck honoring Abraham Lincoln, one might assume that another one would be superfluous. Most of these honor him for his accomplishments as a legislator or as the President. Avard Fairbanks has chosen instead to portray a period in the formative years of the sixteenth President, when he received inspiration reading about the accomplishments of President George Washington.

The medal was struck by the Hamilton-Hallmark Mint about the time of the Bicentennial of American Independence. It commemorates the life of George Washington, his devotion to his country and to the cause of liberty; serving as an inspiration to young Abraham Lincoln and to all Americans. The youth is portrayed exhilarated by the stories of heroic deeds when reading before the dim light of a crackling fire on the hearth of a frontier log cabin. In the background an image of General George Washington rises in the vapors and wisps

of smoke above the blaze, as though rendering counsel and guidance.

Reverse side: Young Lincoln Medallion

Abraham Lincoln statue for New Salem State Park, Illinois.

A LINCOLN STATUE
FOR
NEW SALEM, ILLINOIS

Dr. Fairbanks' second monument to Abraham Lincoln was placed at the New Salem Village in Illinois. It has been highly praised by a dedicated Lincoln scholar, Mr. Thomas I. Starr, late president of the Detroit Lincoln Group. His article in the *Michigan Christian Advocate*, February 11, 1954, is included with permission of that journal.

AT THE CROSSROADS OF DECISION

By Thomas I. Starr

Sons of fathers who were driven from their Illinois homes by mutual misunderstandings with their neighbors, which led to flaming torches of religious intolerance, will return next spring—108 years after their tragic departure—to present to Illinois an heroic bronze statue dedicated to the memory of the State's most illustrious adopted son, who spoke and lived "with malice toward none."

"Sons of Utah Pioneers" is the donor organization. They are Mormons, descendants of forefathers who were burned out of their homes in Nauvoo, Illinois, and driven across the frozen Mississippi, in 1846. Their leaving brought to end the raids and counter uprisings which constitute a sorry and unnecessary page in our national history. The Mormons went on westward to settle in wild, unoccupied lands, where there emerged eventually the state of Utah.

Avard T. Fairbanks, dean of the school of fine arts at the University of Utah since 1947, and for 18 years previous associate professor of sculpture at the University of Michigan, is the creator of the new Lincoln statue. It will be placed in New Salem, the reincarnated little village in Menard County (Sangamon County then), which the Kentucky-born Abraham Lincoln reached by circuitous route at the age of 22. Until this time, New Salem has had no statue of Lincoln. The town itself, in its restored state, is a memorial to him. Were it not that it was his home for four years, New Salem, if ever remembered, would have been forgotten a century ago.

Most Lincoln statues have a name or a title, such Lincoln –the Emancipator, –the Lawyer, –the Debator, –the Railsplitter, –the Mystic, –the President, –the Hoosier Youth; or, as Fairbanks titled his earlier statue: *Lincoln The Frontiersman*. This nine-foot bronze produced by Sculptor Fairbanks a decade ago, while he was associated with the University of Michigan, was a bequest by a former teacher to the campus of the Ewa Plantation School, in the Hawaiian Islands. Critics have acclaimed it, and more than a half-dozen plaster models enhance as many institutional and private collections of *Lincolniana*.

As far as this writer knows, this statue for New Salem, the second to be moulded by the talented mind and hands of this artist, has no title or name. But, to the observant critic familiar with the Lincoln biography, the statute portrays an intelligent and a determined young man of rugged stature, also a thinker, at a cross-road of decision. Furthermore, it *looks* like Lincoln.

Especially appropriate it is that Lincoln thus portrayed should be placed in New Salem. For it was in this humble, pioneer community that he made several important personal decisions—decisions that were to direct his life, eventually into a position of everlasting and world-wide respect and esteem.

Abraham Lincoln discovered New Salem in the spring of 1831. He upset his loaded flat-boat on the rim of the Rutledge mill dam, which clogged the current of the shallow Sangamon river as it ran by the little village. Restoring his cargo, while villagers observed and tossed out friendly advice, he floated on to and down the Mississippi to sell at the market in New Orleans. A determined destiny brought him back to this settlement on the Sangamon to take up residence and become a storekeeper.

It was in New Salem that Lincoln established a reputation as a grocery clerk, a wrestler, a storyteller, an avid reader of every available printed word. For a time he was postmaster, reading every newspaper passing through his office. (His compensation was something more than opportunity to read the papers; he received $55.70 for 28 of the 36 months he held the office, according to the *United States Official Register 1836*.)

Here also he established himself as an honest man. He had been an honest man before he ever heard of New Salem, of course; but several trivial incidents such as the long walk to return small change made it evident and named him "Honest Abe." It was in New Salem that Lincoln cast his first vote in an election. It was there that he became a soldier—a captain in a regiment of militia in the short-lived Indian outbreak of Chief Black Hawk. In New Salem he decided to become a lawyer; also to enter politics, and did… experiencing the only defeat ever received in a public election.

(Let's detour for a moment to examine that defeat—sometimes called "a failure." Lincoln and a Methodist preacher by the name of Cartwright wanted to represent that portion of Sangamon county in the Illinois legislature. Lincoln went off to the Black Hawk war, neglecting his campaigning. Cartwright stayed at home, busily working in the election district, "saving souls for the Methodist Church (bless him for that) and the Democratic Party," and went to the legislature for a single term. But Lincoln won the next *four* elections and served *four* times in the legislature. Then later on, after Lincoln had moved to Springfield, he tangled again with Cartwright before the electorate… and went to Congress. Thereafter 'Church and State' did not mix well for the preacher; he stayed with the Church.)

Fairbank's *New Salem Lincoln* holds a striking similarity to his Hawaiian *Lincoln The Frontiersman* of a decade ago. Yet, it is different, and appropriate to the community where it will remain. The boots and the ax are the same, and the clothing is similar; but the countenance is more mature. The brightness of the eyes and the alertness of the posture are identical. But the ax, held firmly in both hands in a working position on The *Frontiersman,* now rests on the ground, supported loosely by the thumb and fingers. It seems about to fall from Lincoln's left hand; while clutched firmly by the right hand, and held against the body, Lincoln supports a law book.

Tradition tells us that it was in New Salem that Lincoln acquired and read his first law book: a copy of Blackstone's *Commentaries.* But like so many of

the Lincoln 'traditions,' this tradition just is not true. (It is in his own handwriting where Lincoln once wrote in a correction when another 'tradition' was about to commence, "No harm, if true; but, in fact, not true." Lincoln loses none of his greatness when facts tear away some of those traditions.)

Lincoln borrowed and read law books back in Indiana, ten years earlier when still in his teens. He borrowed and read them not necessarily because they were law books, but because he borrowed and read anything and everything that was available within walking distance.

However, Lincoln did *read* Blackstone's *Commentaries* in New Salem. But there is no evidence to sustain the story that he "found it in a barrel left behind by a passing wagon train." He also read the *Revised Code of Laws of Illinois* while laid up with frozen feet in the home of the Macon county sheriff. And from New Salem he walked 20 miles to Springfield to borrow, read, and return Greenleaf's *Evidence,* Story's *Equity,* and Chitty's *Pleadings.*

New Salem was the *crossroad of decision* for Abraham Lincoln. And Avard Fairbanks has perpetuated in bronze the laying down of the ax and the taking up of the law book; …the transition of the rail-splitting frontiersman into the young lawyer.

This significant and unusual gift from descendants of early Illinois Mormons to the State of Illinois, to become a part of its important New Salem State Park, is "a triumph of the spirit of tolerance over the prejudices of history." And it is all just a fragment of the story of America!

Starr, Thomas I., "At The Crossroads of Decision." *Michigan Christian Advocate*, Adrian, Michigan, 11 February 1954.

•

THOMAS I. STARR

Adapted from articles written by Alan Jenkins

Early in Avard Fairbanks's search for information and background about Abraham Lincoln, for the Hawaiian statue, he visited the Detroit Lincoln Club and gave a demonstration lecture, modeling a statuette, a preliminary concept of the monument to be erected. President Thomas I. Starr immediately took great interest in the projects and contributed considerable effort toward finding factual material about Lincoln as a young man.

Thomas Starr's interest in Lincoln started when he was a child attending elementary school in a one-room schoolhouse near Olean, New York. He listened attentively to stories about Lincoln read by his teacher Florence McCarthy. He spent his boyhood in Royal Oak, Michigan, a sparsely populated suburb of Detroit at that time, and attended Royal Oak High School. On occasions the president of the school board gave lectures about the Civil War. After high school, Tom attended Albion College in Albion, Michigan. After graduation, in 1927 Starr was employed by the Michigan Bell Telephone Company, first in publicity, then in the company magazine. In 1935, he became editor, and continued for 19 years in this capacity. The trade journal won many awards for excellence for industrial journalism during his time as editor.

After hearing a lecture by the noted Lincoln author Ida Tarbell in 1929, he returned home with her autographed two-volume book, *The Life of Lincoln,* and became a dedicated collector. His avocation was the study of Abraham Lincoln and the Civil War Period. Starr's basement library, after about 20 years, held more than 2,000 catalogued books, 500 magazine articles, and more than 2,000 clippings. Tom Starr's collection was used by many Lincoln scholars, as well as high school and college students. Among many friends was Carl Sandburg, who often visited his library. Other authors using his resources included James G. Randall, Harry E. Pratt, David Donald, William H. Townsend, Louis A Warren, Emanual Hertz, Ralph G. Newman, Edgar De Witt Jones, and Milton H. Shutes.

At one time, while searching through newspaper files in the Detroit Public Library, he found a file behind some bound news copies. In it was a faded copy of a Lincoln address to the rally of the Republican Young Men of Michigan in Kalamazoo, on August 27, 1856. It had been considered a lost speech. He published a small book about the background of events and included a copy of the speech. His published Lincoln articles totaled eleven. For his publication of the lost Kalamazoo speech, he received an honorary Phi Beta Kappa membership and a national honor by the American Institute of Graphic Arts. He became an honorary associate of the sons of the Union Veterans in 1956. Among numerous honors, he was a specially invited guest at the opening of the Robert Todd Lincoln Collection of Abraham Lincoln Papers, July 1947, in Washington, DC.

Jenkins, Alan. "Thomas I Starr: Courageous Lincoln Scholar." *Lincoln Herald,* Summer, 1963

Jenkins, Alan. "Thomas I. Starr – A Stellar Life." *A Pulpit Message,* Congregational Church, Royal Oak, Michigan, August, 1963

[Author's Note: Avard Fairbanks felt privileged to receive counseling and advice from Mr. Starr, and was honored that Starr should write several splendid articles about monuments that Fairbanks created portraying various aspects of Abraham Lincoln. There was a deep debt of gratitude for the help and encouragement rendered. The sculptor was saddened to learn of an illness that shortened the productivity of this fine scholar. Starr had to resign from his position as editor, but continued his efforts in collecting Lincolniana for several years. Multiple sclerosis caused a disability in walking, but his mind remained clear. For a time he slept on a cot in his basement library. Thomas Starr passed to his reward in 1963.]

Fig. 1. The armature, a wooden frame with wire mesh.

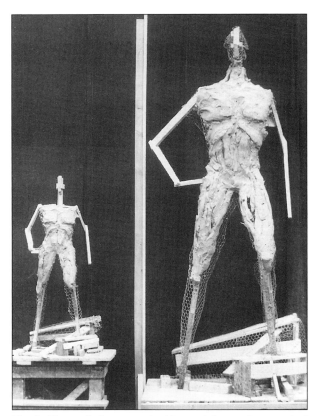

Fig. 2. The preliminary roughed-in modeling and anatomical construction.

The following is a description of the creation of the statue of Lincoln for the New Salem Village, written by the sculptor. Although there may be some repetition of technical information related in the discussion of the previous monument, it is more detailed and is presented with illustrations that give added meaning and interest. It is included with permission of the *Journal of the Illinois State Historical Society,* which originally printed it.

MAKING THE LINCOLN STATUE FOR NEW SALEM

By Avard Fairbanks

The task of creating the heroic statue *Abraham Lincoln for New Salem* has not been accomplished in a short period of time, but was the result of years of study. From my early impressions, from my teachers in elementary school, from a study of American history, and from a close sympathy with Lincoln's pioneer heritage, I have deeply revered his life and his struggles. I have gathered information from many and various sources, and have intimately associated with students of *Lincolniana.* Also, being one who lost his own mother at an early age, I have sensed the spirit of his mother, Nancy Hanks Lincoln, guide of his childhood.

I have made other compositions and other stat-

utes of Lincoln, but since there has not been a study in sculpture of his New Salem period, it was a challenging opportunity to bring to the people of America this phase of the determining years of his life.

To make a suitable statue of such a subject, one must first get in mind a basic concept of the character and qualities of the person to be portrayed. The spirit of the times has to be sensed. One must consider the location of the statue, as well as many other factors. A memorial should be made in a size commensurate with the personage who has achieved eminence and has performed heroic deeds. Therefore a statue that would look well in a public park

Fig. 3. Modeling has progressed with clothing and some details added.

Fig. 4. Sculptor Fairbanks continues modeling, but the ax needs to be added.

or public building should be of heroic size—eight or nine feet high. A life-size statue placed in the open gives the impression of a small man, and such a statue in no way would characterize Lincoln.

When he arrived in New Salem late in July, 1831, Lincoln was 22 years old, a "friendless, uneducated, penniless boy, working on a flatboat," as he later described himself. He soon gave up rail splitting to become a storekeeper, soldier, postmaster, surveyor, and later a member of the state legislature and a student of law. This is the period of his life that I proposed to recreate in a statue of impressive and heroic bronze sculpture. To symbolize it I chose to compose Lincoln with the implement of his past activities, an ax (in his left hand), showing him as a capable, stalwart man of the frontier, and a law book (in his right hand), portraying him also as a man of mental pursuits and capabilities.

I devoted much time to making different studies of the head of Lincoln as he appeared at the age of 28, when he left New Salem to practice law in Springfield. I had excellent reproductions of the life masks of his face and his hands, cast before his elec-

tion to the presidency by the sculptor Leonard Volk. These were invaluable because they gave actual shape to his head, features, and hands. The use of these, along with fine photographs, gave an opportunity to put into that face and those hands the vibrant spirit, personality, and character of Lincoln as a young man.

The sculpture of the *New Salem Lincoln* portrays him as tall, broad-shouldered, and courageous, with the strength and spirit of young manhood. His eyes are deep and far-seeing. There is vision and anticipation in his entire countenance. His whole attitude of mind and body looks outward and forward, as if clearly foreseeing a significant destiny for himself and his fellow men.

The foregoing are necessary concepts to have in mind as one develops them into their physical manifestations; and further, it is a great satisfaction to have others feel that an assignment of this nature has been well performed and that it will uplift beholders to the great ideals of the one portrayed.

The preceding paragraphs tell of the necessary considerations involved in putting the spirit into work. They outline the procedure I used in arriving at the concept, or what is termed the content in art. To give an idea of how those matters are evolved into material form by a sculptor in the completion of a study, the following description of the various activities entailed is presented.

Many constructive processes are utilized in setting up a heroic statue through sketches, enlarging them into a scale size or working model, and then enlarging again from the working model into the final heroic size. Preliminary sketches of Lincoln were made in drawings. After many trials of one study and another, finally the subject matter and the position which seemed to be the most effective and appropriate was to show Lincoln in Illinois in the period of transition in his life, "at the Crossroads of Decision." The time when he saw a new future ahead, and decided on the New Salem location.

After the general position and attitude of the study were agreed on, a preliminary model, 1/4 of the full heroic size or 1/3-life size, was developed. From this was constructed the 1/2-heroic size working model, utilized as the experimental study and in making the large nine-foot-tall model of the size known as heroic. Beyond the drawing sketches, three different models were constructed and carried to completion.

First Model

Only a slight support was required for the first model, which was 1/3-life size, with a figure 18-inches tall. The armature or framework was constructed in a manner similar to the first model for *Lincoln The Frontiersman,* and will not be repeated for sake of brevity.

After the wires were arranged into place, Plastelina (a special clay) was added on them in rolls until the form of the miniature statue took shape. The Plastelina was formed anatomically to get the bodily members into their proper shape and proportions. Afterward the draperies were added. Finally the face, features, and other details were made to express the concepts of the sculptor (Fig. 1). The defect of the horizontal pipe may be retouched after casting in plaster.

Second Model

From the first model, used as a guide, a second model 2/3-life, or 1/2-heroic size, was made in order to gain further details that could not be attained in the smaller study. The armature of this study was built, not like that of the Plastelina sketch, but in much the same manner as that of the heroic study, because it had to be the basis of construction of the latter from the beginning to the end. This second model, known as the scale or working model, was developed as an experiment in the construction of the larger nine-foot statue. While the smaller model was made in Plastelina, the two larger ones were completed in water clay, which has fine qualities for more detailed modeling. Furthermore, instead of using an armature with an "L" support extending in toward the body, the armatures for the clay studies needed construction to be inside.

Accurate measurements had to be made in the enlarging process, for both scale model and heroic size (Fig. 1). In order to do this, two three-dimensional T-squares proportionate to each study were made, with the right-angle crosspiece that could be moved on the stand or floor. The upright members and the horizontal depth measuring rules were ruled for each model, with all measurements computed to be in scale or appropriate ratio to each other. This served as a three-dimensional grid in which height, width, and depth could be proportionately measured.

The experimental or scale model was developed from the first one, following all the movements and contours of each part of the total figure. Thus there was an endeavor to retain the spontaneity and the attitude that was achieved with the freedom of composing put into the preliminary studies. Particular care was taken in making this scale model so that the heroic size statute would also be vibrant and have the same spirit as that achieved in the first composition. This dynamic spirit needs to be maintained right up to the completion of the work.

Third Model—Heroic Size

In the heroic model the armature was arranged to fit within the completed form of the statue. Wire mesh over wooden supports was used to make the shape, not only of the body, but of the logs at Lincoln's feet as well. All of the construction had to

Fig. 5. Statue near completion; sculptor Fairbanks (left), with sons Justin (left) and Elliott (right) assisting.

be measured and formed one inch smaller than the surface of the clay model in the finished statue which was to be. Figuring this out was an engineering job.

After the final development of the armature, the water clay that had been mixed and prepared was put on in rolls, making first the anatomical construction (Fig. 2); and later adding the clothing and further details (Fig. 3). The heroic statue nearing completion needs an ax to be added (Fig. 4). Finally the character and likeness had to be accomplished.

Sculptor Fairbanks was assisted by sons during the creation of the heroic statue (Fig. 5).

Water clay is preferred by many sculptors because finer detail may be modeled. One reason for a thoroughly constructed armature is the fact that clay does not support itself very well. It is a very difficult problem for the sculptor to keep the clay from falling, particularly in large studies where thousands of pounds of moldable material are hanging and ready to drop at any time.

Another problem is how to keep the clay wet.

Fig. 6. A fence (multiple sections of two-inch-wide tinned sheet metal) is applied to separate sections of the mold.

Soaked cloths may be kept over the study, but these often mar the sculptor's work by rubbing the surface. At present, a new very lightweight plastic cloth that keeps out air is available to prevent drying of the clay. Such a cloth was used to cover the Lincoln study between periods of modeling.

The heroic-size model, twice the height of the half-heroic, contained eight times its bulk. Thus the armature had to be more rigid, to support eight times the amount of clay. Calculations showed that a ton of powdered clay would be used, and the addition of one-third more water would make the

heroic size statue weigh about 3000 pounds. Further adding to this the weight of the armature and the weight of the plaster when casting it, a possible 4000 to 5000 pounds had to be anticipated.

Clay Modeling

Preparing a ton of clay was a considerable undertaking. When it was mixed and made to the right consistency, it was formed into large rolls; these were made into smaller ones, then added piece by piece to the large armature. The body was molded first, then the legs and arms, and finally the head.

Fig. 7. The application of the blue coat of plaster is begun; Avard Fairbanks (upper left), Rex Faust (lower left), Delamar Fairbanks (upper right), and Elliott Fairbanks (lower right).

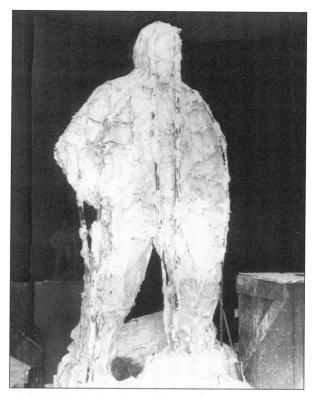

Fig. 8. Reinforcing iron bars add strength.

All the skill and artistic training of the sculptor came into play in this part of the work. The body had to be anatomically correct. Research was necessary to make the costume according to the period. To gain the true spirit and character of Lincoln, research and consultations had to be carried on so that the right impression of the man and the ideals for which he stood could be adequately and correctly portrayed.

Casting in Plaster

After the model was fully developed in the studio and approved, the work was ready to be cast in plaster. It needed to be cast in a hard semipermanent medium so that it could be sent to the bronze foundry. This plaster casting was discussed in an article about *Lincoln The Frontiersman*, entitled "Engineering in Sculpture," and would be repetitious. The same casting process was used. However, a series of diagrams are included with a brief description to help demonstrate the process in stages.

The choice of a *waste mold* limits a sculptor to one cast. It is accurate but time consuming, and seldom used after the last three decades of the 20th

Fig. 9. Anterior mold framework applied. Avard Fairbanks (left), Elliott Fairbanks (center), and Mr. Meunier (right).

Waste Mold diagrams help to demonstrate this process in stages.

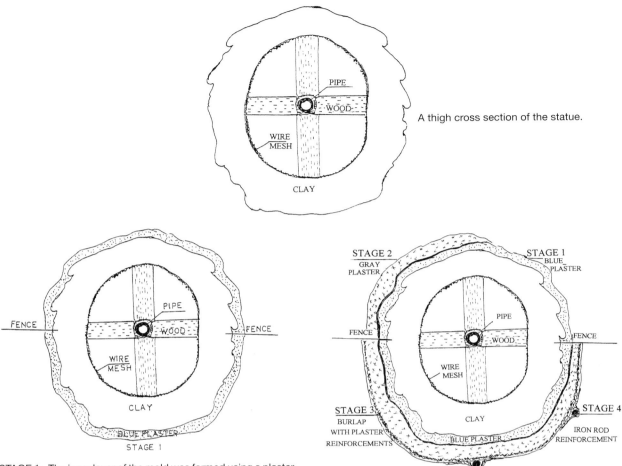

A thigh cross section of the statue.

STAGE 1: The inner layer of the mold was formed using a plaster slurry with bluing added, in three applications (Fig. 7), to serve as a warning when later chipping away plaster.

STAGE 2: Gray plaster was applied by hand on the blue plaster.

STAGE 3: The mold was reinforced with burlap strips dipped in the plaster slurry.

STAGE 4: Reinforcing iron bars added strength (Fig. 8), when held in place with burlap-plaster strips.

STAGE 5: A frame reinforcing was added to the anterior, master mold (Fig. 9). After two days the reinforced plaster has sufficient hardness and strength to be lifted off the model. The fence was also removed. The clay was rapidly excavated and remaining bits were washed out with wet sponges.

STAGE 6: After drying, the blue inner layer was shellacked to seal pores and greased to facilitate separation later from the cast (Fig. 10).

STAGE 7: While the anterior section serving as the master mold was horizontal (Fig. 11), prior to application of plaster, internal reinforcements were formed. White plaster was carefully applied in several layers that fused; re-inforcements were placed, and attached with plaster-saturated burlap strips.

STAGE 8: The anterior section was lifted to a vertical position (Fig. 12), and other sections that have been cast and reinforced were lifted in place. The seams were filled and joined with plaster and reinforced with saturated burlap strips and iron rods.

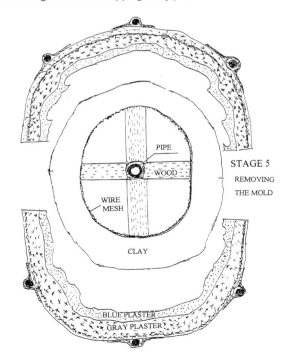

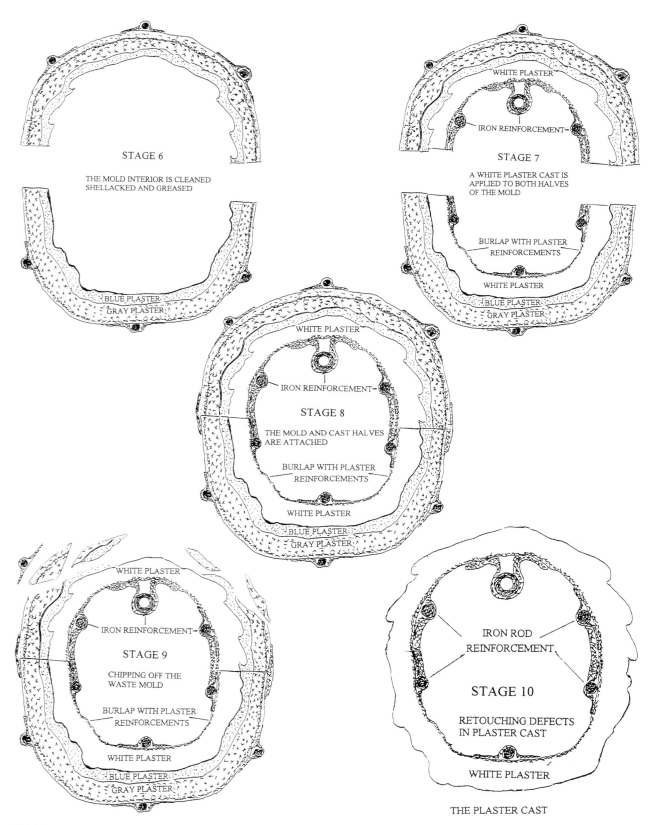

STAGE 6

THE MOLD INTERIOR IS CLEANED
SHELLACKED AND GREASED

STAGE 7

A WHITE PLASTER CAST IS
APPLIED TO BOTH HALVES
OF THE MOLD

WHITE PLASTER

IRON REINFORCEMENT

BURLAP WITH PLASTER
REINFORCEMENTS

WHITE PLASTER

BLUE PLASTER
GRAY PLASTER

BLUE PLASTER
GRAY PLASTER

WHITE PLASTER

IRON REINFORCEMENT

STAGE 8

THE MOLD AND CAST HALVES
ARE ATTACHED

BURLAP WITH PLASTER
REINFORCEMENTS

WHITE PLASTER

BLUE PLASTER
GRAY PLASTER

WHITE PLASTER

IRON REINFORCEMENT

STAGE 9

CHIPPING OFF THE
WASTE MOLD

BURLAP WITH PLASTER
REINFORCEMENTS

WHITE PLASTER

BLUE PLASTER
GRAY PLASTER

IRON ROD
REINFORCEMENT

STAGE 10

RETOUCHING DEFECTS
IN PLASTER CAST

WHITE PLASTER

THE PLASTER CAST

STAGE 9: The initial effort to removing the mold is to cut away the external iron reinforcement. The gray plaster was then boldly chipped off with large chisels (Fig. 13), down to the blue layer of plaster. The blue layer is a warning that the cast is near, and small chisels are used with caution.

STAGE 10: When the last of the mold has been removed (Fig. 14), bubbles and chip marks need to be retouched with plaster. This is also time consuming (Fig. 15), but there is a sense of gratification when the cast appears perfect.

Fig. 10. Elliott Fairbanks fits a section of mold to master mold prior to casting.

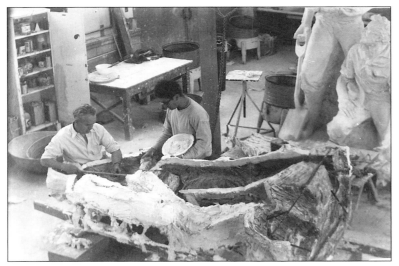

Fig. 11. Avard Fairbanks (left) and son Elliott (right) prepare internal reinforcing.

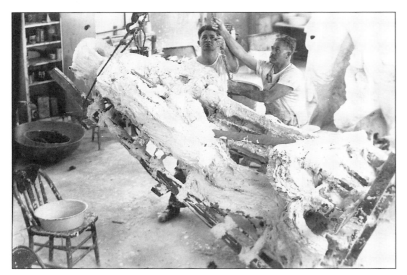

Fig. 12. Cast mold sections are assembled and the mold with cast are lifted to upright position by Elliott Fairbanks (left) and Delamar Fairbanks (right).

century, since new flexible mold technology became practical. When the figure was modeled to the artist's satisfaction, a fence, to separate sections of the mold, was made (Fig. 6), with multiple sections of two-inch-wide tinned sheet metal.

Illustrations are included to demonstrate needed modifications of the waste mold technique. After the plaster cast was retouched, it was sent to the bronze foundry in three sections.

Three models in all had been made, and the last of these—the heroic size—had gone through three processes, the modeling in clay, the waste mold, and the cast, in order to have it in semi-permanent form. The plaster positive was now ready for crating and shipping to the Roman Bronze Foundry in Corona, New York.

The Casting in Bronze

Bronze foundry work is done by men who have spent a lifetime in the particular mechanics of reproducing sculpture in bronze. Two processes for sculpture are generally used, the sand process and the *cire perdue* or lost wax process, the latter meaning that the wax is lost while making the casting. The Lincoln statue was cast by the lost wax process, which renders fine detail.

To get a wax casting, glue (actually a tough gelatin) molds are made from sections of the plaster model. A large statue must be cast in sections of not more than two feet in either dimension, since bronze shrinks unevenly as it cools.

Molten wax is brushed over the surface of the glue molds, then later poured over them repeatedly to build up a uniform layer of wax, much like the buildup of wax when

Fig. 13. Avard Fairbanks (left), Delamar Fairbanks (center), and Elliott Fairbanks remove frame and reinforcement.

Fig. 14. Avard Fairbanks chipping off the waste mold.

Fig. 15. The cast emerges from the waste mold.

Fig. 16. Portrait details of the statue.

dipping candles. This will determine the thickness of the bronze—about 3/8 inch. The glue mold is then removed, and the wax cast reveals the same details as the original clay and the original plaster cast.

Composition material is poured into the hollow or interior of the wax sections to form the core. Nails to support the ceramic mold are next partly driven through the wax into the core on very flat surfaces which can be easily retouched. These nails help to maintain the intended thickness of the space into which heavy molten bronze will soon be poured.

Then on the outside of the wax a composition material called *luto* is applied to form a ceramic investment, creating a firm, heat-resistant mold. This mold is made into a barrel shape. When completed it is placed in a kiln for drying. During the drying, which takes weeks to accomplish, the wax melts out or evaporates as a gas, leaving a 3/8-inch thick image where it was.

The large barrel-shaped composition *luto* mold is then placed in a pit and packed about with special sand and heated to a high heat so that the molten bronze will flow evenly, fill every space, and reproduce all fine details. The molten bronze is then poured into funnel shaped openings at the top of the mold, which are arranged to receive the molten metal.

The numerous sections of the statue follow this same procedure. When the bronze sections have cooled, the *luto* is removed, the nails knocked out, the bronze is welded in spots and retouched (or chased), and finally sections are bronze-welded together.

After seams are retouched, it is sandblasted and has a golden color. It is then ready for the patina or coloring by acids. This is done to give the effect of aging or weathering, which would occur in nature, but which is hastened in the foundry. Men have spent many years in training at this specialty of applying patinas for bronze casting.

As Lincoln was the great spirit who maintained the unity of the North and South in a crisis, it is hoped that his spirit and likeness in bronze may keep alive his great ideals, and be a factor in the constant unity of the East and West, as well as the North and South.

Granite Base

Not only can the statue itself have meaning, but the base may also carry significance. Granite was chosen for the base of the *New Salem Lincoln* because it is solid and sturdy, as was the character of the Emancipator. The particular type of stone called rainbow granite was selected because the rainbow is a symbol of hope for the people of today, as it was in ancient days, and as it was when Lincoln lived at New Salem and formed his hopes for America.

On the upper portion of the pedestal, a band is sandblasted completely around it with an inscription quoting the "Second Inaugural Address,"

"With malice toward none
"With charity for all
"With firmness in the right
"As God gives us to see the right."

On the lower portion, in a smaller but similar band, is the statement that the memorial, which was dedicated on June 21, 1954, was a gift to the State of Illinois by the National Society of the Sons of Utah Pioneers.

These inscriptions express the good will and bond of friendship of the people of the two states, whose history was so closely linked together in the pioneer days of our great nation and who today earnestly seek closer cooperation through the ideals so clearly expressed by one of the sons of Illinois, Abraham Lincoln.

Fairbanks, Avard T., "Making of The Lincoln Statue for New Salem." *Journal of the Illinois State Historical Society,* Summer Issue, 1954. Reprinted by permission.

THE RESOLUTE LINCOLN

By Dr. Louis A. Warren,
Curator of the Lincoln Museum, Lincoln National Foundation, Fort Wayne, Indiana

The major decision of Abraham Lincoln's early life, which changed his entire occupational viewpoint, has been visualized by Avard Fairbanks in a heroic bronze statue which might well be designed *The Resolute Lincoln.* There is no spot offering an environment more appropriately located for the dedication of the statue than New Salem, Illinois, where the momentous question of his future employment confronted him.

The supreme importance of this crisis can best be recreated by the use of Lincoln's own words found in an autobiographical sketch that he had prepared in the third person. After participating in the Black Hawk war and upon returning to New Salem in July 1832… "without means and out of business," apparently he gave himself an aptitude test. He observed:

> "Studied what he should do—thought of learning the blacksmith trade, thought of trying to study law, rather thought he could not succeed at that without a better education."

The perplexing problem which confronted him might be put in this simple form, Blacksmith vs. Blackstone. Was he to continue manual labor to earn his livelihood, or would he venture the more difficult task of preparing himself for a profession? We are happy indeed that in this exigency he chose the more exacting course.

Sculptor Fairbanks has utilized two symbols to illustrate the dilemma in which Lincoln at New Salem found himself when he was but 23 years old—the ax, which Lincoln holds in his left hand and in such a position as if he were about to stand it against a fallen tree, and a large book, which he grasps in his right hand as if he were anxious to delve into its contents. The laying aside of an instrument of manual labor and the acquiring of an analytical volume present almost a perfect visualization of the extremely important decision he was about to make.

Writing in later years about his early occupation, he said, "I was raised to farm work, which I continued until I was 22." He then elaborated on this experience in his third person autobiography as follows:

> "Abraham, though very young, was large for his age (eight years), and had an ax put in his hands at once; and from that 'til his twenty-third year he was almost constantly handling that most useful instrument, less of course in plowing and harvesting seasons."

After making other corrections in a campaign biography of 1860, he left standing, without change, this statement about an important episode at the beginning of his legal apprenticeship.

> "He bought an old copy of Blackstone one day at an auction in Springfield, and on his return to New Salem attacked the work with characteristic energy."

The book which Fairbanks has placed in the hands of Lincoln in the interpretative bronze study is a large one, not a school text of small dimensions, but in form typical of the Blackstone, which, as far as recorded, was the first book directly purchased by Lincoln.

Not only has the sculptor interpreted with appropriate symbols the transition period at New Salem, but in the poise of Lincoln's body one observes the 'characteristic energy,' and in the expression of his face the determination to achieve, which invites one to think of him at New Salem as "The Resolute Lincoln."

Warren, Dr. Louis A., "The Lincoln Statue at New Salem." *Lincoln Lore,* June, 1954: No. 1316, Fort Wayne, Indiana.

THE DEDICATION

By Bryant S. Hinckley

The Sons of the Utah Pioneers have journeyed far to join with you today in these impressive ceremonies. We unite with you and with all America in honoring Illinois' great citizen and one of the greatest leaders of men of all times. Majestic in character and intellect, lofty in purpose, sublime in his faith and forgiveness, Abraham Lincoln stands as the tenderest memory of the ages.

One hundred seventeen years ago Lincoln bade farewell to his neighbors and to this quaint village, as you see it today, and turned his face toward a new world, little knowing where time would take him or the colossal tasks which he would face. As these sculptured features show, his gentle heart was strong and warm, and his faith in the future unfaltering. This man of destiny was on his way to an everlasting place in the affections of the world.

Eighty-nine years have gone since his gentle heart was stilled by an assassin's bullet; and more books have been written about him, more eulogies have been spoken over him, more tributes have been paid to him than any son of American soil.

He was born on the hard edge of the frontier—

"Wouldn't you like to turn time backward and see Lincoln at 12, when he had never worn a pair of boots? …the lank, lean, yellow, hungry boy—hungry for love, hungry for learning—tramping off through the woods 20 miles to borrow a book, and spelling it out, crouched before the glare of the burning logs." *

He had six months in school. It started him in reading, writing, and arithmetic, and that was enough, absolutely enough for a man endowed as he was. No man ever went to the White House better prepared for its tasks and responsibilities than Lincoln. He spoke always with an eloquence that few mortals are ever given to speak. No matter how high his hope or no matter how sanguine his faith in the future, when he left New Salem, he could not have had a premonition of the warmth he would find in the hearts of the people of the world or of the imperishable place given to his words; or of the monuments in granite and marble that would be erected to his memory. No one at that time could have believed how often his form and features would speak to coming generations in bronze, or that his name would go down in history as the tenderest memory of the ages.

•

"God gave to man the rainbow in heavens as a symbol of hope and promise. A statue of Abraham Lincoln in bronze on a base of rainbow granite—the most imperishable materials of the earth—shall be symbolic, for the peoples of the world, of those enduring hopes and promises to be gained through adherence to those guiding principles given by Lincoln."

~ Avard Fairbanks

* Elbert Hubbard

Heroic statue in clay of Abraham Lincoln, campaigning for presidency.

THE CHICAGO LINCOLN
A HEROIC MONUMENT IN BRONZE

*Erected at Ravenwood's Lincoln Square in Chicago North Side
Confluence of Lincoln, Lawrence, and Western Avenue*

THE MAKING OF A LINCOLN STATUE

An address by Avard Fairbanks, Ph.D.

A tall man of the frontier, alone in the world, came to Illinois around a century and a quarter ago. He settled in New Salem. While there he determined upon his career. He saw before him the serving of his fellow men through the process of law and public service.

Near this same time my grandfather came from New England and settled in the largest city of the State of Illinois. It was called Nauvoo the Beautiful. He later moved on to the West with other pioneers.

Two years ago, the Sons of Utah Pioneers erected at New Salem a monument to Abraham Lincoln in the spirit of warmest of friendships from one State to another. The inscription on the base is in Lincoln's own words in the concluding paragraph of his second inaugural address.

Lincoln always has been a tradition in our home, and as an ideal to emulate he was upheld before the growing children. Particular emphasis was stressed that the struggles of a frontier make men strong, courageous, and capable… . Thus through my pioneer background and heritage, I feel a deep kinship to the hopes and ideals of the man we honor today.

We are here gathered to dedicate, in as imperishable material as man can fashion, a bronze portrayal of our beloved Abraham Lincoln. I feel deeply appreciative of the opportunity to have had a part in its development and erection. As a sculptor, when confronted with the responsibility of creating the expression of a great character, one faces many things not generally realized. The work is not just the forming of the cut of the coat, the shaping of a hat, the buttons and wrinkles on the vest, nor the mole on the face, nor the part in the hair. To be sure, all external details one must be aware of… and make correct. The particular proportions of the person, and also mannerisms and costume of the time, need to be utilized. Photographs deserve to be studied, and all available material should to be employed to give the right form.

However, the inner soul and spirit must be known and expressed. These above all else make a work of art live down through the ages. These same qualities which make for character in life give character to art, and we look upon a work of art as some-

thing that lives. One must strive to be closely associated and acquainted with the individual one portrays, the same as one comes to know his most intimate friends… .

It is the work of a creative sculptor to give soul and spirit to form so that it lives on. So here before you is Lincoln campaigning for the presidency of the United States. How appropriate even today.

Can you sense both the anxiety of Lincoln and the nation in his time! Rugged in appearance, profound in his thinking, yet common to all, could he be given the position to serve those he loved and hoped to uplift to the realization of the greater opportunities through government?

Realizing such situations, with what convictions did he give utterance to the thought in the Chicago Speech?

> "Free society is not
> and shall not be a failure."

A sculptor has to project himself into the period of his subject. I made a sketch of Lincoln, which was approved by the commission. We all felt it was the one to use. It faced north and was centered in this plot. Suggestions were given that the statue should face south, as Lincoln's attention at the time was on the South. This idea had merit. It was studied. To design this it became necessary to place the statue at the north apex of the triangular plot. This was worked over and developed.

Then instead of an extended arm, a podium was placed at his right, with his hand firmly gripping the draping cloth. As the work developed it became more vigorous and strong… . The creation of this statue has been a great experience, and I trust I have made it worthy of the man.

Members of your commission… visited my studio to give approvals… I know that they experienced something of outstanding significance. Students and all who have watched this work progress have come close in feelings to Lincoln and to Illinois.

May I state that the statue is but an expression. It is in bronze, but it stands as a testament that in the hearts of free men everywhere the spirit of Lincoln lives on. His greatness and love of freedom, whether reflected in words, in pictures, in stone, or in bronze, are guides to the destinies of a better world.

Liberty, A Magazine of Religious Freedom,
Vol. 53, #1, 1st Quarter 1958, p. 19.

•

One of the enthusiastic promoters of the Lincoln Square monument was Leo Lerner, editor of the *Lerner Chicago Northside Newspapers.* His brother Robert, an associate editor at the time, has written a descriptive narrative of the groundwork and organization that preceded the creation of the monument. It serves as a tribute to the many civic leaders who generously donated both time and money to secure an impressive memorial.

It is included here to demonstrate that all great monuments have an impressive background story that is often not told. The dedication is the culmination of sincere efforts, often with considerable personal sacrifice, by many highly motivated individuals. There have been many committee meetings, research, technical planning, and promotional efforts to insure a significant masterpiece is placed to represent the desires and expression of the people.

Reference Article

LINCOLN MEMORIAL, ONCE A DREAM

How the Statue Became a Reality.
Many Community Leaders Combine Their Efforts to Achieve the Goal.

By Robert Lerner

Abraham Lincoln, destined to become the 16th President of the United States, was born 147 years ago [in 1809].

More than three years ago, on March 10, 1953, the Illinois Memorial Commission had its official birth upon creation by the state legislature.

On this Saturday, October 16, 1956, *The Chicago Lincoln,* Dr. Avard Fairbanks' great Lincoln statue, will be unveiled in Ravenwood's Lincoln Square.

Thus, after three years and seven months of labor and persistence, the dream to have erected on the North Side one of the world's finest statues of Lincoln will be fulfilled. How did this commission get its start? Who were the people responsible for this destined-to-be-famous statuesque addition to Ravenwood's Lincoln Square?

Credit for conceiving the idea for *The Chicago Lincoln* is given without reservation to Alderman John Hoellen. For every statue there is someone who has the idea and someone who persistently campaigns for its becoming a reality. The 47th Ward Alderman was both.

"I had the idea back in 1950," says Hoellen. "I got to thinking about what would really give Lin-coln Square a reputation. What would 'Fountain Square' in Evanston be without a fountain? Can you imagine 'Logan Square' without a statue of General Logan? What about Lincoln Square? I didn't want the main item of attraction in Lincoln Square to be a lamp post, a fire hydrant, or a traffic signal. So I decided that we needed a statue of Abraham Lincoln, the namesake of the square.

"I proposed the idea to the Lincoln Square Chamber of Commerce back in 1951, and from there, with the support of the Chamber and other business and community leaders of the North Side, the idea grew until it became a reality."

On March 10, 1953, House Bill 338, which established the Illinois Lincoln Memorial Commission, was introduced by the then 6th district state representatives, William E. Pollack, Charles H. Weber, and W. Russell Arrington. The bill was passed by the Legislature and was signed by Gov. William G. Stratton. Leo A. Lerner, editor and publisher of the *Chicago North Side Newspapers,* State Senator William G. Knox, and Pollack were appointed to the commission.

On January 21, 1954, the commission elected

Harry Spellbrink, president of the Commercial National Bank, as executive secretary. The commission, at the January meeting, named the following to the advisory committee: Alderman John J. Hoellen, Herbert Heidkamp, George Brumlik, George Pfaff, Edward O. Fahner, Charles Gutsell, Nathan Rattner, Lloyd Miller, Ralph Newman, Michael Lerner, Charles McPartlin, and Frank Jerger, Sr.

It is important to note that during the entire history of the statue, the Lincoln Square Chamber of Commerce has supported the venture to the fullest and has taken a leading part in bringing the project to fulfillment. The Lincoln Square Chamber of Commerce concentrated interest and effort on the building of the Lincoln statue from the moment it was suggested.

Led by Arthur Sallas, general chairman of the statue committee, for months they planned the dedication ceremonies and the publicity for the event. Hoellen proposed his idea for the statue while Herbert Heidkamp, Jr., was president of the chamber. Since then, Nathan Ratner, Charles McPartlin, and Dean Adinamis have "carried the ball" for the statue during their successive terms as chamber leaders. Interest of chamber members is exemplified by the number of them that took an active part. Also included were Charles Gutsell, James Loukas, Harry Spellbrink, George Brumlik, George Pfaff, Clara Bruhn, Arthur Lukas, Edward Fahner, Sam Rosko, Byron Brahos, Fred Fargeson, Seymour Amsel, Don Glassman, Dr. E.J. Callahan, George Rafel, Al Surlin, Myron Gordon, and Frank Jerger, Sr.

Once the commission was authorized and allocated $1000 to choose a site and pick an artist and sculptor, the actual work began. The first thing to do was to choose the site. The triangle formed by the junctions of Lincoln-Lawrence-Western was chosen. This location, for decades known as "Lincoln Square," was regarded as a natural. It was widened to permit erection of the statue.

It was then important for the commission to find an idea for the physical statue. To do this, the commission offered a $1000 prize for the best suggestion. This contest was publicized nationally, and in the community it was promoted by local newspapers, including the *Chicago North Side Newspapers*

and the *Midweek News*. The $1000 was donated by the Lincoln Square Chamber of Commerce.

Hundreds of entries were received. The winner was Lloyd Ostendorf, a young freelance illustrator from Dayton, Ohio. The 34-year-old Ostendorf conceived the idea of a youthful Lincoln, "beardless and strong," the way he appeared in Chicago from 1849 to 1860. After adoption of the Ostendorf suggestion, the Illinois House passed an appropriation bill allowing $35,000 to the commission.

State Representative William E. Pollack, vice-chairman of the Illinois Lincoln Memorial Commission, is conceded to be the number one spark plug that brought *The Chicago Lincoln* into being. His perseverance, not only in the legislature, but on much of his own free time, was the backbone of *The Chicago Lincoln.*

When Alderman John J. Hoellen and the late Herbert Heidkamp, Sr., first got the idea for the statue, they contacted Bill Pollack. The legislator carried the ball for them. He introduced both bills in the state legislature: the bill to establish the Commission, and the appropriations bill. Bill Pollack took many a trip to Springfield on behalf of the commission. Pollack later went to Salt Lake City to check on the statue's progress. Bill Pollack did immense amounts of paperwork, telephoning, and letter writing. His office was the office of the Commission. In short, Representative Pollack was the workhorse of the Illinois Lincoln Memorial Commission.

The bill was drafted by Representatives Pollack, Elroy Sandquist, and Erwin Martay. The cash grant was approved unanimously after the appropriations committee met with Charles McPartlin, Sam Rosko, Arthur Lucas, and George Pfaff, Lincoln Square merchants. The house committee voted, 29-0, to support the bill. It was then passed unanimously on the floor of the House. On July 1, 1955, the Senate voted, 38:5, in favor of the appropriation.

Without the Governor's personal aid, *The Chicago Lincoln* wouldn't exist. Illinois Governor William G. Stratton backed the campaign for *The Chicago Lincoln* to the hilt. Many other statue bills have been pending before the legislature in the past five years, and many were sidetracked, at Stratton's insistence, so that *The Chicago Lincoln* could be erected.

Stratton's interest in the statue is shown by the speed in which legislation for the statue was passed. Ordinarily a bill to establish a committee like The Lincoln Memorial Commission would lie dormant in committee for many months. However, Stratton's personal interest in the erection of the statue assisted in its early passage. Even though the Lincoln statue idea is five years old and the commission only three, the commission was established at the very onset of the first legislative session at which it was proposed.

All during the activities of the commission, and through the appropriation of funds for the statue, Stratton was the key man. When commission members made their trips to Springfield, the governor himself was their host.

With the appropriation from the state legislature, the commission was set to locate a sculptor who would do the job. They chose Dr. Avard Fairbanks, professor of arts and humanities at the University of Utah in Salt Lake City.

In the summer of 1956, when the statue was nearing completion, the Chamber of Commerce stepped in to perform its valuable functions publicizing the event. Not satisfied with simply promoting through these regular channels, they made special arrangements for city-wide publicity, via the mediums of radio and television and newspapers. The chamber, with the assistance of Alderman Hoellen, and with cooperation with city, park district, and police officials, planned the parking facilities and rerouting of traffic for the unveiling.

As the date of the unveiling grew closer, the city began its work—the removal of public utilities that would obstruct the construction of the statue.

Included in the work of the commission were frequent meetings, often only weeks apart, from 1953 'til now (1956). They also made a trip to Salt Lake City to check upon Fairbanks' progress with the statue.

The original plan for the statue, calling for Lincoln's right arm to be extended, palm upturned, was altered, and the position of Lincoln's right hand was changed to rest on a podium.

Commissioner of Streets and Sanitation Lloyd Johnson played an important part in the prepara-

tion of the triangle at Lincoln Square for installation of the Lincoln statue. His department moved three traffic signals and one 'electrical vault,' an underground coordinator of lighting activity, to a different location. This was necessary so that the *The Chicago Lincoln* could be put in place. There was much to be done.

Chicago is a city 'underground.' Under most intersections are sewers, electrical wiring, and traffic controls. To build on these intersections means the relocation of these public utilities, a job that requires a great deal of effort. To move traffic signals is a tedious job. The signals have to be relocated, rewired, and then tested often to make sure that the lights are working in the proper order.

To further complicate things, they could only work at the same time the state architect's office widened the street. Both departments, municipal and state, worked together smoothly and had the job finished in two days.

Special recognition goes to Chicago's Mayor Richard J. Daley, one of the project's biggest boosters. When funds for the project were low and money was needed to remove electrical conduits from underneath the triangle at Lincoln-Lawrence-Western, the Mayor made a special attempt to get money for the job. Finally, after using every available means, he convinced the Department of Public Works to use its funds for the project. Since its inception, the statue has benefited from his support. More than once he used his authority to get things ready with haste so that the dedication would not be delayed.

It was at Daley's urging that the triangle was widened four feet into Western Avenue. With many departments of the city having something to do with the statue, it was extremely helpful to have the Mayor's interest and to have him assist in coordinating the efforts of the departments.

Credit for the *The Chicago Lincoln* statue idea must be given to many people. Its completion was with the cooperation of many others.

Lerner, Robert. "Lincoln Memorial Once a Dream, How Statue Became a Reality." *Lerner Chicago North Side Newspapers,* Week of October 14, 1956: Sec. 2, p. 2.

THE CHICAGO LINCOLN: A CHANCE TO PORTRAY LIBERTY

By Avard Fairbanks

Lincoln has become so universally admired and accepted by all people of all nations as the symbol of FREEDOM that a monument to him evokes our profound veneration and strikes a responsive chord from all liberty-loving people everywhere.

To make a statue of this great character and to erect it in that part of the country which gave him his early development and growth into public life is an honor; and to be selected by a commission of the great state of Illinois is indeed an opportunity for a sculptor. Of course, such recognition brings forth from an artist the very utmost in creative efforts and his technical skills.

In giving utterance to a sculptor's inner reactions and the impressions of his mind as he works upon such a project, one must say that the challenge is awe-inspiring. It captures the very heights of imagination and causes one to want to prove his capabilities, which he has spent his life's efforts in developing. And such a realization comes in the heroic portrayal in bronze of Abraham Lincoln in Illinois.

The Ideals and Significance of a Monument in General

No masterful work in sculpture is ever developed without one's total efforts and intense feelings being completely involved in a presentation of a great historical character, whether it be a Moses of Ancient Israel, a Lycurgus of Greece, a Joan of Arc of France, or a Lincoln of America. The spirit of a nation which such a person assists in building, and the hopes, the ideals and aspirations of a people whom he or she served need to be sensed and compressed into a moment of action of one figure.

Thus the pose and the attitude of the total composition must express an expanse of time and vibrate to the sympathetic reactions of millions of people who will capture in a moment's glance the beliefs, the hopes, and all those finer impulses to heroic deeds and actions which elevate our cultural objectives for a finer civilization, to be the inspiration of all mankind.

All great works of art are universal. In becoming known they traverse all boundaries, and their influences are not confined to a particular locality. Nevertheless, as the human spirit finds its expression through a particular individual, likewise a spirit in finding its self-expression in permanent materials of bronze or stone deserves to be focalized and is located so that it may have place and standing in our world.

Lincoln Square in Chicago, as a location on an intersection of main thoroughfares in the City of Chicago (one avenue being named to honor Lincoln), was an appropriate setting for something heroic.

Here, in an area known as Lincoln Square, the thought had developed that there was an opportunity, by erecting a monument at this site, to give recognition to one of the World's Champions of Freedom. What an opportunity, particularly in these times of uncertainty, to arouse people to the consciousness of Lincoln's efforts, his struggles, and what he left to us as a heritage! He loved all the people and was concerned with their uplift and well-being. Truly he was a character deserving of a heroic stature in every way, physically and mentally. Now, such qualities are to be made evident in a statue.

Lincoln of Heroic Stature

This personage of lowly and humble nature, but exalted in spiritual and mental capabilities, has the qualities to make the rocks of the hills to breathe in unison with his lofty purposes. So with the granite mountains of the Black Hills of South Dakota, Mount Rushmore, sculptured by Gutzon Borglum—they do this. The marble from Georgia in the colossal seated figure of Lincoln carved by Daniel Chester French, which is centralized in the edifice known as the *Lincoln Memorial* in Washington, DC, also has such powers. This international shrine has an all-pervading influence over the capitol city of our country. It causes fellow countrymen to stand in awe and reverence. Statesmen and lowly immigrants from all nations may also stand in awe and reverence. In the presence of this masterpiece, one feels in accord and can almost sense the reverberations of harmonious soul-gripping emanations from the great emancipator.

Even the metals from the depth of the earth are caused to fuse into formal rhythms and speak out the never-ending messages which are echoed in our minds as we behold our brave and trusted friend and brother. And this we shall sense in the heroic bronze, *The Chicago Lincoln*.

In beholding a Lincoln of the campaign period, all our own as well as those experiences of Lincoln will respond. We will sense the uncertainty of successes or failures, and the struggles, the hopes, and the obligations to accomplish worthy goals, particularly those for public benefits, devoid of selfish desires and interests.

To feel the magnitude of Lincoln's aspiring to the position of President, one has to sense the struggles and the possible reactions that Lincoln might have felt, and also how his whole being might have been tense to the situation.

In Lincoln there was the problem—did he have the backing, the strength, and the courage to meet the situation of whether a people might succeed in being united, or fail? To him, this was no question. National leaders realized that in Lincoln there was the answer. And the people arose to elect him and likewise to share their strength and courage in the great cause that succeeded.

In campaigning for the highest position of the land—which we present Lincoln as doing—what anxiety must have been deep in his inner consciousness. Rugged in appearance, profound in his thinking, yet common to all, could he be given the position to serve those he loved and hoped to uplift to the realization of the greater opportunities through government? Could he bring about those ideals he envisioned and for which he stood with firmness? Could our nation continue facing the crisis confronting it in this period of its growth as a world influence?

Realizing such situations, with what convictions did he give utterance to the thought in the Chicago Speech? "Free Society is not and shall not be a failure." The "House Divided Against Itself" address and other determining messages of the times were all awaiting the opportunity to be voiced and become documents of universal import.

The Sculptor's Background and Traditions

Because I am of pioneer descent and have experienced the frontier during my own childhood, the traditions of Lincoln have been very much a part of my early training. They have given me a sense of close relationship to that American frontier youth—one as rough-hewn as the trees he felled or the rails he split for his fellowmen's use, but also some dreams for the improvement of conditions for his fellow beings.

Also in the depths of his thinking and understandings, he had a culture well developed in 'the humanities' (courses in these subjects are now being stressed in universities). Stories of him and his dealings with his neighbors and those in close associations with him have always been guides and inspirations in my life. And, as in my own attitudes and ambitions, I can see that youth everywhere takes renewed courage in the example of the simple life of a lonesome boy of the pioneer lands whose future was one of self-determination against many odds. Though he might have been placed in situations to seek personal gain in the developing new country of the West, still the concern for his fellowmen he always placed above his own acquisitions. Youths in every country see in Lincoln ideals for their own lives. In him they find the great character for emulation.

The foregoing and many other considerations need to be sensed as a sculptor endeavors to characterize them in a statue worthy of the man. All the ideas, the ideals, and the meaning embodied in a work of art are called the content. To these must be given the expression through technical skills. In such a project the creator of the monument senses the obligation that the study through which expression is to come must stand the test of the ages, along with the individual he portrays.

In the book *History of Esthetics* by Katharine Everett Gilbert and Helmut Kuhn, they state:

> "There is an element of making in all artistic creation. Out of the communion of impulse and thought arises the intelligent action which alone is able to bestow perfection on the work. Therefore esthetic thought is an element of the creative life, and the thinker shares the burden of responsibility for what happens in practice."

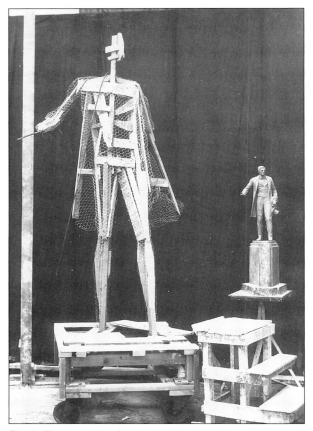

Fig. 1. The armature of wood and wire mesh.

Fig. 2. The heroic figure was modeled in clay with anatomical construction.

Therefore the composer of an important artistic creation, when taking on the production and erection of a masterful and heroic bronze in a monumental work of art, gives to it intelligent action and bestows perfection upon the work. With the people who are influenced by it and are aware of its significance in our civilization and also our cultural heritage, the sculptor shares the burden of great responsibility; namely, whatever happens in practice becomes uplifting and inspiring.

A true work of art is the accumulation of the hopes of many. Such was a situation in Chicago. When the Abraham Lincoln Memorial Commission of the state of Illinois called me into conference with it; of course, I felt that a great opportunity and responsibility confronted me.

Though a work may be heroic in size in its final stage, still the beginnings are small. A sketch was made, then many others in drawings and in clay, and still others until something of the spirit and action I was hoping to achieve seemed to evolve. When a study seems to strike the sympathetic chord

or feeling sense, then it is worked upon and developed.

Later a small model was made in the full round in clay. This was improved, adjusted, arranged, and rearranged. In order that it may stand up of itself, the clay was put upon a wire framework called an armature. A ridged iron rod was bent in an appropriate shape to support the aluminum wires.

[Author's Note: The armature was described in the preparation of *Lincoln The Frontiersman* and will not be repeated here.]

The future of a masterpiece is dependent upon the formation of constructions with purposeful intent. The beginnings were earnest and replete with great responsibilities.

The space at the intersection of three avenues—Western, Lincoln, and Lawrence—forms a triangle in which the statue was to be erected. The problem of adjusting this study to the location required the designing of a base and pedestal with its contours in keeping with the triangle shape of the plot. Thus

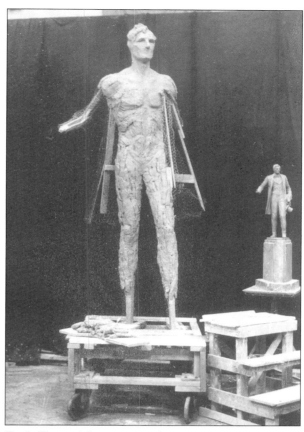

Fig. 3. The modeling progressed.

Fig. 4. The progress continued. Additional modeling is evident.

the granite base stone, the die stone, and statue were so designed with a curvilinear, convex, equilateral triangle form to harmonize with the space. The commission approved this coordinated design.

With all items progressing well, approvals made and model design acceptable, the small model, developed to scale, became the working model for the final one. When it was enlarged, many details and solutions to technical problems needed to be repeated.

The heroic size is larger than life, and in the Chicago statue is 1-1/4 of Lincoln's own proportions. The work was done in moist clay. (It is rather strange that the clay comes from Illinois and is the same clay used to form the Lycurgus statue, the founder of constitutional government in the 9th Century BC, and the forerunner of Hellenic Laws and peoples' liberties.)

It is an impossibility to build up moist clay upon wires and irons as on the small model. The heroic size has to be made with an internal support that conforms with all the shape of the large model even

before it is made. It is built with metal or wooden framework; various structures are made to conform to the shape and contours of every detail that has been developed in the 'working model.' These need to be accurate in their measurements.

After the sculptor makes the wooden structure, wire netting is placed and formed into the shape, which is to hold the clay. This wire netting is measured so that its surfaces come to within an inch or 1-1/2 inch of the finished surfaces to be made. This is really a very demanding and complicated process, and were it not for the small working model scaling it to the heroic size, such could not easily be accomplished.

With the wire netting being secured to the supporting structure, the total is called the armature or the framework (Fig. 1). Upon this armature then the sculptor begins to add the clay. The putting on of this material is done with the consideration of the movement of the body and with regard for the structural forms of a person's being, such structures as bone and muscles (Fig. 2).

Fig. 5. The modeling advanced with more details.

The figure was built up anatomically, and as the sculptor feels that there is a proper proportion and good action to the bodily form, further details are applied (Fig. 3). Clothing and articles were added afterwards, conforming to body contours (Fig. 4).

The work thus proceeds to the extremities and accessories, as formed in the small model. These details have to be constructed in the large armature from its beginning. They cannot be added afterwards. The work continues in a methodical manner towards the completion (Fig. 5).

Even in the large and heroic size, the work is sketched in a rugged manner. During the application of the clay, the sculptor stresses correct proportions, the importance of giving rhythms, lines, and movement to render action of the figure. Under the hand of one with technical skill, all items added to a work become a part of the total composition, including its meaning and significance. Thus they are all necessary elements of the design.

In accordance with the approved suggestions and models and during the production of the heroic size model, Mr. Ralph Newman, an eminent Lincoln authority in Chicago and owner of the Abraham Lincoln Book Shop, gave information that

another statue existed with an arm in a similar position. A sculptor creating an original composition strives to produce a work which is without precedent. I knew nothing about and had never seen the other statue. However, I felt that it would be better to alter the composition, even though it was already approved.

In a review of numerous photographs of Lincoln during the presidential campaign period, he was frequently shown with a pedestal or podium to his side, and upon it were placed books or papers. An addition of a podium to the composition gave an opportunity for some stronger and more sweeping lines. This allowed a new balanced feature that added coherence to the total effect, particularly with the draperies placed over the podium. Lincoln could grasp these in his hand, which added power and strength to the work.

As the heroic size study was in the process of change, new photographs were made and sent to the commission in Chicago for approval. The widening of the statue study required the widening of the statue base, and this required the widening of the granite base. New designs had to be made. Together with the relocation of all of these items on the plot, they occurred right in the midst of the progress on the large study. Nevertheless, total readjustments were worked out and approved, and the work continued. The alterations have come to be very effective improvements, and a more impressive monument will be the result.

Not only did these suggestions on the Lincoln pose render improvement, but other comments came forth. Interested citizens who heard that the statue and base were designed so that the Lincoln, as placed in the triangle, would be facing North, voiced further criticisms. They said that Lincoln's political endeavors required his attention to the South. This idea was symbolic in its meaning and quite apart from the requirements of the location, which were planned in accordance with the shape of the area. The monument was designed to be centered in the triangular plot.

The sculptor, however, has always worked with the theory that people voice their comments because they feel there is merit in what they have to offer. He then took under advisement the possibility of these changes and the values in the Lincoln statue

Fig. 6. The completed statue modeled in clay was approved by the committee from Chicago. Avard Fairbanks and Mrs. Maude Fairbanks (upper left); Mike Lerner, Committee Technical Assistant (light suit); and Leo Lerner, Chairman of the Commission (lower left). At right are Dr. Homer Durham, Vice President, Univ. of Utah; Mr. John Hollen, Alderman City of Chicago (dark suit); and Mr Paul Hodson, Assistant to the President, Univ. of Utah.

facing in the southern direction. The more it was given consideration, the more it was felt that those who had offered suggestions had ideas worthy of utilizing in a new design.

The ensuing consideration necessitated a complete reversal of location of the statue. It could be placed on the northern apex of the triangle. This was a worthwhile solution. Lincoln in facing south could also face the open area. There was a need for people to have an opportunity to contemplate the statue, and there would be many photographs taken of it; if they were to be taken with the statue in the center of the plot, the people would need to be out into the route of traffic. Nor could they even get a view for contemplation without having to be there.

The placing of Lincoln at the end of the triangle made it less hazardous. It also made the design less formal. Lincoln, himself, in his character was less formal and more informal, so that this item added values to the alteration. All these considerations were worked over and the proposition submitted to the commission. It was disturbing at first because the plans had been confirmed, and now a reconsideration of the total memorial was required.

Fig. 7. The application of the piece mold was started in sections.

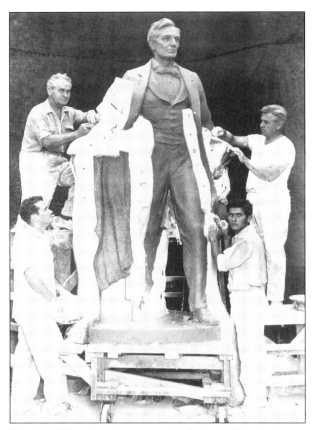

Fig. 8. Additional sections were added. Avard Fairbanks (upper left), Justin Fairbanks (lower left), Jonathan Fairbanks (lower right), and caster Clarence Curtis (upper right).

The commission gave careful deliberation to the new suggestions, and after weighing the former plans along with the new ones, the latter were approved, and the work toward development was resumed.

The sculptor, after much diligent work, completed the large-size, 1-1/3-life-size model in clay. The commission was notified and representatives came to the studio of the sculptor to give final approvals (Fig. 6).

A Chicago newspaper's comments on the approvals gave statements as follows. The front-page headline read: "Lincoln Committee Thrilled at Mighty Emancipator Statue."

The news article continued: "One of the greatest Abraham Lincoln statues will be in existence." The three committeemen agreed the Lincoln statue approaches perfection in the arts. "Illinois will be proud of the representation of its great son."

Casting the Statue in Plaster

Approvals do not constitute the climax of a great story in a sculptor's studio. The work must be transformed into the permanent statue. Plaster is semipermanent and a transitory medium, one also that can be handled and shipped. (The clay cannot be moved from the studio without falling apart.)

Various casting processes can be employed, namely a waste mold, a flexible glue (tough gelatin) mold, or a piece mold.

[Author's Note: More recent technical advances include flexible molds of rubber or silicone.]

When creating *Lincoln The Frontiersman* for Ewa, Hawaii, and the Lincoln statue for New Salem, Illinois, waste molds were used. Glue (gelatin) molds are difficult in the studio on large size statues.

Unlike the other Lincoln statues, *The Chicago Lincoln* statue was cast with a multiple piece mold (Fig. 7). This involves more time and details creat-

Fig. 9. Statue seen from behind with additional sections of mold. Avard Fairbanks (upper left) and caster Clarence Curtis (left), son Grant Fairbanks and daughter Maria Fairbanks (right).

Fig. 10. Additional sections have been added to the piece mold. Clarence Curtis (upper left), Avard Fairbanks and student Don Cramer (lower left), David Fairbanks (upper right), Grant Fairbanks (middle right), and Justin Fairbanks (lower right).

ing the mold, but saves considerable time and effort by not needing to chip off the mold from the cast. Another advantage was that more than one cast can be made from the mold. The description and illustrations are included to demonstrate another technique of casting (see next two pages for illustrations of this process).

In describing this work, the sculptor must keep in mind that the model was a positive. From it a mold was made, which was a negative. From this mold a casting was made, which was a positive and a replica. Fortunately, a skilled caster was available who had considerable experience with this more complicated mold.

Sections had to be arranged so that certain parts of the mold would draw or release from the model without binding in recesses or undercuts. It was a time-consuming and tedious work. Aluminum shims were cut and pressed into the clay edgewise, creating a fence to arrange the separations. Small

sections were made first to eliminate the undercuts. Larger sections were then planned and separating shims were added.

The entire mold was made of plaster. Casting plaster comes in a powder form, and it is mixed with water to a creamy consistency. The plaster slurry hardens in about 20 minutes. This slurry was applied to the model first with several thin coats. Additional coats were reinforced with plaster-saturated burlap until a thickness of one inch or more was accumulated; each section was made separately (Fig. 8).

More than a ton of plaster was used for this mold-making. Almost 70 sections in all were made, and of these, nearly 50 sections were needed for the anterior half (Figs. 9, 10).

After smoothing the surfaces of the small piece molds in place, indents like small cups were carved to act as keys to insure accurate fit when the mold was to be reassembled. The small sections were

A Piece Mold

The Chicago Lincoln was cast with a piece mold that would allow more than one plaster cast to be made with the mold. A series of diagrams is included for the reader to better understand this casting process.

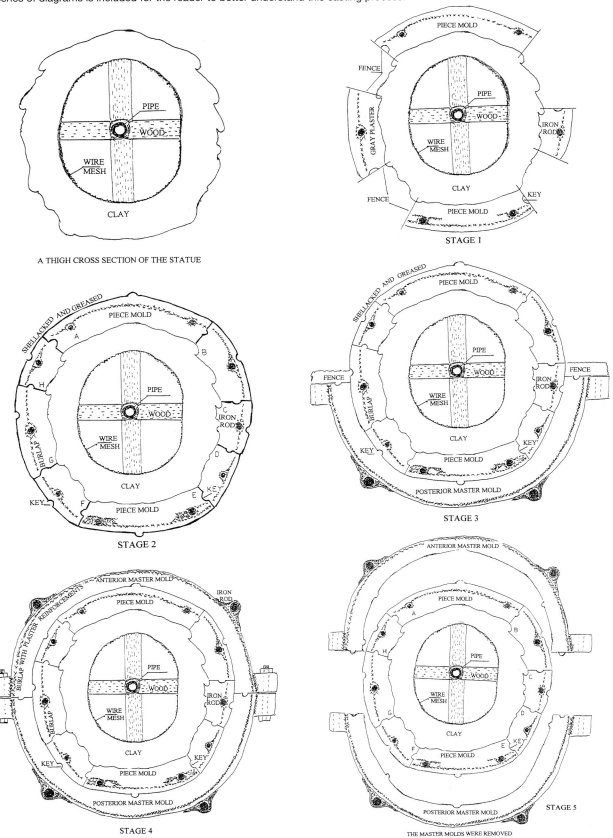

A THIGH CROSS SECTION OF THE STATUE

STAGE 1

STAGE 2

STAGE 3

STAGE 4

STAGE 5

THE MASTER MOLDS WERE REMOVED

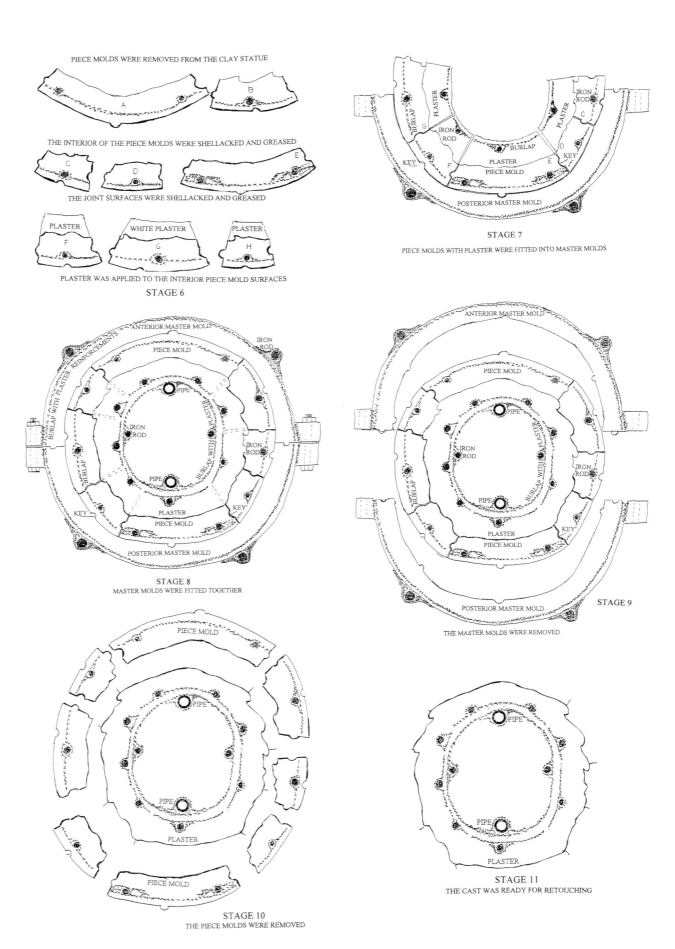

PIECE MOLDS WERE REMOVED FROM THE CLAY STATUE

THE INTERIOR OF THE PIECE MOLDS WERE SHELLACKED AND GREASED

THE JOINT SURFACES WERE SHELLACKED AND GREASED

PLASTER WAS APPLIED TO THE INTERIOR PIECE MOLD SURFACES

STAGE 6

STAGE 7
PIECE MOLDS WITH PLASTER WERE FITTED INTO MASTER MOLDS

STAGE 8
MASTER MOLDS WERE FITTED TOGETHER

STAGE 9
THE MASTER MOLDS WERE REMOVED

STAGE 10
THE PIECE MOLDS WERE REMOVED

STAGE 11
THE CAST WAS READY FOR RETOUCHING

67

Fig. 11. The anterior master mold was cast over piece mold sections. Avard Fairbanks (top left) and sons Jonathan Fairbanks (right) and Justin Fairbanks (left).

Fig. 12. Reinforcing irons were applied to the anterior master mold. Avard Fairbanks (top left) and sons Jonathan Fairbanks (left) and Justin Fairbanks (right).

made smooth on the outer surfaces, except for button-shaped nubs or keys for accurate fitting.

The surface was shellacked and greased prior to applying plaster for the exterior or master section of the mold. The front master mold section was formed on the outside of all of the smaller sections. It contained and supported all those within it (Fig. 11).

The master section was further well-reinforced and braced by irons and pipe (Fig. 12). On the outside a heavy wooden framework was arranged for stability (Fig. 13). A similar process was then used on the back of the statue, excepting that the back master mold was divided into about seven or eight horizontal pieces. There were fewer recesses and undercuts. This was also convenient for filling the mold from the back, step by step from the base up to the head. The master mold sections were first removed by help of a chain hoist.

The removal of the mold from the clay model was very strenuous, requiring a small derrick, with a block and tackle, and other mechanical devices. The plaster adheres firmly to the clay. It is also very tedious to avoid damage, and each section has to be handled with great care.

The clay study remained intact as the molds were drawn away from the model (Fig. 14). Each section had to be carefully cleaned of all excess clay. No line or shape should be marred in any way. The surfaces of all pieces and borders were allowed to dry and were thoroughly shellacked and lubricated. This gave an increased surface hardness to each section and sealed the porous plaster. They were fitted, numbered, and refitted into the master sections many times, for trials and to prove good fitting before the final placement for casting.

Since the front section of the master mold is very large and is difficult to handle for casting, it was

Fig. 13. The frame reinforcement was applied to the anterior master mold; Avard Fairbanks (top left), Jonathan Fairbanks and Grant Fairbanks (left), caster Clarence Curtis (top right), and Justin Fairbanks (right).

Fig. 14. The anterior master mold and several sections of piece mold were removed.

laid down horizontal with the hollow side facing up. Each piece-mold section was then carefully arranged into position.

A medium to assist separation of the mold sections and the mold from the intended cast was applied. It consisted of a mixture of stearic acid and kerosene. After a generous application, it was then brushed clean, so as not to leave any excess material in the mold that might alter the surface or diminish the detail.

Liquid plaster slurry was then applied to the mold sections laid in place in the master mold. The plaster slurry was applied, creating layers until the coating of about 1/4-inch surface accumulated.

Again strips of burlap saturated with liquid plaster were added to give reinforcement. Iron rods were added and tied in by burlap and plaster reinforcing. After the front sections were filled with plaster and fiber reinforcing to about one-inch thick, the

back sections were added (Fig. 15). The fitting together of the mold surfaces of these sections was done as previously described for the large front section.

The front half of the mold and cast was raised by a block and tackle to a vertical position. The posterior base section was added first. Of course, there was an unplastered strip in between the castings of the front and the back molds. Liquid plaster was added by brush and by hand to these chinks, first with plaster mix and later with burlap soaked in plaster slurry for reinforcement across the joints to hold sections together. The plaster casting inside the section molds were united, by these means, progressively into one piece.

The second back section to be added was the one next above the base section. These were first filled, reinforced, and then fit onto the front and base sections in the same manner. Each plaster casting's

Fig. 15. Cast sections of piece mold were fitted into the horizontal anterior master mold. Left to right are David Fairbanks, Avard Fairbanks, Grant Fairbanks, Elliott Fairbanks, and Justin Fairbanks.

sections (inside of the sections of the mold) were united in this manner, eventually creating a cast of the statue in one large piece.

Each back section placed vertically was about one foot to 18 inches high. From side to side they varied as their edges fit to the front master mold width. One was filled, then added to the front master section, and sealed. The next was filled and made ready for fitting. This continued until all sections were added, one stacked against, and on top of, the next section below.

Removing the Mold

When the mold was completely filled, with the casting inside, and allowed to harden about two days, the mold sections were removed one by one, very cautiously. The first to be removed were sections of the master mold. This work required the utmost care so as not to chip or break away any part of the casting. With all sections removed, the casting in white plaster came out of the mold complete as it was in the clay. The head was cast separately in a similar manner and later fitted in place.

The Finished Casting

Where each section fitted against another a thin line, or mold seam, called a fin, was left. This was retouched away, cutting with steel modeling tools. The plaster casting was then finished (Fig. 15). For ease in shipping to the bronze foundry, the statue was separated into sections. These were crated separately and sent as a group.

[Author's Note: Since the bronze casting was performed in the same manner at the bronze foundry as outlined in the description of the procedures in the Lincoln statue for New Salem Village, Dr. Fairbanks' description will therefore be omitted from this monument's description.]

The chosen material, Rainbow Granite, for the stone base of *The Chicago Lincoln* was a type of Minnesota granite. The sculptor selected this particular granite because of its significance and meaning. In ancient times the rainbow was a symbol given to Noah as a promise of hope, peace, and new opportunities in the world.

After the great crisis of Lincoln's time, he suffered death as a martyr. This recalls his letter to Mrs. Bixby, in which he said, "The solemn pride that must be yours to have laid so costly a sacrifice upon the altar of Freedom."

In sorrow our nation took on hope and a new life in its determination to fulfill the ideals of being united to work for human good. Lincoln also wrote, "From these honored dead we take increased devotion to that cause."

As then, so it is now; we still look to his great leadership and to the 'Rainbow of Hope' for a new and better life after deluges. These need not be floods of water. For destructive influences that are overbearing may become deluges. Whether they are by force of arms, adverse ideologies, subversive influences, intrigues, or other forces that threaten to engulf the world and deprive man of human liberties, they may be considered deluges. We strive for strength to brave these storms.

The spirit of Lincoln in immortal bronze and placed upon a 'Rainbow' granite pedestal is inscribed with his quotation, "Free Society Is Not and Shall Not Be A Failure." It will be a constant testament to the world of his greatness and his faith in humanity (Fig. 17).

Fig. 16. Portrait bust details.

"Why shouldn't there be a patient confidence in the ultimate justice of the people?" All who look to Lincoln take renewed courage in knowing that his intellectual direction still lives on to guide the destinies of free men everywhere. This spirit, in all its vigor, is embodied in a masterful study *The Chicago Lincoln*.

The import of his messages to all mankind, the meaning of the metal of his figure, together with the significance of the foundation upon which they are based, shall stand forth as imperishable as bronze, as solid as granite, and as secure as GOD'S PROMISES.

Adapted from: Fairbanks, Avard T., *Lerner Chicago North Side Newspapers,* week of October 14, 1956: p. 8. Reprinted with permission.

Fig. 17. The heroic bronze statue of Lincoln was erected on a rainbow granite pedestal with an inscription, "Free Society Is Not And Shall Not Be A Failure." It was located in Ravenwood's Lincoln Square, at the confluence of Lincoln, Lawrence, and Western Avenues, Chicago, North Side. (Photo by The Lewellyn Studio, Chicago.)

Avard Fairbanks modeling the finishing details on *Lincoln The Friendly Neighbor.*

LINCOLN THE FRIENDLY NEIGHBOR
A Heroic Monument in Bronze
Erected at The Lincoln Federal Savings and Loan Association, Berwyn, Illinois

"The better part of one's Life consists of his Friendships." Abraham Lincoln wrote these words in a letter to Judge Gillespie.

Inscribed at the base of this monument is the quotation from our sixteenth president, which emphasized his warm interest in the life of the community and especially the children of the community.

Frank Kinst, a student of Lincoln lore and president of The Lincoln Federal Savings and Loan Association of Berwyn, Illinois, wanted to make his bank one of the suburban showplaces. A new bank building was planned with attractive modern architecture. Several years previously he had arranged for The Lincoln Federal Savings and Loan Association, a banking company, to commission Avard

Fig. 2. A 2/3-life-size statue is modeled to refine details for the heroic statue whose armature has been started.

Fairbanks to create a colossal portrait in marble. It stands in the lobby of the bank now, entitled *The Enduring Lincoln*.

However, Mr. Kinst, a member of the Civil War Round Table, was still intent on improving the community of Berwyn. He decided that a large statue of Lincoln was something the whole town could admire with pride. He contacted Dr. Fairbanks, since he knew the sculptor had already completed three major Lincoln statues. Ralph G. Newman, proprietor of the Abraham Lincoln Bookstore in Chicago, was called in as consultant. Together they helped, by idea and suggestion, as the working model developed under the sculptor's masterful hands.

Years ago humorist Ogden Nash said, "Bankers are just like everybody else, only richer." Banker Frank Kinst was having a lot of fun proving that "Bankers are just like everyone else, only a little more civic-minded." One might even say a lot more civic-minded in his case. Besides duties at the bank, he has served as a member of the Board of Trustees of Lincoln College, The Civil War Round Table, and The Illinois Historical Society. He served on Berwyn, Yorkfield, and Elmhurst district school boards. He has membership in the Berwyn Kiwanis, Elks, Moose, and Yorkshire Woods Association. He has been active in Boy Scout work. His promotion of a Lincoln monument was another manifestation of being "a little more civic-minded." He has in fact taken many of the attributes of Lincoln to heart.

Fig. 3. Avard Fairbanks (left) and sons Justin Fairbanks (right) and Jonathan Fairbanks (right front) model finishing details.

The Board of Directors of The Lincoln Federal Savings and Loan Association concurred that as a tribute to their namesake they would erect this statue. They wanted to create a landmark that would symbolize the dedication of the Association to the life and principles of Illinois' greatest son. They also felt that a statue of Lincoln as a friendly neighbor would best reflect their own attitude and spirit of the community.

After the small model was approved, the commission was granted and preliminary work on the large statue was begun in the studio at the University of Utah. A second and larger model, 2/3-life size, with more detail was made (Figs. 1, 2).

The creation of a heroic monument takes many days, and progress on the large heroic statue continued (Fig. 3). After the heroic statue had been accepted by the committee and sculptor Fairbanks decided the modeling was complete, preparations for casting were begun. A cast was made in plaster when the modeling was finished on the 2/3-life-size model. This casting was accomplished with a waste mold in a manner similar to that described in the article entitled "Engineering in Sculpture," for *Lincoln The Frontiersman*.

The cast was shipped to the Roman Bronze Foundry in Corona, Long Island, New York. The creation of this statue took two years to complete. The final monument stands 13 feet high. The granite base is three-feet, ten-inches tall, and weighs

13-1/2 tons. It was placed on the lawn in front of The Lincoln Federal Savings and Loan Association. A resolution adopted by the City of Berwyn re-named the intersections of Cermac Road, Riverside Drive, and Wesley Avenue as Lincoln Circle. (See color section.)

This unveiling ceremony was held July 4, 1959. The dedication speech by Illinois Senator Paul H. Douglas commemorated the 150th year of Lincoln's birth. The Governor of the State, William G. Stratton, was invited and regretted being unable to attend. Participating also in the dedication were Mr. Frank Kinst; Mr. Ralph G. Newman as Master of Ceremo-nies; William I. Kriz, Mayor of Berwyn; Judge Rob-ert F. Jerrick, Police Magistrate; Dr. Raymond Dooley, President of Lincoln College; and the sculp-tor, Avard Fairbanks.

[Author's Note: When there was a change of ownership and name of the bank, the bronze monument was no longer ap-propriate. A new Lincoln School was constructed at 16th and Elmwood Streets and the statue was contributed to the school. It needed a new and taller pedestal. A campaign of pennies contributed by the students amounted to $11,000, enough for a rose-colored marble pedestal and moving costs. The school is now proud of its statue placed on the school grounds in 1997.]

LINCOLN THE FRIENDLY NEIGHBOR

A Guest Editorial by Avard Fairbanks, Sculptor

Throughout Lincoln's life, he had close touch with individuals of everyday life. His heart was al-ways with them. His experiences were akin to their struggles and their sorrows, and he knew their hopes. Such understanding has endeared him to all of those who are termed the common people. After 100 years we again sense the anxiety of the times and feel the Lincoln spirit.

Following my statue of the "Chicago Lincoln," I was commissioned to create another heroic monu-ment to "Lincoln the Friendly Neighbor" for The Lincoln Federal Savings and Loan Association, to be placed at the Lincoln Circle in Berwyn, Illinois.

To make great memorials of this nature, one has to put himself into the scenes of our nation's heri-tage. To objectify situations in permanent bronze, we must bring out the finest of our ideals that we hold dear. Those of Lincoln are worthy to have con-stantly in public view. Lincoln, to be sure, is the cen-tral figure of the group. He is as heroic in size as he is in character, and he is as strong and secure as the metal of the monument. At his right side is a boy with a dog, who awakens in the great Lincoln his own childhood. In looking back to the frontier of his own youth, Lincoln again feels the joys of the open fields, the woodlands, and the brooks. He also remembers the sorrows that came with the loss of his mother. In this monument he looks down upon the boy with great depth of feeling and senses in him the potentialities of every young American. In Lincoln's own situation of aspiring to the presi-dency, he is conscious that any American boy could be chosen and elected. Whoever is selected becomes the representative and the servant of all. Youth must therefore be looked upon as the spirit of a promise that God and a free people have given to every young American heart: leadership.

In the statue, Lincoln places his great hand upon the shoulder of youth as if on every young boy in our country, in every walk of life and in every ac-tivity. Thus, symbolized in bronze, his guiding hand inspires every boy to greatness in the field he will choose for the future. The young lady holds onto the arm of Lincoln as she looks up to him. There must be someone to guide our people in the time of stress and dissension. Such is her expression of con-fidence in this great man. She sees in this stalwart person the strength of character needed. Her admi-ration is that of a nation.

Freedom, liberty, justice, and other universal qualities of people's ideals are frequently symbol-ized in feminine characterizations. So in this me-morial the lass at the side of Lincoln is symbolic. Her countenance represents the trust, the hope, and the admiration of America. In an emblematic sense, such feelings are timeless. They are what we all sense in Abraham Lincoln and his ideals. We, the living, are the youths whom Lincoln looks down upon, and Lincoln places his hand upon our shoul-ders in friendship and in faith.

Fairbanks, Avard T., *Lincoln Herald*
(Harrogate Tennessee) 62.3, (Fall 1960): 97.
Reprinted by permission.

Fig. 1. Avard Fairbanks modeling the colossal portrait, *The Enduring Lincoln.*

THE ENDURING LINCOLN
Colossal Portrait Bust in Marble
Erected at The Lincoln Federal Savings and Loan Association, Berwyn, Illinois

The sculptor had oftentimes desired the opportunity to create a large masterpiece of Abraham Lincoln as the President. The opportunity was fulfilled along with the commission for a heroic bronze statue of *Lincoln The Friendly Neighbor*, for a colossal portrait of Lincoln the president was also requested.

This great historic personality presents many possibilities for portrayal. Abraham Lincoln was an eloquent speaker, a Commander-in-Chief of the Armies of the United States, an executive directing his cabinet and the affairs of the nation. Yet he was also a humanitarian, a friend to many, and a loving husband and father. The sculptor chose to portray

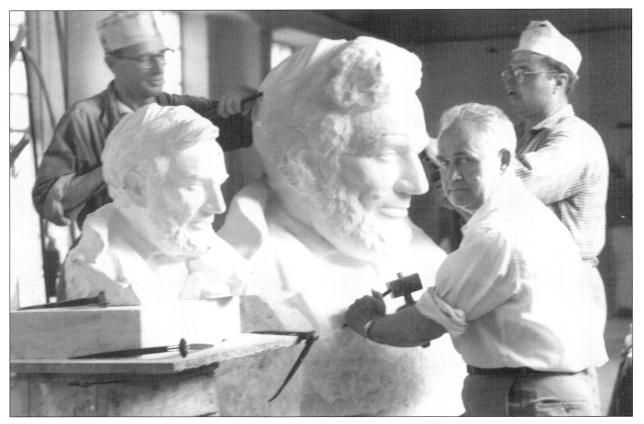

Fig. 2. The colossal portrait, *The Enduring Lincoln*, is illustrated as it was being carved in Carrara marble at the stone carving studio in Pietrasanta, Italy. A heroic plaster image is used as a model to carve from in a three dimensional enlargement process. Avard Fairbanks is in the foreground finish carving with mallet and chisel, while technicians in the background use pneumatic chisels.

the President in contemplation, in a moment of reflection, externally calm, but inwardly seeking a solution to many of the momentous problems of the times.

Since the schedule was critical, every effort was made to expedite the completion of the colossal marble bust. When approval of the committee was obtained, the portrait was modeled in clay (Fig. 1). It was then cast, retouched, and shipped to Italy. It arrived in Pietrasanta, a Tuscany village near to the Carrara Mountains. A suitable block of the finest white marble was chosen.

Although one may assume that the marble of these mountains is pure white, such is not always the case. The marble strata actually have streaks and bands of gray. For every ton of prime white stone, acceptable for sculpture, more than 50 tons of unsuitable stone must be discarded.

The selected block was quickly roughed out. The skilled marble carvers, with diligent care, carved the features to within 1/64-inch accuracy. They use pneumatic chisels, but the pointing device, to in-

sure accuracy for three dimensional reproduction, is of a design that has been used for several centuries.

Sculptor Fairbanks flew to Italy to complete the carving. It is essential that the artist finish the details. While the expert craftsmen can skillfully recreate the form, it requires the sculptor to refine and to give expression to the face. Fine pneumatic chisels are used to accentuate the subtle features (Fig. 2). When the carved stone finally met his satisfaction, the colossal marble portrait was crated and shipped to Illinois.

There were some anxious moments awaiting the arrival of the marble portrait from Pietrasanta, Italy. The ship from Genoa finally arrived in New York City. A rush priority was requested for it to clear customs. Several phone calls were made to the company to speed the transportation, in the hope that it arrive with sufficient time for the erection prior to the dedication of the new building.

The marble portrait arrived at the express office on the afternoon before the ceremonies (Fig. 2, 3).

Fig. 3. *The Enduring Lincoln* carved in Carrara marble, anterior view.

Fig. 4. *The Enduring Lincoln* carved in Carrara marble, left lateral view.

It was delivered to the grounds of the bank the morning of the dedication. Power equipment was available to handle even heavier loads than the half-ton colossal marble bust. However, the new bank's terrazzo floor had recently been laid and polished. The contractor dared not bring in heavy equipment, for the floor would surely crack.

Soon the sculptor arrived and was presented with the dilemma. Fortunately, he had experience in the Italian marble quarries, where they often worked without the benefit of heavy power equipment. It was necessary to resort to age-old methods in order to move and place the marble.

A pile of used lumber, about to be hauled away, was put to use. A cradle was formed about the bust, with stout planks serving as long handles. All available manpower was recruited. The sculptor and 16 able-bodied men including laborers, newsmen, bank executives, and carpenters grasped the handles. The marble crew slowly carried it in through hallways, up several steps to the pedestal, and set it down.

The next problem was to place it on the pedestal without damage. The cradle was removed. The marble portrait was slowly raised by rocking side to side, forward and backward, as three foot sections of 2x4 boards were alternately inserted under the free edges, gradually building up a platform for the pedestal height, much as a log house is built.

When the proper height was achieved, the marble was gradually eased onto boards on the pedestal. These boards in turn were removed by the same gentle rocking procedure. Only a short time remained for the sculptor and those assisting to make themselves presentable for the dedicatory services.

The heroic bronze statue of *Lincoln The Friendly Neighbor* was placed prominently in front of the new bank building. The colossal marble portrait *The Enduring Lincoln* was elegantly displayed in an appropriate room within the building. Both of the statues were dedicated during the same ceremony.

[Author's Note: When there was a change of name and ownership of the bank, this marble portrait was no longer appropriate at that site and it was sold to a private party.]

Reference Article:

The following address was presented by Dr. William W. Haggard to the Rotary Club of Bellingham, Washington, in February 1970, commemorating Lincoln's birthday. Dr. Haggard was President Emeritus of Western Washington State College (now Western Washington University) at Bellingham. Although his primary discipline was Education, Dr. Haggard was a serious student of Abraham Lincoln's life and history. He had given many speeches on various aspects of the life and career of Lincoln. The following address presents Lincoln's image with an interesting perspective, a complement to the colossal portrait bust of *The Enduring Lincoln.*

WAS ABRAHAM LINCOLN A CONSERVATIVE OR A LIBERAL?

By William W. Haggard

This month (February, 1970) we celebrate the birthday of our greatest president. On the 12th of February, 161 years ago, Abraham Lincoln saw the light of day in a Kentucky log cabin, 17' x 12'. It has been almost 105 years since he died at 56 in a tiny bedroom of a boarding house across the street from Ford's Theater in Washington, DC, our first martyr president.

My subject today is, "Was Abraham Lincoln a Conservative or a Liberal?" I shall not attempt to answer the question flatly. Rather my aim is to present relevant words and deeds of Lincoln and let you answer for yourself. I shall not attempt to define terms, but I do find that Lincoln defined conservatism in his October 16, 1854, Peoria, Illinois, address, to quote, "What is conservatism? Is it not adherence to the old and tried, against the new and untried?" It seems appropriate to examine Lincoln's view of man, government, his political party, capital and labor, and Americanism.

First, what was Lincoln's view of man?

When he came to New Salem, Illinois, at 22 years of age, he wrote of himself as a piece of driftwood that had floated in on the Sangamon River. In announcing himself as a candidate for the Legislature here, his first sentence was, "Fellow Citizens: I presume you all know who I am—I am humble Abraham Lincoln." A favorite poem of his was, *Why Should the Spirit of Mortal Be Proud?* At dusk one day as Lincoln left the courthouse in Bloomington, Illinois, Jesse Fell took him by the arm and guided him to his brother's law office.

Fell had just returned from the East. Abraham Lincoln could be a formidable presidential candidate, he said. Lincoln was not impressed. What was the use of talking when such men as Seward, Chase, and others were in the running? Jesse Fell was the founder of the *Bloomington Pantagraph* (a famous newspaper) and had other important interests. A few months later Lincoln wrote Thomas J. Pickett, editor of the Rock Island, Illinois, *Register,* "I must in candor say that I do not think myself fit for the presidency." One may easily deduce that Lincoln thought every man his equal or better. He harbored not one iota of arrogance toward his fellow man throughout his entire life.

Lincoln once said that Thomas Jefferson was our greatest statesman. Jefferson wrote the *Declaration of Independence,* in which he said that all men were created equal. Lincoln certainly was no disciple of Alexander Hamilton, who said to Jefferson, in a George Washington cabinet meeting, that his (Jefferson's) 'people' were a beast. Recall the first sentence of the Gettysburg address, "Four score and seven years ago, our forefathers brought forth upon this continent, a new nation, conceived in Liberty, and dedicated to the proposition that all men are created equal."

Lincoln's letter of 1855 to Josh Speed, his most intimate personal friend, tells much about his view of man. May I quote an excerpt?

"I am not a know-nothing, that is certain. How could I be? How could anyone who abhors the oppressing of Negros be in favor of degrading classes of white people? As a nation, we began by declaring that 'all men are created equal.' We now practically read it, 'all men are created equal except Negros.' When the know-nothings get control, it will read, 'All men are created equal except Negros, foreigners, and Catholics.' When it comes to this I should prefer emigrating to Russia."

When Lincoln obtained control of the German-language newspaper in Springfield, Illinois, he wrote Theodore Canisius, the editor,

> "Understanding the spirit of our institutions to aim at the elevation of men, I am opposed to whatever tends to degrade them. I have some little notoriety for commiserating the oppressed Negro. I should be strangely inconsistent if I could favor curtailing the rights of white men, even though born in different lands."

You may not have read or heard of this. When General Grant issued an order expelling "all Jews" from the lines of his military department late in 1862 or early in 1863, Lincoln revoked the order. This matter had something to do with peddlers, according to Carl Sandburg. James G. Randall encloses the words "all Jews" in quote marks. But Lincoln did revoke the order.

Lincoln's compassion for the poor and the unfortunate, even the deserter, is without parallel among our presidents. Richard Current in his book *The Lincoln Nobody Knows,* has a chapter entitled "The Tenderhearted."

Following Lincoln's re-election in 1864, a crowd gave the White House a serenade. Despite the fact that he had been the most bitterly criticized of all of our presidents, in the course of his remarks he said, "So long as I have been here, I have not willingly planted a thorn in any man's bosom."

Sherwood Eddy once said that Lincoln was the most unorthodox and the most saintly Christian of our presidents. Henry C. Deming, congressman of Connecticut, asked Lincoln why he had not joined a church. The reply was,

> "When any church will inscribe over its altars, as its sole qualification for membership, the Savior's condensed statement of the substance of both law and gospel, 'Thou shalt love the Lord thy God with all thy heart, and with all thy soul and with all thy mind, and thy neighbor as thyself' that church will I join, with all my heart and all my soul."

Parenthetically, the Baptists have claimed Lincoln because his parents were Baptists, and the Unitarians because of his liberal views. So much for Abraham Lincoln and man.

Second, what was his philosophy of the state or government?

In 1854 he formulated a very concise, some would say limited, definition of the purpose of government. It was found among some notes for a law lecture. It is,

> "The legitimate object of government is to do for a community of people whatever they need to have done, but cannot do at all, or cannot do so well, for themselves in their separate and individual capacities."

A much earlier example of a concrete interpretation of this purpose of government may be found in his advocacy, as a member of the Illinois Legislature, of extensive internal improvements. In *The Lincoln Reader* by Paul Angle, an eminent scholar, there is a long chapter captioned, "The DeWitt Clinton of Illinois." DeWitt Clinton was governor of New York in the 1820s and was largely responsible for the Erie Canal.

As a member of Congress from 1846-1848, Lincoln was a strong advocate of internal improvements by the federal government. James G. Randall, some would say our most eminent Lincoln scholar, writes of Lincoln's scathing criticism of a "do-nothing government."

You will be interested in two very significant bills, historically and presently speaking, Lincoln signed as president. They are the Homestead Act and the Morrill Act, both of 1862. Carl Sandburg has this to say of the former,

> "Lincoln signed the Homestead Bill on May 20, 1862, giving a farm free to any man who wanted to put a plow to unbroken sod. Immense tracts were thrown open in the Western territories. A citizen of the United States or anyone asking for the first papers declaring intention of citizenship, paying a registration fee of $10., and staying on the same piece of ground five years, could have title papers making him the owner of 160 acres. Tens of thousands of Britons, Irish, Germans, and Scandinavians came, many exclaiming, 'What a good new country where they give away farms.' As a war measure touching enlarged food supply and as an act fulfilling a Republican Party pledge, Lincoln found it easy to sign the bill. Later Lincoln agreed that the law

should be modified to favor Federal soldiers and sailors."

What was the Morrill Act? In short, it created the land-grant college. The act provided, on the basis of each senator and representative in Congress, for a land grant of 30,000 acres or its equivalent in scrip to the several states for an endowment, the interest from which was to furnish "instruction in agriculture and the mechanic arts without excluding military tactics."

According to the last statistic I have seen, there are now 68 land grant colleges and universities in the United States. Washington State University is a land grant institution.

I wish I had time to tell you about Jonathan Baldwin Turner of Illinois as related to this movement, and his buttonholing Lincoln and Stephen A. Douglas. Turner was a teacher of the classics in Illinois College who came to see the necessity of the practical arts. Moreover, the Department of Agriculture was established by the Lincoln administration with Isaac Newton, Lincoln's friend, as the first commissioner. This Isaac Newton was from New Jersey, unrelated to Sir Isaac Newton who lived in England in the 17th and 18th centuries. It is clear that Lincoln did not accept the *laissez faire* philosophy of government.

May we consider another aspect of Lincoln's philosophy of government. In his address before the Young Men's Lyceum of Springfield—which followed the mob action killing Elijah Lovejoy, the abolitionist editor of Alton, Illinois—he declared,

"Let reverence for the laws be breathed by every American mother to the lisping babe that prattles on her lap; let it be taught in schools, in seminaries, and in colleges; let it be written in primers, spelling books, and in almanacs; let it be preached from the pulpit, proclaimed in legislative halls, and enforced in courts of justice, and in short, let it become the political religion of the nation; and let the old and the young, the rich and the poor, the grave and the gay of all sexes and tongues and colors and conditions, sacrifice increasingly upon its altars."

Twenty-two years later, in the Cooper Union speech in New York City, Lincoln had this to say of John Brown:

"That affair, its philosophy, corresponds with the many attempts related in history at the assassination of kings and emperors. An enthusiast broods over the oppression of a people until he fancies himself commissioned by Heaven to liberate them. He ventures the attempt, which ends in little else than his own execution."

Only the William Lloyd Garrisons declared John Brown a martyr. Lincoln repudiated John Brown, and again condemned violence and stressed the necessity of law and order.

May I quote from the First Inaugural?

"I hold that, in contemplation of universal law and of the Constitution, the Union of these states is perpetual. Perpetuity is implied, if not expressed, in the fundamental law of all national governments. It is safe to assert that no government proper ever had a provision in its organic law for its own termination. Continue to execute all the express provisions of our national Constitution and the Union will endure forever—it being impossible to destroy it except by some action not provided for in the instrument."

Lincoln believed in a "do-something" government and a government that provides security for its citizens, but most of all he believed in a democratic government. He said in his 1854 Peoria speech,

"No man is good enough to govern another man, without the other's consent. I say this is the leading principle, the sheet anchor of American republicanism."

He does not capitalize "r" in republicanism. He wrestled with this concept of government in his July 4, 1861, message to Congress when he wrote,

"Must a government, of necessity, be too strong for the liberties of its people or too weak to maintain its existence?"

Third, to what political party did Lincoln belong?

He said repeatedly he was a Whig. He was a Whig until he joined the new party—Republican—in the middle 1850s. Lincoln was the Whig leader in the Illinois House of Representatives; he was a

Whig congressman; he campaigned for the Whig candidates for the presidency.

The Whig party developed as an opposition party to Andrew Jackson (King Andrew they called him). It favored sound banking, the protective tariff, internal improvements, and divided on the slavery issue, which contributed to the party's doom. Daniel Webster and Henry Clay were the great Whigs. You may be interested in the election of two Whig presidents: first General William Henry Harrison in 1840, son of Benjamin Harrison, a signer of the Declaration of Independence, and grandfather of Benjamin Harrison, the 23rd president; and second, General Zachary Taylor in 1848. The former President W. H. Harrison died one month after taking office, and the latter 16 months after inauguration.

Stephen A. Douglas, senator from Illinois, rammed the Kansas Nebraska bill through the Congress in 1854, which repealed the Missouri Compromise. This stirred Lincoln to political activity as nothing before. It involved several years of debate with Douglas, including the famous Seven Joint Debates in 1858. In 1856 Lincoln received 110 votes in the Republican National convention as a vice presidential candidate to run with John C. Fremont.

In 1860 Senator William H. Seward of New York was regarded as the most eligible Republican candidate for the presidency in the Wigwam convention in Chicago. He led on the first and second ballots but, because of the fear of his controversial image and the astute Illinois delegation, Lincoln was nominated to lead in the opposition to the extension of slavery in the territories.

According to Richard Hofstadter, "in the social climate of Illinois Lincoln ranked as a moderate conservative." He was conservative enough and liberal enough, and gradual enough in his approach to the solution of the slavery problem, to weld many diverse elements into a winning Republican party. As president, Lincoln, of course, was too slow for the Republican anti-slavery extremists and too lenient with the secessionists for the Republican Vindictives.

As a great party leader Lincoln kept the people's minds and hearts on his central war aim, the saving of the Union; hence the Republican party was the Union party in Lincoln's campaign for re-election in 1864. You recall that Andrew Johnson, southern Democrat, implacable Unionist, and military governor of Tennessee, was the candidate for the vice-presidency. In the 1864 campaign the 13th amendment to free the slaves replaced the prevention of extension of slavery in the territories plank of the 1860 platform and the Emancipation Proclamation of 1863.

Listen to a brief excerpt from Lincoln's December 1862, message to the Congress. Note he uses the words *this administration.*

"The dogmas of the quiet past are inadequate to the stormy present. The occasion is piled high with difficulty and we must rise with the occasion. As our case is new, so we must think anew and act anew. We must disenthrall ourselves, and then we shall save our country. We cannot escape history: We of this Congress and this administration will be remembered in spite of ourselves. We—even we here—hold the power and bear the responsibility in giving freedom to the slaves, we assure freedom to the free, we shall nobly save or meanly lose the last, best hope of earth."

Upon returning from Virginia to Washington following the surrender of Robert E. Lee, Lincoln found celebration the thing. A crowd gathered at the White House the evening of April 10 for a typical 'hurrah' speech. Lincoln had developed a great fondness for the Rebel war song "Dixie." The Union had now rightfully captured it, he said, and he had the band play it. He asked the crowd to return the next evening for a speech.

On this occasion he made his last speech. He spoke on reconstruction and reconciliation, a disappointment to the celebrators, in which he was out in front of his party, especially the radical leaders. Had Lincoln lived, many believe the country would have been spared the disastrous reconstruction era.

Fourth, what was Lincoln's view of capital and labor?

Recently I found this quote from him on the walls of the outer office of a real estate company in Seattle,

"Property is the fruit of labor; property is desirable; it is a positive good in the world. That some should be rich shows that others may become rich, hence is just encouragement to industry and enterprise. Let not him who is houseless pull down the house of another, but let him work diligently and build one for himself, thus by example, assuring that his own shall be safe from violence when built."

This is from the address to the Workingmen's Association of New York, indicating his grateful acceptance of membership.

In his message to the Congress, December 1861, he wrote,

"Labor is prior to and independent of capital. Capital is only the fruit of labor and could never have existed if labor had not existed. Labor is the superior of capital and deserves much the higher consideration. Capital has its rights, which are as worthy of protection as any other rights."

He further wrote in the message,

"There is not, of necessity, any such thing as the free hired laborer being fixed to that condition for life. Many independent men everywhere in these states, a few years back in their lives, were hired laborers. The prudent penniless beginner in the world labors for wages a while, saves a surplus with which to buy tools or land for himself, then labors on his own account for a while, and at length hires another new beginner to help him."

I have mentioned the Cooper Union speech of February 1860. In connection with this trip to New York he visited his son, Robert, who was in Phillips Exeter Academy, New Hampshire, preparing for Harvard. He made several speeches while in New England. At Hartford, Connecticut, where the shoemakers were on strike, he said, "I am glad to see that a system of labor prevails in New England under which laborers can strike." At Manchester, New Hampshire, Lincoln was introduced as the next president.

In the South, one George Fithurgh, a lawyer of Virginia, advocated that both the Negros and the poor whites of the United States should be enslaved, thereby providing a better condition for society.

As against this philosophy, Lincoln stated repeatedly that the cause of the preservation of the Union was the common people's cause. Had it not been for Lincoln's effective advocacy of this point of view, England might have recognized the Confederacy.

James G. Randall says that one of Lincoln's finest presidential papers is his letter to the workingmen of Manchester, England, in response to a laudatory address that had been sent to him. A photograph of John Bright, a great English liberal, hung in Lincoln's outer office.

"The basic tenet in Lincoln's economic thinking was equal opportunity for all. Living a part of his life in an age of craftsmanship and a part of it in an age of burgeoning industrialism, with cheap land always available, he saw perseverance, thrift, and enterprise rewarded. Under a system of individualistic enterprise it seemed of first importance to him—it seemed sufficient—merely to keep the road to high attainment clear of inequitable obstruction," says Benjamin P. Thomas, author of the best single-volume biography of Lincoln and other books.

You will find this in the essay on Lincoln in Richard Hofstadter's *The American Political Tradition*, "The Democratic Party he (Lincoln) charged in 1859 abandoned the Jeffersonian tradition by taking the position that one man's liberty was absolutely nothing when conflicting with another man's property. Republicans, he added in an utterly characteristic sentence, are for both the man and the dollar, but in case of conflict the man before the dollar." How do you account for the pro-labor strain in Lincoln?

Fifth and finally, Lincoln and Americanism.

James G. Randall writes that Lincoln is known as much as anything else for a basic Americanism, but that he was not a patrioteer. James Russell Lowell in the "Commemoration Ode" at Harvard University on July 21, 1965, called Lincoln the first American.

To the Young Men's Lyceum in Springfield, Lincoln said as a young man,

"We find ourselves in the peaceful possession of the fairest portion of the earth, under a system of political institutions conducing more to the ends of civil and religious liberty than any of which history of former times tells us."

In the same address he declared that the pillars of the national temple should be, "hewn from the solid quarry of sober reason against passion which could be our enemy."

In Lincoln's tribute to Henry Clay we find,

"He loved his country partly because it was his own country, but mostly because it was a free country; and he burned with a zeal for its advancement, prosperity, and glory of human liberty, human rights, and human nature."

These words are Lincoln's about Henry Clay, but Richard Current says these words can be applied fittingly to Lincoln himself. Some say Lincoln was really speaking of himself.

In the 1854 Peoria address, rebutting Stephen A. Douglas, he said, "I love the sentiments of these old-time men," meaning the Revolutionary Fathers.

At the outset of his presidency Lincoln showed the utmost fervor in underlining, "our national fabric, with all its benefits, its memories, and its hopes."

Speaking again of Lincoln's passion and fervor in connection with saving the union of the states, John Nicolay, his senior private secretary, tells of seeing tears running down the cheeks of Lincoln one day. Nicolay found that Lincoln was reading this stanza from Longfellow:

Thou, too sail on, O Ship of State!
Sail on, O Union, strong and great.
Humanity with all its fears,
With all its hopes of future years,
Is hanging breathless on thy fate!

I shall never forget hearing Winston Churchill use this stanza in one of his compelling radio addresses during World War II. Nicolay revealed that he as a schoolboy had memorized the entire poem. Lincoln asked him to recite it, which he did. Lincoln did not speak for some minutes, but finally said, "It is a wonderful gift to be able to stir men like that." Sail on, O Union, strong and great!

(Address by W. W. Haggard, at Bellingham, Washington Rotary Club, February 9, 1970. Printed by permission of Dr. W. W. Haggard, President and Professor Emeritus of Western Washington State College, Bellingham, Washington.)

THE LINCOLN – DOUGLAS DEBATES

The city of Galesburg, Illinois, is proud and deeply conscious of its history. It holds the honor that the only remaining building used in the historic Lincoln-Douglas debates, Old Main of Knox College, is still maintained intact. As the 100-year anniversary of these debates approached, impressive ceremonies were planned.

Anniversary celebrations of the great debates were not new to this community. In the year 1896, Knox College President John Houston Finley promoted the first of the celebrations. It was the 38th anniversary. Among the speakers were Chauncey M. Depew, President of the New York Central Railroad, ex-governor Bodes of Iowa, and Robert Todd Lincoln, son of the President. When an opportunity developed in 1898 to schedule President William McKinley and his entire cabinet to visit Galesburg, Dr. Finlay organized another impressive celebration for the next year, 1899.

The semi-centennial was held October 7, 1908, sponsored by Knox College and Galesburg. Prominent among the dignitaries attending were Clark E. Carr, who had known Abraham Lincoln and had been active in previous celebrations; Adlai E. Stevenson (former Vice-President of the United States, elected in 1892 in Grover Cleveland's Administration); Theodore E. Burton, who spoke on Lincoln; Honorable William Howard Taft, who spoke on the debate; and Robert A. Douglas, the grandson of Stephen A. Douglas.

Again, on the 70th anniversary in 1928, 10,000 people attended a condensed re-enactment of the debates. Forty men and women who had attended the original debate were invited to sit on the platform as honored guests. Frank McGlynn, an actor, impersonated Abraham Lincoln, while Galesburg attorney, A.B. Pierson, took the part of Stephen A. Douglas. Other speakers included Dr. Albert Britt, a nationally known Lincoln authority and president of Knox College; Dr. William E. Barton of Oak Park, Illinois; Carl Sandburg, native of Galesburg, poet and Lincoln biographer; and Dr. Edgar J. Goodspeed of the University of Chicago.

The 1958 centennial celebration commemorating the Galesburg Lincoln-Douglas Debate began October 4th with the joint efforts of Knox College,

City Officials, Illinois State Historical Association, Civil War Round Tables, and many other organizations. The calendar of events continued four days. High school and junior high school bands, as well as high school choruses and college choirs, participated. The Theater Arts Department presented a play, "The Baffling Eyes of Youth," and an opera, "Young Lincoln." A centennial dance festival was held. Even the Knox County Bar Association rendered an historical dramatic skit.

Many noted statesmen, scholars, educators, and Lincoln authorities participated in the programs. Prominent among these were Dr. Sharvey G. Umbeck, President of Knox College; Hon. William H. Small, mayor of Galesburg; Dr. Allen Nevins of Columbia University; Willard L. King, a Chicago attorney and Lincoln scholar; and Herman R. Muelden, Professor of History and Dean of Knox College.

October 6th was designated Carl Sandburg Day in honor of Galesburg's native son, who had been a student of Knox College. He was hailed as a poet and as author of *Lincoln–The Prairie Years* and *Lincoln–The War Years*. The unveiling and dedication of the Lincoln and Douglas Commemorative bas-relief panels made an impressive climax to the events of that day.

On October 7th, the centennial day of the program began with the convocation. Mr. Bruce Catton, editor of *American Heritage* and author of many books about the Civil War period, gave the centennial convocation address. Hon. William G. Stratton, Governor of Illinois, discussed the debates. Senator Everett McKinlay Dirksen spoke about Abraham Lincoln, while Senator Paul H. Douglas spoke about Stephen A. Douglas.

In the afternoon a historic pageant progressed from downtown to the campus. A re-enactment of the original scene at Old Main was performed. Arthur Barlow took the part of Abraham Lincoln, while Richard Francis Sokup portrayed Stephen A. Douglas. The assembled people, interested in history, and curious as to how the past still lives with us, witnessed a re-enactment of a great event. Their lives have been enriched by the actors and speakers, and those who participated also gained by the experience. Now the audience has dispersed, just as an audience dispersed 100 years before, yet many young people have an event to recall, history made real and living.

Old Main stands, much as it did a century before. The commemorative panels, cast in bronze, have been permanently placed on the building. They portray not only the personages, but also the moment, the feeling of the men, and the impact of the event for those who visit this historic site. It is entirely appropriate that such events as these be memorialized by sculpture modeled with historic correctness and projecting the personality of the characters. The Sculptor chose to portray Abraham Lincoln with his head higher on the plaque in order to convey the impression of his tall stature. The inscriptions were adjusted accordingly. Stephen A. Douglas' face is nearly centered. Lincoln was a foot taller than the "Little Giant." They partly face each other, yet look out as though ready to speak. These two great statesmen had succeeded as national leaders, by outstanding ability, tenacious determination, by diligent application, and by heroic effort. Fate was unkind, indeed, for neither survived a decade.

The bas-relief plaques were modeled in Plastelina about three-by-five feet with relief portraits in heroic proportions, about 1-1/2 times life size (Figs. 1, 2). Simple plaster molds were made directly from the modeled plaques. The molds were reinforced with iron rods and allowed to harden. After lifting the molds off the clay image, adherent modeling clay was removed and the interior of the mold was shellacked and lubricated.

A plaster image was created by pouring the liquid slurry into the mold. This was reinforced with irons in the same manner as the mold. When it had hardened sufficiently, the cast was lifted off the mold. This requires considerable lifting and insertion of wedges in the borders. Suddenly the mold and cast would separate and the cast could then be retouched for sending to the bronze foundry.

In this case, not sufficient time had been allowed for bronze casting. The plaster casts had to be painted like a bronze patina for display and dedication. The plaster casts with a bronze-like patina were used for the dedication and unveiling ceremonies, while second copies were sent to the bronze foundry to be cast in bronze. The bronze casts were placed on the Old Main Building the next year, and few people knew the difference.

The Great Debates*

Lincoln had actually spoken in reply to Douglas on six occasions before the first debate at Ottawa. Douglas had little to gain and much to lose in the debates, but he could not refuse the challenge without creating the impression that he feared to meet Lincoln on equal terms. Douglas is reported to have said, "Should I win, I shall gain but little; should I lose, I shall lose everything." He readily recognized that Lincoln was the strong man of the Illinois Republicans, "full of wit, facts, dates, and the best stump-speaker in the West with his droll ways and dry jokes. He is as honest as he is shrewd, and if I beat him my victory will be hardly won."

The seven formal debates between Lincoln and Douglas are not remembered because of the eloquence of the speakers, nor because of the lasting interest in their contents. All seven of the debates were concerned primarily with one subject: the status of slavery in the territories of the United States.

Actually Lincoln and Douglas agreed more than they differed concerning the issue of slavery. Their biggest difference was in their opinions concerning popular sovereignty as a basis for settling the question of slavery in the territories. Douglas championed popular sovereignty, while Lincoln was opposed to it.

From *The Chicago Tribune:* July 22, 1858: *The Tribune* suggests a series of joint debates between Douglas and Lincoln:

> "Let them agree to canvass the state together in the usual western style. We have reason to believe that this would meet with Mr. Lincoln's views. In this manner, the people can make up their minds as to which candidate is right. If Douglas should refuse to be a party to such an arrangement, it will be because he is a coward. We are well aware that so long as he accomplishes his purpose, he cares not how he accomplishes it. But he must either go with Lincoln now, or run away from him as he did in 1854."

---

* From a pamphlet published in 1958 by the State of Illinois.

Fig. 1. A bas-relief portrait of Abraham Lincoln commemorating the Lincoln-Douglas Debate at Galesburg, Illinois.

October 5, 1858: The Galesburg Debate. A word to the Committee on Arrangements:

"We desire to say a word to the Committee of Arrangements for the debate. At none of the pre-vious discussions have there been any adequate accommodations for reporters. It is not a fact that two chairs and a washstand 18-inches square are sufficient furniture for half a dozen men to work

Fig. 2. A bas-relief portrait of Stephen A. Douglas commemorating the Lincoln-Douglas debate at Galesburg, Illinois.

on, nor is it always convenient to make a battle against a mob of excited politicians, when the fighting editor is at home. On behalf of ourselves and such other representatives of the press as may be represented, may we request that arrangements be made for at least six reporters— that the chairs and tables be placed where they will not be jarred or overthrown by the people on the platform and where there will be no room for persons to crowd between the reporters and the speakers—that somebody with authority and physical strength enough to secure obedience be appointed to keep loafers out of the reporting corner. These things are absolutely essential to the accuracy of the reports."

LINCOLN AND DOUGLAS

Excerpts were made from an address Mr. Claude G. Bowers was expected to deliver in Galesburg during the centennial, but his death intervened. The address was first delivered Feb. 12, 1929, to the Lincoln Centennial Association in Springfield, Illinois. Mr. Bowers served as Ambassador to Chile and Spain, and among his historical books are *The Struggle for Democracy in America* and *The Revolution After Lincoln.*

"It is a remarkable fact that the ability, the genius, the breadth, the depth, and the power of Lincoln were less appreciated by his political associates than by his lifelong rival, Stephen A. Douglas. On the eve of the struggle of 1858, Douglas knew he was girding his loins for a supreme effort, when many of the followers of Lincoln were reconciling themselves to the political burial of their leader.

"Stephen A. Douglas is one of the most majestic figures in all our history. He had a genius for statesmanship. He had constructive capacity of a very high order. He was a master in the management of men and of conflicting forces. In the Senate of Webster, Calhoun, and Clay he met the greatest on equal terms and without dipping of his colors. He caught the popular fancy as few men have, and his followers were legion in every quarter of the land. It was his statesmanship that molded many States from Territories and ushered them into the council chamber of the Nation. It was his prescience that planned the binding of the East and West with bands of steel, and he led the way. His devotion was to the Constitution, his passion for the Union.

"He fought throughout his life for one, and for the other he died, at length, as literally as Lincoln."

~ *Claude G. Bowers*

The information presented has been extracted from publications obtained from the Special Collections and Archives, Knox College Library, Galesburg, Illinois.

MR. BRUCE CATTON'S CONVOCATION ADDRESS, OCTOBER 7, 1958

By Bruce Catton

We are met here today in the lengthening shadows of two great men, who stood here one century ago to grapple with an issue that had become intolerable in a society of free men. That issue revolved about the continued existence of Negro slavery and the effect that institution was likely to have on the growth and destiny of the American democracy. The issue itself has long since disappeared. It was removed by a violent and convulsive effort of the whole nation, at a tragic and shattering cost. Negro slavery no longer exists, and the arguments which Abraham Lincoln and Stephen A. Douglas made here have a dim, far-off sound today, like the echoes of a great battle fought long ago over some point which has long ceased to disturb the conscience or the emotion of mankind.

Yet today's commemorative exercise is in no sense a dry antiquarian glimpse at something long since laid away to rest. The great debates of 1858 have a curiously contemporary ring to them. They touched upon issues which are eternal; the line between the profound underlying cause of the Lincoln-Douglas debates and the great still-unsolved problems of today is direct and unmistakable. When we re-examine the Lincoln-Douglas debates we are not so much going far back into the past as taking a fresh look at our own times.

We tend to attach a dignified, stately, almost saintly quality to the separate chapters of these debates. Lincoln and Douglas—we assure ourselves, quite correctly—were great Americans. Because they were genuinely great, we assume that they met on a very high plane; that they behaved and spoke as if they were constantly aware that history was looking over their shoulders. We assume that they never really got down into the dust and heat of the arena and slugged one another with the gusto and zest of two men who, above everything else, were personal rivals for a high office which each man very much wanted to attain.

This is all very well, except that it does give us an unreal view of these two great rivals. It makes us forget that dedicated patriots may also be men who can get angry and who, having become angry, may strike at one another with any weapon that may be available.

Lincoln and Douglas were men of their own time—and it was a robust, virile, uninhibited time, all things considered—and what they said to and about each other has a direct relevance to the angers and passions of today. The historians, who by nature tend to be rather pious, full of dignity, and given to impartial judgments, have perhaps taken a little of the blood out of the debaters who argued here before any of us were born. Lincoln and Douglas did not meet here to conduct a high school class in civics. They were fighting for a seat in the United States Senate, they were arguing about a point that meant a great deal to each of them, and they pulled out all of the stops. They would understand to the full the arguments which today disturb our peace of mind so greatly.

Consider, for instance, the following diatribe, addressed to a man who failed to see any particular sanctity in a highly controversial decision of the Supreme Court which bore on the race problem. Says the complainant, of the dissenter:

"Suppose he succeeds in destroying public confidence in the Court, so that the people will not respect its decisions but will feel at liberty to disregard them, and resist the laws of the land, what will he have gained? He will have changed the government from one of laws into that of a mob, in which the strong arm of violence will be substituted for the decisions of the Courts of justice… He is going to appeal from the Supreme Court of the United States to every town meeting in the hope that he can excite a prejudice against that Court, and on the wave of that prejudice ride into the Senate of the United States when he could not get there on his own principles or his own merits."

These words were not addressed—as one might easily imagine they addressed—by the editor of the *Arkansas Gazette* to Arkansas Governor Faubus in this year 1958. They were uttered in this place, 100 years ago today, by Stephen A. Douglas, and Senator Douglas was referring to Abraham Lincoln.

There is a present-day quality to these old debates. We can still learn something by listening to them again. They were no mere exercise in political rivalry; taken as a whole, they constitute one of the most profoundly significant and moving chapters in American history. We today share fully in what was said here and in the deep emotions that here gripped the American electorate. If those who spoke here and those who listened here were standing in the presence of something incalculable, something that went to the very heart and soul of America's bright destiny, we ourselves are in the presence of the same thing; because the far-reaching problem which tormented the decade of the 1850s torments our own time as well, and still demands its solution.

To understand what that problem is, let us begin by trying to get a little better understanding of the great Lincoln-Douglas debates themselves. It sometimes seems to me that few experiences in American politics are more persistently misunderstood than those debates.

We live by politics, in this country. We place the utmost confidence in the scope and flexibility of our political machinery—a confidence which, by and large, considering most of the experiences of the past, is pretty well justified. We are fond of saying that what our political life needs more than anything else is free and open debate regarding its most lively issues. If candidates for office, we tell ourselves, could only meet face to face and thresh these issues out where all could hear—if, doing so, they could get the rapt attention of all the electorate, and so bring the voters' minds to bear on all aspects of the day's most pressing concerns—then, we believe, our democracy could work with full efficiency. Then an informed electorate, after complete ventilation of the issues before it, could and would make the kind of decisions that would settle things once and for all and settle them properly.

Precisely what we are always demanding actually happened here in Illinois in 1858. The two candidates for the United States Senate—one of them an obvious candidate for the Presidency at the next election, the other a man whose "dark horse" potentialities for such a candidacy were steadily becoming more apparent—arranged a series of meetings and, from the same platform, subjected the dominant issue of the day to the most thorough, thoughtful, and intelligent analysis.

That dominant issue was of course the question of chattel slavery. More specifically, it was the question of permitting or prohibiting the existence of slavery in the territories; but constantly visible back of this one question were the larger questions of whether slavery itself was right or wrong and whether the institution should be allowed to continue into the indefinite future or should be so hemmed in and limited as to put it in the course of ultimate extinction.

It was an infinitely disturbing question. When Lincoln declared, in his famous "House divided" speech, that the nation could not continue to exist half free and half slave, he was bitterly criticized—by Senator Douglas, among others—for seeming to advocate destruction of the Union; yet he said no more than most men then were consciously or subconsciously thinking. The great dispute over slavery was a dangerously divisive force. All men were somehow aware that unless it could presently be settled the nation might in sober truth be torn apart in bitterness and in violence.

And so, in 1858, the most trusted remedy in our whole political arsenal was applied. Two candidates for office met on the same platform, up and down and across the entire constituency, and debated the matter. They were brilliant men, able thinkers, politicians whose technical skill at the devices of politics never caused either man to lose sight of his larger responsibility for the welfare of the country as a whole. They gave to this dangerous issue exactly the sort of treatment which we believe is above all other things needed in a time of crisis—and what happened?

Within three years the two sections of the country had gone to war. The Lincoln-Douglas debates, admirable as they were in purpose, completely failed to do what they were supposed to do. They did not bring a settlement of a difficult issue. They did not solve the crisis which was upon the country. Looking back on them from this distance, we can see that this profound exercise in political statesmanship was, tragically, no more than the prelude to the Civil War. It certainly did not bring on the war, but it certainly did not prevent or even postpone it. The best our political ingenuity was able to do was, somehow, not good enough. The war came, and neither of the two great men who spoke here

lived to see it brought to its final conclusion.

So what must concern us today, as we commemorate that part of the long debate which took place on this ground, is the deep, baffling question: Why did this failure take place? What meaning is there for us, in 1958, in the fact that the fearful calamity of the Civil War did finally come upon us in spite of the flexibility of our political institutions and our genius in using those institutions? Just wherein did Stephen A. Douglas and Abraham Lincoln fail?

Perhaps one answer—only a partial answer, but valid within limits—is the fact that our political machinery can handle anything on Earth except a deep moral issue. There was a moral issue involved in the slavery question, and it made the issue one that could not be resolved by the processes of free discussion. That there were many causes for the Civil War is of course obvious. Modern scholarship has made it abundantly clear that the motivating forces were uncommonly complex and involved. Clashing economic interests, different theories about government, deep loyalties that went beyond the reach of argument, varying concepts of nationality itself, profound misunderstandings about other men's viewpoints and intentions—all of these existed, and all of them, in one way or another, had their place in bringing the two sections into combat. The mere fact that such a man as Robert E. Lee, who believed neither in slavery nor in secession, should feel that his duty required him to go with his state rather than with his nation, is abundant evidence that the causes of this war were very far from simple.

Yet the fact remains that slavery was at the base of everything; that the war would never have taken place if it had not been for slavery; that every other issue might have been worked out, or compromised, or finally dispelled altogether, if the slavery issue itself could have been settled. And slavery, after all, was a profound wrong. Its continued existence in the middle of the 19th century did pose a moral issue. With that issue our political machinery was finally unable to cope. And the war came.

But there is a great deal more to it than that. If there were not, we could simply look back upon the Civil War experience as one of the tragic, all but ruinous chapters in our life as a nation, give it the mournful attention which is properly bestowed on tragedies of the long ago, and then go on about our business. But we cannot do that with the Civil War. It demands continuing attention, not because it was an experience by turns hateful and inspiring, ugly and romantic, heartbreaking and uplifting—although it is all of that—but because it was a point of departure rather than a conclusion. If it ended one era it also began another—the era with whose infinite complexities we are grappling today—and what began there was ever so much more important than what ended there.

It is hardly going too far to say that ultimately the Civil War compelled us today to face up to the great underlying problem which neither Douglas nor Lincoln was prepared to face up to during those great debates of a century ago. That is to say that it left us required to perfect that dream of brotherhood, freedom, and democracy which is the basis of our existence as a nation. It left us utterly and finally defenseless against the deepest challenge of our time: the requirement that privilege and distinction between man and man—between race and race—be finally and completely blotted out.

Slavery was the moral issue of the 1850s. But never forget that in a very real sense slavery served to conceal the underlying race issue itself. It was not so much an economic system as it was a system of racial adjustment and social control. Its existence relieved people of the necessity for coming to grips with the race issue itself; and dimly, uneasily, in the back of their minds, the men who debated the slavery issue were aware that a larger issue lay back of it.

If you have Negro slavery you really have no race problem. The man who can be bought and sold, owned from the cradle to the grave, compelled by all the power of government and public opinion to serve your will as long as he may live—he may indeed be a problem, but the problem does not involve the question of how the different races of men are going to get along with each other. Perhaps that is the real reason why slavery lasted so long in this country. It offered a handy way—the only way men could think of—to dodge the race question. Remove slavery and you still have the two races, living elbow to elbow in a land which professes to believe in unvarnished democracy. What do you do then?

That was the unspoken question that lay back of the issue which was central to the Lincoln-Douglas debates. It was the question which neither this country nor its leaders was then prepared to answer. By the same token, it is the one question above all others which we ourselves, today, have got to meet. What do you do then?

Slavery was not universal in the United States a century ago. In the Northern states all men were free—many of them colored men. In the Southern states, also, there were many free Negros. Yet the status of the free Negro in the 1850s was not actually much better than the status of the slave. Both Northern and Southern states had sharply restrictive legislation which put him unmistakably in the ranks of second-class citizens. As Ulrich B. Phillips has pointed out, the status of the free Negro in those days was that of "a third element in a system planned for two." He simply did not fit in, and the reason he did not fit was that he was considered to be an inferior sort of person.

Bear in mind that the very abolitionists themselves began as a group which hoped to see Negro slaves freed and then transported bodily to some far-off land—Liberia, or Central America, or some place else—where they might work out their own destiny as best they could. Lincoln himself clung to a lingering faith in this colonization proposal even after the Civil War had begun; and the basic motive in all of this, obviously, was not so much to give freedom to the slave as to rid American society of an element which was considered deeply and permanently inassimilable.

Here at Galesburg, Senator Douglas spent a substantial part of his allotted time elaborating the charge that Lincoln stood for equality between the races. The Negro, said Douglas, was entitled to certain rights—which the senator did not bother to specify—but he was not, could not be, and ought not to be a citizen.

Answering this charge, Lincoln, undeniably went on the defensive. In a curiously roundabout locution, he remarked, "I have never manifested any impatience with the necessities that spring from the actual presence of black people among us." He was firmly and unequivocally against the oppression of the Negro, but once the oppression was ended he was little more ready than Douglas to welcome the Negro to full membership in the American society.

Nobody was ready in 1858; not too many people are ready in 1958; and in those facts lies the tragedy and the challenge of the Civil War. For the challenge that nobody was quite prepared to talk about then was a challenge to the idea that the basic rights of free men are inviolable and eternal. It was a challenge to the notion that in a society dedicated to the proposition that all men are created equal there can be no ranks or grades of citizenship; a challenge, finally to the belief in the brotherhood of man under the fatherhood of God.

We are no longer living in the world that saw the American Civil War. The world has moved, since then—and it has moved out from under the ground on which the men who listened to Lincoln and Douglas stood. In our own generation we have, at a very high cost, gone to war with men who announced that there was a Master Race which would control the world through all visible future time. We beat them, precisely as in the 1860s we beat the men who stood for eternal enslavement of the subject race; and we are left with nothing but the obligation to understand that there are no master races or subject races on all the earth. There are nothing but a lot of people, the children of an ever-living God who, as we are told in Holy Writ, is no respector of persons.

And it was this fact which the debaters of a century ago avoided. They could not face up to it; it was too radical an idea for that generation, and sometimes it seems too radical an idea for today. But it is an idea which we have got to understand and accept, because if it is not accepted our whole American way of life is based on error and falsehood. We began by announcing that all men are created equal; we fought a terrible war to prove that we meant it; now we have to live up to it.

All men; not just the men of our own color, religion, racial origin, or habit of thought; all men. The dream we have dreamed is broad enough to include them; this infinite Earth of ours spinning through space on its eternal journey from the incomprehensible to the final embodiment of the best that we have imagined it, also, is wide enough and great enough to accept this idea, which is the most powerful idea that has ever taken hold of the mind of man. There are no separate, inherent classifications in human society; man, as we say when we recite our creeds, was born a little lower than the Angels, and crowned with glory and honor—and the family of man is at last a unit.

The debaters who stood where we are now pleaded for justice, as they understood justice. They spoke eloquently and with power, but they left something for us to do, because they saw things with the eyes of their own generation. Their generation trusted them, followed them, and at last went to war to work out a part of the proposition which the debaters had found themselves unable to state. The Civil War was fought, and its final heritage is the everlasting obligation to go on from the point where the leaders and the fighters stopped.

Standing here, Senator Douglas extolled the principle that each state in the Union ought to mind its own business; he went on to say that, "Under that principle the United States can perform that great mission, that destiny which Providence has marked out for us." We do have a mission, we do have a destiny marked out by Providence—yet it goes a little beyond the matter of minding our own business. It goes beyond justice to brotherhood, beyond fair play to understanding. Far beyond anything that anyone who was here a century ago could see, there is the undying ideal of the lasting unity of human society, the idea that freedom is for everyone without qualification, the picture of a human society in which the color of a man's skin simply does not matter at all. The Civil War compelled us to face up to this ideal. It committed us, once and for all, now and forever, to the task of working for its attainment.

(Reprinted by special permission
from Mr. Bruce Catton.)

Bruce Catton

Among the eloquent speakers present at the Galesburg Centennial celebration was Mr. Bruce Catton. He was invited to give the convocation address above, included with his permission.

Mr. Catton, a native of Michigan, had demonstrated very early in his career that he was fascinated by Civil War history. His narratives of that period very promptly received popular attention. Among these were *The War Lords of Washington, Mr. Lincoln's Army,* and *Glory Road.* These were followed by *A Stillness at Appomattox, The American Military*

Tradition, Banners at Shenandoah, and *The Hallowed Ground.* Others include *America Goes to War, Grant Moves South, Two Roads to Sumpter, Terrible Swift Sword,* and *Never Call Retreat.*

He was honored in 1954 for his historical writings by the award of the Pulitzer Prize. He also received the National Book Award that same year. The Ohioana Library Association presented him the nonfiction award for 1954. For many years he has been the senior editor of the magazine *American Heritage.* He is also a member of the American Academy of Arts and Letters. He has contributed many articles to *This Week, Holiday,* and *Life* magazines.

His convocation address illuminates the conditions and problems which generated these famous debates. He presents the historic events as dynamic antecedents to our present concepts of national conscience and philosophy of government.

AN ADDRESS ABOUT STEPHEN A. DOUGLAS

By Senator Paul H. Douglas (D. IL.) for delivery at the Quincy, Illinois, Celebration Commemorating the 100th Anniversary of the Lincoln-Douglas Debates, October 13, 1958. It was very similar to the address he presented at Galesburg.

In a natural desire to magnify the qualities of our noble politician-saint, Abraham Lincoln, there has been an unfortunate tendency to disparage and depreciate Stephen A. Douglas, his opponent. As Lincoln has been properly cast in the role of hero, what is more inevitable for those who love sharp contrasts than to assign Douglas the part of the villain? So in discussing these memorable debates in which a century ago the two ablest sons which Illinois has produced struggled across our hot prairies and into the cold and rainy autumn, and which were, in fact, the prelude to the Civil war, many writers and orators swayed by a sense of drama and, at times, by partisan feeling have generally drawn a sharp comparison between Douglas, who is pictured as squat, arrogant, morally obtuse and none too bright, and the tall, majestic, all-comprehending Lincoln.

This is a grave distortion of the truth. Without disparaging Lincoln in the slightest, I hope that in the few minutes at my disposal, I may put the debaters in a more accurate perspective.

In the first place, Douglas' energy and ability was such as to make him a foeman worthy of Lincoln's steel. No neutral can study the debates—including the preliminary Chicago, Bloomington, and Springfield species—without concluding that Douglas was very often the superior, and it is well to remember that it was Douglas and not Lincoln who won the election.

Born in Vermont in 1813, Douglas came to Illinois at the age of 20 with but a single dollar in his pocket. After teaching school at Winchester for a few months, he was admitted to the bar shortly before he was 21. A few months afterwards, he was chosen State's Attorney of Morgan County. Elected to the Legislature at the age of 23, he served with Lincoln, where he made a distinctly better record than the latter. At 27, he became Secretary of State for Illinois, and shortly afterwards, the youngest judge ever to serve on our State Supreme Court. Douglas took up his residence in Quincy soon after his election to the Supreme Court in 1940. Then in 1843, at the age of 30, he was elected to Congress, and three years afterwards, to the Senate of the United States. As Clay, Calhoun, Webster, and Denton faded from the scene, Douglas became the intellectual leader of the Senate—the voice of young America and of western expansion. He was chairman of the Committee on Territories of the House and Senate, and brought five states into the Union. He barely missed being nominated for the Presidency in 1856, and when he appeared in Quincy, Illinois, an even century ago, he was the foremost statesman of the Nation.

Douglas was, as I have said, the advocate of western expansion. He had supported the Mexican War and the acquisition of what is now New Mexico, Arizona, California, and Nevada. He had worked aggressively for an Oregon treaty, which brought the Pacific Northwest under the American flag, and he looked forward to the day when all of North America, including Canada and Mexico, would be joined to us in political union, with continental free trade and with democratic institutions prevailing for all. To cement such a union, he put through the Illinois Central Railroad, running from Elena and Chicago in the North to New Orleans in the South. This was designed to tie the middle west together with the Mississippi and Gulf states and which, in the process, built up many cities along its way. In doing so, he avoided the later abuses and scandals of the railway grants of the '60s and '70s, and gave to the State of Illinois a share of the revenues of the road and a voice in its control. Then he pushed through legislation for a railroad from Chicago to the Pacific Ocean to connect the middle and far west.

It was here that, unfortunately, he helped to set in play the forces which were his ultimate undoing. For the immediate question of the late '40s and '50s was whether the new territories which were being acquired were to be slave or free. The ultimate issue was no less than the fate of the Nation as a whole. The Southern fire-eaters wanted to extend slavery into the North, and Toombs of Georgia boasted that he was going to call the roll of his slaves from the foot of Bunker Hill Monument. The Northern abolitionists, on the other hand, wanted slavery to be abolished in the South. If either of these groups were to fail in their objectives, each preferred secession and separation to union in a divided country.

Midway between these groups stood Douglas. As a compromise, he proposed that the people of the newly established territories should have the right to decide whether or not they wished to legalize slavery, and that the Federal government should preserve strict neutrality. To obtain Southern support for his Western railway, he got Congress in 1854 to pass the Kansas-Nebraska Act, which repealed the Missouri Compromise of 1820. This compromise had prohibited slavery in new territories north of the extension of the southern boundary of Missouri, but Douglas' impetuous and unwise decision now opened them up to local option on the question.

While disclaiming in public any moral concern over the question of slavery, and in his speeches stating that he did not care whether slavery was voted up or down, Douglas nevertheless insisted on the right of the people of the territories to make a free choice and the duty of the Federal government to be neutral in fact as well as in word. When the Buchanan Administration violated this principle and with the aid of armed bands from Missouri tried to jam the pro-slavery Lecompton constitution down the throats of the people of Kansas, Douglas broke with Buchanan and fought with all his strength for fair play and free elections. Douglas was in no sense a defender of slavery, and his private correspondence indicates that he wanted the popular referendum to reject slavery. There are certainly few more courageous acts in American political history than his defiance of Buchanan and the South and his insistence that the Kansas elections should be fair and above board. He knew that if this were carried out, the territory of Kansas would vote against slavery and the issue would be settled by local rather than national action.

In the Senatorial election of 1858, he was, therefore, being opposed by the Buchanan Democrats from the right, as well as by the newly founded Republican Party under its leader, Lincoln, from the radical left. These latter two groups, widely divided as they were in their ultimate aims, were never-the-less united in a common effort to end the political career of Douglas.

Lincoln's opposition was, of course, deeper than any personal rivalry. Like Douglas, he occupied a middle ground between the two sets of extremists. He, too, was opposed to abolishing slavery by force in the South. But, unlike Douglas, he maintained that the Federal government should not merely be neutral. He contended that since slavery was wrong, it should instead prevent its extension into the territories. By thus preventing the spread of slavery into new territory, he believed that the economic wastes of that institution would ultimately lead to the freeing of the slaves in the South. But he wanted this to be done peacefully, voluntarily, and with full compensation to the owners.

These, then, were the momentous issues which a century ago were being threshed out on the prairies of our beloved State and which faced the debaters.

At Freeport, on the 27th of August, Lincoln had asked Douglas the crucial question as to how he could reconcile the Dred Scott Decision that slave owners could take their slaves into free territories, and possibly even into free states, with his doctrine of the supremacy of popular sovereignty. Douglas' instant reply was that by local police ordinances and by the sentiments of the people, the Dred Scott decision could be made inoperative in the territories. This won for him the Senatorial election of 1858. But his answer split the Democratic Party between its Northern and its Southern wing and led to his own defeat in 1860 as the Presidential candidate of the Northern section.

Part of the debate at Quincy, as elsewhere, was taken up with not very productive charges and counter-charges as to how radical Lincoln and the Republican party had been in 1856 and whether Lincoln had not falsely accused Presidents Pierce and Buchanan, the Supreme Court, and Douglas himself of a conspiracy to extend slavery not only into the territories but also into the free states themselves.

Lincoln was, however, under some embarrassment by Douglas' comparison of his speeches in Chicago and Freeport before anti-slavery audiences and those in Jonesboro and Charleston before audiences primarily composed of men and women from the South. In Northern Illinois Lincoln had stressed the Declaration of Independence with its noble Jeffersonian Preamble that "all men are created equal and are endowed by their Creator with certain inalienable rights; that among these are life, liberty, and the pursuit of happiness."

Douglas had hit hard at Lincoln and had accused him of changing his position according to his audience. Lincoln's reply was that there was no contradiction between what he said in Northern and in Southern Illinois, and this was probably true. Yet it is also true that he did stress a different emphasis in different portions of the state. But Lincoln had recovered his equilibrium at Quincy, and at the end of his opening speech properly stressed the moral wrong of slavery and his hope that it might ultimately disappear, although by peaceful and legal means which he did not venture to define.

Douglas, in his speech, demanded to know precisely how Lincoln would prevent the spread of slavery, and asserted again the right of the people of the territories and states to choose whether or not they wanted slavery. He said he had defended this principle against Buchanan and the slavocracy, and he was defending it against Lincoln and the Republicans. If this were done, the Union could stand with both types of states and go on to greater triumphs.

It was in the election of 1860 that Douglas, however, rose to true greatness. Seeing that his defeat for the Presidency was inevitable, he toured the South and begged the Southerners not to secede. If they would only let the issue of slavery be freely decided on the frontier, he argued that this divisive issue could be insulated from the mainstream of the nation's political life so that the Union could thus be preserved. This had always been implicit in his policies, but it now became his main theme.

As I have said, Douglas was in no sense an apologist for slavery. He was instead a passionate American patriot. He was trying to prevent not only his party, but also the Union, from breaking up, and he sought to effect this by a political compromise which would prevent a fight to the death over a moral issue. In this way he hoped to avoid secession and a bloody civil war.

There are still many who argue that Douglas was right and that if his advice had been taken we might have avoided the Civil War and that, in the long run, the Negros would have been as well off. He was certainly seeking a peaceful political solution to avoid disunion and to obtain time during which the question of slavery might be settled peacefully.

But by 1858 slavery had properly become a moral issue. The conscience of the North had been touched, and the publication of *Uncle Tom's Cabin*, the Dred Scott Decision, and the struggle over Kansas were fanning these sentiments. The attempt to find a political solution for a moral issue failed. For neither the North nor the South would accept Douglas and his compromise. The South rejected him at the Charleston convention of the Democratic Party in 1860 and formed a separate party of its own with Breckenridge as its nominee.

The split in the Democratic Party in the spring of 1860 led to the firing on Fort Sumter in the Spring of the following year, and hence to the Civil War. For the North would not accept Douglas' compromise, either, and Lincoln was elected although he polled only a minority of the popular vote. Then the South seceded rather than live under the presidency of a hated Northerner. When this issue was presented to the nation, Douglas did not hesitate for a moment. He pledged his support to his rival, Lincoln, and went on an extended speaking trip through Southern Ohio, Indiana, and Illinois to rally the Democrats behind the Union cause. In this he was largely successful, and he even brought over such violent Southern sympathizers as John A. Logan and John A. McClernand, who became Union generals. But worn out by heat, over-exhaustion, and strain, he succumbed to a fever and died more or less penniless on June 3, 1861, at the early age of 48. He was as much a war casualty as those who died on the field of battle.

Looking at the period in perspective, it is apparent that one of the tragedies of American history was the failure of Douglas in 1856 to be nominated and elected as President instead of James Buchanan. For had Stephen A. Douglas been President from 1857 to 1861, it is possible that the Civil War might have been prevented. Douglas would have seen to it that the people of Kansas had complete freedom to deal with slavery as they thought best. He would not, like Buchanan, have tried to force a pro-slavery constitution upon the unwilling voters of Kansas. Kansas would then have voted slavery down, and John Brown would have had no urge to take revenge. If the South had threatened to secede, Douglas—unlike Buchanan—would have acted to prevent it. With his fairness and firmness guiding the nation, we might have avoided the Civil War and ultimately have set the slaves free.

By the fall of 1858, however, matters had probably gone too far. A weak President was in the White House, and the South was refusing to follow the middle course mapped out by Douglas. It was proper, therefore, for the country to have elected Lincoln in 1860, and the 1858 debates were instrumental in doing just that. But Douglas had been the man for 1856.

A fighter for American unity, Douglas' body lies near the shores of Lake Michigan, and into the coolness of his tomb the stormy waters of the inland sea send at times their clangor. Atop an excessively high pedestal, his protégé Leonard Volk fashioned a figure in marble of his beloved patron. Perhaps Volk designed the high pedestal in reprisal against the neglect which the Illinois Legislature in its partisanship had accorded to the second most eminent son of our State. But as an eminent historian has remarked, it might perhaps have been more appropriate for Douglas' statue to have faced West, rather than East. For it was the West which he loved and which he wanted to bring into the Union with institutions of its own choosing. For his better nature always inclined there, rather than towards the East and his vain hopes of the White House. But his proud and patriotic spirit would have rejoiced at the carving of his last words to his children, at the base of the monument, "Tell them to obey the laws and support the Constitution of the United States."

(Reprinted by permission of Senator Paul H. Douglas. A copy was obtained by courtesy of the *Chicago Historical Society*.)

Senator Paul Howard Douglas

The Centennial Committee at Galesburg requested statesmen, scholars, and historians to discuss the many facets of these historic debates. The address by Senator Paul H. Douglas was selected to complement the memorial bas-relief plaque of Stephen Arnold Douglas and to present to the reader an appreciation of the admirable qualities of the man Abraham Lincoln chose to challenge.

Senator Paul H. Douglas was three times elected to the United States Senate by the State of Illinois, and served from 1948 to 1966. Prior to his first election, he served as a university professor. He began his career in 1917 as an economics instructor at Reed College in Portland, Oregon. He advanced to an assistant professorship at the University of Washington in 1920. In 1923 he moved to Chicago, where he was appointed to the faculty of the University of Chicago. He was also honored by the appointment as visiting professor of Amherst College in 1927. He received a Guggenheim fellowship in 1931. He served as a professor of Industrial Relations at the University of Chicago until 1948. Later, after his terms in the Senate, he was appointed to the faculty of the New School of Social Research of New York College.

During World War II he served in the United States Marine Corps, from 1942 to 1946, advancing from an enlisted man to Colonel. He saw action in the occupation of Peleliu and Okinawa. He was awarded the Bronze Star.

He is the author of many publications regarding Economics and Industrial relations. His books include: *Wages and the Family, Real Wages in the United States, The Coming of the New Party, The Theory of Wages, Controlling Depressions,* and *Ethics in Government.*

He has demonstrated a lifelong interest in United States history, with a special attention to the history of Abraham Lincoln and the State of Illinois. This address, presented at Quincy, Illinois, is included by special permission of Senator Paul H. Douglas.

Fig. 1. *Portrait of Carl Sandburg*, author, poet, and Lincoln historian.

A PORTRAIT OF CARL SANDBURG
Author, Poet, and Lincoln Historian

One can hardly speak of Carl Sandburg without recalling his voluminous contributions to the Lincoln story. A bond of sympathy exists between Lincoln and Sandburg, since this poet also came from meager circumstances and secured an education by his own means and determination. He was born in Galesburg, Illinois, in 1878, of immigrant Swedish parents who came to this country with practically no education. Knox College in the same city was the site of one of the famous Lincoln-Douglas debates. Abraham Lincoln was considered a hero in this community, and young Sandburg was duly impressed with the abundant stories about the president. At the age of 13 he had finished the eighth grade and went to work to earn a living, but he continued to read poetry and the Bible. He worked at any odd job he could find. He was a milk wagon driver, a porter in a barber shop, and a truck driver for a brick kiln before he was 17. Adventure called, and he rode the rails west. He gained experience working in wheat fields, washing dishes in cheap hotels, and as a carpenter's apprentice. He returned to Galesburg and was employed as a helper to a house painter.

When the Spanish-American war broke out, Sandburg enlisted in the Army and saw active service in Puerto Rico. He served as a war correspondent for the *Galesburg Evening Mail*. After the cessation of hostilities, he returned to Galesburg and Lombard College with the little money he had saved from his soldier's pay. This he augmented by work as a tutor, a bell ringer, and a janitor while in college. Here the influence of an inspiring teacher encouraged him to further achievements in literature.

His first publication, *In Reckless Ecstasy*, was written during his college years. For the next two years, he roamed the country, taking temporary jobs on newspapers. He became acquainted with the people of America and learned many of the customs and folksongs of the different regions. Strumming his guitar, he traveled North, South, East, and West.

On his return to Illinois, he accepted an editorial position with the *Chicago Daily News.* Later he moved to Milwaukee, where he served as secretary to the mayor for two years. There he married Lillian Steichan in 1908. For support of a growing family, his interest turned to advertising, feature articles, and occasional free verse. Returning again to Chicago, in 1912, he continued writing free verse. He published his *Chicago Poems* in 1916 and *Cornhuskers* in 1918.

When the United States entered World War I, Carl Sandburg went to Sweden as a special correspondent for the Newspaper Enterprise Association. Returning from Europe after the War, he joined the staff of the *Chicago Daily Mail.* He published *Smoke and Steel, Slabs of the Sunburnt West,* and *Rootabaga Stories.* During this time he was collecting information for a biography of Abraham Lincoln. About three months out of the year he spent on speaking engagements, with special preference for cities where he could study and collect Lincoln material. In 1926 he published the two-volume compendium, *Abraham Lincoln: The Prairie Years.* The literary critics were enthusiastic in their praise of this book written for the common man.

With the proceeds of this publication, he was able to concentrate his efforts on the continued biography. In the process he collected and studied every book, article, scrap, or bit of Lincoln material he could secure. He read more about the subject than any other person living or dead. Sixteen years later he published *Abraham Lincoln: The War Years* in four volumes. Although it was written in much the same style, a greater attention to factual details earned him the praise of historians as well as literary critics. This publication won for him the coveted Pulitzer Prize for history.

He also wrote a Civil War book entitled *Storm Over the Land,* and he continued to compose poetry during this period. *The American Song Bag* was published in 1927, *Good Morning America* in 1928, and *The People Yes* in 1936. *Always the Young Strangers,* coming off the press in 1953, was a narrative of his life in Galesburg.

He won many prizes for his poetry and received many honors for his contributions to Lincoln lore. At the Centennial of the Lincoln-Douglas Debates at Knox College, he was honored by a Carl Sandburg day.

In modeling the portrait, Dr. Fairbanks has embodied the personality and the character of this poet of industrial America. This author often wrote using slang and the language of the street with a colorful frankness, sometimes gentleness, but occasionally with intense vigor. The face conveys an impression of the courageous honesty of a man who portrays, without embellishments, the conditions as they exist. He was a poet of the worker.

The original plaster cast of the portrait was placed in the Chicago Historical Museum. A bronze cast of the portrait bust of Carl Sandburg was donated to Knox College by Joseph Halle Schaffner of Santa Barbara, California; Max Goodsill of Galesburg, Illinois; and Harold Szold of New York. It was unveiled at the 115th Commencement of the College.

Fig. 1. *Abraham Lincoln The Youth*, anterior view.

THE FOUR AGES
OF ABRAHAM LINCOLN
Portraits in Marble

The Four Ages of Abraham Lincoln

Broadcast Music, Inc., commissioned the distinguished American sculptor, Avard Fairbanks, to create four heroic size portraits in marble of Abraham Lincoln that were later presented to the National Government for the Lincoln Sesquicentennial. These measured 21-inches tall, 10-inches wide, and 9-inches deep, depicting Lincoln at various stages of his life: *Lincoln The Youth, Lincoln The Pioneer, Lincoln The Lawyer*, and *Lincoln The President*.

In ceremonies at the Ford Theater, Lincoln Museum, February 1, 1960, the four marble heads of the Great Emancipator were unveiled. Participating in this unveiling were Senator John Sherman Cooper, Chairman of the Lincoln Sesquicentennial Commission; Carl Sandburg, noted poet and Lincoln biographer; Earl H. Hardin, prominent Lincoln collector; and the sculptor, Avard Fairbanks.

The original commissioning of these busts was undertaken as part of the art work to accompany a series of radio scripts prepared by Broadcast Music, Inc., for distribution among the nation's broadcast stations as a public service during the Lincoln sesquicentennial year. The scripts, entitled "Abraham Lincoln 1809-1959," are a part of the Broadcast Music, Inc., prize-winning series, "The American Story."

The first two portraits, cast in plaster, were presented February 19, 1959, at the headquarters of the Lincoln Sesquicentennial Commission in the National Archives. These were *Lincoln The Youth* and *Lincoln The President*. Presiding at that unveiling were Senator John Sherman Cooper (R. Ky.), chairman of the Sesquicentennial Commission, and Representative Fred Schwengel (R. Iowa), president of the Lincoln Group for Washington, DC. Copies of these plaster casts, along with the casts of *Lincoln The Frontiersman* and *Lincoln The Lawyer*, were later sent to Pietrasanta, Italy, where they were carved in Carrara marble.

Official presentation of the four marble portraits of Abraham Lincoln to the Federal Government was made on February 11, 1960, at the Willard Hotel. Miss Bertha S. Adkins, chairman of the executive committee of the Sesquicentennial Commission, accepted these portraits from Mr. Carl Haverlon, president of Broadcast Music, Inc., at the annual Lincoln Day dinner sponsored by the District of Columbia Lincoln Group.

A duplicate of the portrait bust of *Lincoln The Frontiersman* carved in marble was placed in a hall of The International Copyright Bureau, honoring great statesmen of the world, in Geneva, Switzerland. The four heroic marble portraits were planned to be placed in the Ford Theater Museum where Abraham Lincoln was assassinated. *Lincoln The Youth, Lincoln The Frontiersman,* and *Lincoln The President* were placed there. *Lincoln The Lawyer* was appropriately chosen to grace the Temple of Justice, the Supreme Court Building in Washington, DC.

A cast of one of the Lincoln portraits was presented to President Dwight Eisenhower at a Republican breakfast in July, 1960, by Governor William Stratton of Illinois as a gift from his state.

Lincoln The Youth

Lincoln The Youth was modeled by the sculptor after comprehensive study of books and articles relating to boyhood experiences. For much of the information about Lincoln at this age, the nation is indebted to William Herndon, his law partner. Mr. Herndon visited the villages and countryside where Lincoln spent his youth. He recorded anecdotes, personal impressions, and events of Lincoln's boyhood activities, as told by former friends and neighbors.

Although no photographs are available prior to his age of 37 years, the sculptor, by expert knowledge and observation of changes in aging, has used the Lincoln features but softened them. Brows and nose were less prominent; the cheeks were rounded; and wrinkles were eliminated. The pleasantness of his countenance reflects many of the qualities of his actions and personality (Figs. 1, 2).

At Gentryville in Indiana, towns-people remembered Abe for being kind and helpful. A man or woman in trouble never failed to receive all the help Lincoln could give them. He wrote essays against cruelty to animals and protested whenever he saw wanton abuse. This gentle attitude, along with his stature and physical strength, made a profound impression on his friends.

Besides gentleness, the sculptor has modeled into the portrait a vigor of youth. In 1826, Lincoln served

Fig. 2. *Abraham Lincoln The Youth*, left oblique view.

Fig. 3. *Abraham Lincoln The Youth*, right lateral view.

as a ferryman at the mouth of Anderson Creek, where passengers and luggage were rowed to or from steamboats plying the Ohio River. Later Mr. Gentry hired young Abe, then in his 16th year, to serve as bow hand, to work the bow oar on a boat loaded with produce bound for New Orleans. He earned $8 a month and passage back home (Fig. 3).

There is a quality of alertness and quick wit about the portrait. Although few books were available to him, he knew them thoroughly. Besides the scanty books in his home, he had in time borrowed and read nearly all the books within a radius of 50 miles. Every lull in his daily labor he used for reading.

He had also gained a reputation as a wag and storyteller at the village store. He recited poems and speeches, and he even imitated the sermons of itinerant ministers. His fondness of public speaking attracted him as a spectator to the trials in court at Boonville, 15 miles distant.

In addition to these many admirable qualities, he was also a dutiful son. He gave the money he earned to his father, as was the custom of the times. For his willingness and ability to perform work about a farm, he was the most sought-after hired boy in the community.

The sculptor considered all these personal characteristics as he created first the form of Abraham Lincoln, using well-recorded details. He then erased the effect of time, transposing to the visage of youth, and he gave the portrait the qualities of expression befitting a young man with these and many other commendable attributes.

Lincoln The Frontiersman

This portrait of *Lincoln The Frontiersman* recalls Dr. Fairbanks' first heroic monument, *Lincoln The Frontiersman*, at Ewa, Hawaii. Before modeling this portrait, he reviewed much of the research material collected during the modeling of the statue. He studied more Lincoln history to increase his familiarity with the background, the character, and the experiences of Abraham Lincoln, so that he might better mold animation and expression of the subject into the lifeless clay.

Abraham Lincoln was born and reared on the frontier, and this sculptured head portrays him as a frontiersman about the time he came of age, before he started the practice of law.

He was 21 when his father, Thomas Lincoln, after 14 years of hard labor, recognized that the farm and the area of Buckhorn Valley were unpromising. He decided to leave Indiana and move to Illinois. Milk sickness had claimed the life of Abraham Lincoln's mother and several relatives. Cattle also periodically died of this malady. The Illinois prairie appeared to be more promising, and a relative had given good reports of Sangamon Valley.

In March 1830, with two other families, Thomas Lincoln moved his family from Pigeon Creek near Gentryville, Indiana, to new land near Decatur, Illinois. It took two weeks of travel in harsh weather over muddy roads and swollen streams. Young Abe drove one of the teams. At the new farm, the young Lincoln helped erect a log cabin. He also split rails for a fence that enclosed ten acres. In the spring of 1831, with the help of his cousin and stepbrother, he built a flatboat and loaded it with produce. After adroitly passing over the dam at New Salem, they navigated the Sangamon and Mississippi rivers, floating down to New Orleans.

On his return he became a clerk of a village store at New Salem, Illinois. He was noted for his comical stories, and his scrupulous honesty became legend. His friends boasted of his physical strength, and on more than one occasion, he had to show he could out-wrestle a powerfully built opponent.

When the Black Hawk war alarms sounded, Lincoln enlisted and was elected captain of a company. Later he enlisted as a private in a company of independent rangers. Although they encountered no hostilities, they covered much of the territory of northwest Illinois. After mustering out of military service, Lincoln returned to New Salem, where he again served as a store clerk and part owner. Later he was postmaster and then became a surveyor.

He read and studied whenever a spare moment presented itself, and it was at New Salem that his political career started. His political speeches, given usually from a convenient stump, invariably attracted an attentive audience. His interest in public speaking led him to join in a debating group. In athletic contests, he often served as umpire or arbiter, and was effective as a peacemaker.

The sculptor has modeled in this a more rugged young man than the portrait of the youth. This portrays the most physically vigorous period of

Fig. 4. *Abraham Lincoln The Frontiersman*, anterior view.

Lincoln's life. Sturdiness of purpose, scrupulous honesty, friendliness, alertness, and possession of a knowledge-hungry mind, all mellowed by his poignant wit, were some of the attributes considered as the portrait progressed.

Even as Dr. Fairbanks built up the rough form, he felt he had a personal acquaintance with this backwoods politician, scout, and businessman. He sensed Lincoln's personality as he applied rolls of clay with bold strokes of his thumb. Excess clay was cut away with a coarse modeling tool. Clay was re-applied in thin rolls, smoothed with the finger, then carefully stroked with a fine tool.

The strong, vigorous features of the finished portrait took many hours to perfect, through days of careful work. The sculptor often reviewed his work, reassessed it, and made alterations accordingly. The casual observer would be impressed with the likeness long before the sculptor was satisfied that he had created the desired mood and animation in the features. The finished details were worked and reworked during periods of creative endeavor, when the artist was imbued with a feel-

Fig. 5. *Abraham Lincoln The Frontiersman*, left lateral view.

ing for the man and his character. True masterpieces require diligence, study, and inspiration.

Lincoln The Lawyer

The creation of a portrait of *Lincoln The Lawyer* required considerable research by the sculptor to develop an understanding of this great character, as he served in the courts of law. Many descriptions by authors were studied, anecdotes by acquaintances were considered, and photographs were reviewed. The sculptor read much Lincoln lore, often re-reading it aloud at the studio in the evening, in order to better understand the feelings and the motivations, thereby modeling Lincoln's personality into clay.

Whoever views this portrait unconsciously assumes the position of a juryman, a witness, or a judge. One may then sense the spirit or animation of this tall, personable, friendly, and often witty advocate as he would plead a case. Lincoln could use pathos or emotion to his advantage, but more often he appealed to reason. He used plain terms that even the dullest juryman could comprehend.

His attitude to a witness was friendly and kind, in such a manner as to bring out the whole truth. His cases were prepared with scrupulous accuracy. The salient points were brought out repeatedly until they were firmly impressed on the jury's memory.

The young Lincoln had started primarily as a self-taught frontier attorney, encouraged by John T. Stuart, one of the leading lawyers and politicians of the state. Many of the law books he studied during the last year he lived in New Salem had been borrowed from Stuart's office.

Soon after Lincoln was admitted to the bar, he gave up surveying, moved to Springfield, and became a partner with John Stuart. This association lasted four years, during which time he gained experience and reputation. He followed the circuit courts of the Eighth Judicial District of Illinois, an area that included 15 sparsely settled counties.

A subsequent partnership was made with Stephen T. Logan, a highly respected, well-educated attorney, who had formerly served as a judge. Logan was meticulous and exact in his preparation, while his presentations were concise and lucid. Lincoln benefited greatly in experience with this able adviser. However, the partnership was dissolved in four years, as Stephen Logan took his own son as a partner.

During Lincoln's third partnership with William Herndon, the law practice continued, interspersed with politics, which included one term in Congress. He decided to abandon politics and concentrate on the practice of law. The years of 1849 to 1855 were his most productive period. He had become a lawyer's lawyer, as the larger part of his cases were referrals from attorneys; he was also sought by them as counsel. During this period, he continued his program of self-education, studying Euclidean geometry and astronomy. He also studied Shakespeare and the Bible, as he strove for greater literary excellence.

Many of his cases were in the Illinois Supreme Court and the Federal Courts. The coming of the railroad not only made travel faster and easier, but brought his firm a new type of business. As the railroads were in the pioneering phase pushing their tracks across the prairie, several railroads retained him as an attorney, and he contributed many legal principles to this industry. His services were also

Fig. 6. *Abraham Lincoln The Lawyer*, anterior view.

Fig. 7. *Abraham Lincoln The Lawyer*, left lateral view.

sought by banks, mercantile institutions, manufacturers, and insurance companies.

The law practice was increasingly active, even though his initial effort for a client was to arrange to settle matters, if possible, to avoid a suit.

He is reported to have once said in a lecture:

"Discourage litigation. Persuade your neighbors to compromise whenever you can. Point out to them how the nominal winner is often the real loser in fees, expenses, and waste of time. As a peacemaker, the lawyer has a superior opportunity of being a good man."

Abraham Lincoln had many other admirable qualities. Foremost of these were diligence, careful and meticulous preparation of cases, and integrity. Mary Lincoln once said, "My husband was truth itself." He was resourceful through the knowledge he gained in various occupations and self-study. He deftly used illustrations and comparisons in order that the jury could more easily comprehend. His wit and humor were nearly always evident before the bar. He was conscientious in accepting cases and

charging fees and he never expected more from a client than the services were worth, or more than the client could pay. He was a humble and modest man, imbued with a sense of fairness. Nevertheless, he had an ability to command in court in the same persuasive manner he assumed to command at the rostrum. In defending a case he would often concede point after point, until he would concentrate the attention of the jury on the crucial issue, emphasizing it repeatedly. His courtroom strategy was legend.

The sculptor has portrayed Abraham Lincoln as a man, not only as a politician of considerable stature, but as an attorney at law, one of the most able and convincing in the State of Illinois. Honesty, humility and integrity are simultaneously manifest with a convincing, commanding countenance.

Lincoln The President

During extensive study for the portrait of *Lincoln The President*, Dr. Fairbanks considered various moods of Abraham Lincoln. He chose at length to model him in a moment of reflection, of deep

Fig. 8. *Abraham Lincoln The Lawyer*, right lateral view.

Fig. 9. *Abraham Lincoln The President*, anterior view.

thought, of pondering the evidence for a far-reaching decision, or deliberating on the problems of the Army or easing the burdens of an individual soldier. He was saddened by the countless casualties of dead and wounded. A genuine humility and compassion were to be molded into the face.

A great source of sorrow during the Civil War was the necessity of punishment. Crimes common to other segments of society were committed, as well as crimes common to military organizations. These included desertion, sleeping at guard duty, disobedience, and supplying information to the enemy. Desertions mounted to alarming proportions and undermined efficiency. It became necessary to punish desertion with great severity, but lives of many condemned men were spared by telegrams from the President suspending sentences.

During the heaviest fighting, one general wrote to President Lincoln requesting permission to execute 24 deserters. At a later interview with the President, he said, "Mercy to a few is cruelty to many." Lincoln answered, "There are already too many weeping widows in the United States. For

God's sake do not ask me to add to the numbers, because I will not." "Must I shoot a simple-minded soldier boy who deserts," he said, "while I must not touch a hair of a wily agitator who induces him to desert? This is none the less injurious when effected by getting a father, or brother, or friend into a public meeting, and there working upon his feelings until he is persuaded to write the soldier boy that he is fighting in a bad cause, for a wicked administration of a contemptible government, too weak to arrest and punish him if he shall desert. I think that in such a case, to silence the agitator, and save the boy, is not only constitutional, but withal a great mercy." Another time he is quoted as having said, "The severest justice may not always be the best policy."

Another source of sorrow was the sight of the sick and wounded about Washington, DC. He visited hospitals as often as he could, speaking personally to men as he passed, giving friendly greetings, showing his genuine interest in the welfare of the soldiers. When passing to another section of the hospital, he gave the same personal

Fig. 10. *Abraham Lincoln The President*, right lateral view.

Fig. 11. *Abraham Lincoln The President*, left lateral view.

attention to wounded Confederate prisoners. This sensibility and sympathy for the suffering of the men and of the nation he set forth in all sincerity in his second inaugural address: "Fondly do we hope, fervently do we pray, that this mighty scourge of war may speedily pass away."

Through 1863 and 1864 the effect of the conflict had caused his face to grow more haggard, its lines deepened with sadness. During these times consumed with sorrow, he once said, "I think I shall never be glad again."

The sculptor has added years to the face of Lincoln by cutting in wrinkles and making character a little deeper. Into the marble he has carved a sense of grief, softened by a hope for peace.

Near the end of the conflict, the city of Richmond, Virginia, had become indefensible. It was abandoned by the Confederate government and civil authorities. When the military withdrew to the West, the mobs took over to loot and pillage. Some order had been restored, and fires destroying a considerable part of the city were quenched by the Union troops. The next day, an unexpected visit was

made by President Lincoln, escorted by Admiral Porter, some officers, and 12 sailors. He was greeted by tumultuous crowds, spontaneously rejoicing. He visited the Confederate White House recently vacated by Jefferson Davis, and spent two days discussing the situation of the city and how to restore Union authority. A tour of the city left Lincoln very depressed. Vandals had wrecked the legislative chambers of the stately columned capitol building designed by Thomas Jefferson. The desolation of one city in the wake of victory gave an insight into the enormous task of reunion and reconstruction.

Lincoln pondered ways to deal with those active in the insurrection, how to make liberal terms, yet hold in check the vindictive forces in his own government who would forget the admonition stated in his second inaugural address: "With malice toward none; with charity for all; with firmness in the right as God gives us to see the right, let us strive to finish the work we are in."

Fig. 12. *Abraham Lincoln The President*, clay.

Speech by Avard T. Fairbanks

The following address by Dr. Fairbanks was presented in nationwide radio broadcasts by Broadcast Music, Inc., of New York City. It was subsequently included with addresses by 75 other distinguished American statesmen, historians, and Lincoln scholars in a book titled *Lincoln for the Ages*, edited by Ralph G. Newman. It is included with permission of Broadcast Music, Inc.

The Face of Abraham Lincoln

By Avard T. Fairbanks

The face of Abraham Lincoln stirs people in all walks of life to a better understanding of mankind. In that face depth of thought, of feeling, and of understanding have outward expressions which become significant of American ideals. Presentations through masterful works of art of the features of Lincoln give to all who behold them greater awareness of the inner character of that unique and great individual.

Lincoln's face shows his true character to be full

Pencil Sketch

of compassion for the sufferer, with a deep sense of love for those who have devotion to duty, and a determination that right shall prevail—and that mankind will have a better world because of that right. He is the son for whom every mother can hope. Misunderstood and opposed by those primarily interested in self-gain, he was the devoted servant of the deprived, the hungry, the oppressed. In the world-wide sense, he is the ideal of those who struggle.

In the monuments and paintings dedicated to this humble man, the features of his face are symbolic to liberty-loving people throughout the world. For in a face can be found the secret of the power of communication with others, in times past as well as our own: here are the hopes, understandings, feelings, attitudes, and aspirations toward which one strives in life's pursuits. As we come to know those of Abraham Lincoln, we draw even closer to a great friend.

John G. Nicolay, his private secretary, observed

Lincoln on many occasions and in many moods. He described him as follows:

"Large head, with high crown of skull; thick, bushy hair; large and deep eye caverns; heavy eyebrows; a large nose; large ears; large mouth, thin upper and somewhat thick under lip; very high and prominent cheekbones; cheeks thin and sunken; strongly developed jawbones; chin slightly upturned; a thin but sinewy neck, rather long... ."

The distinguished correspondent for the *London Times,* William Howard Russell, met Lincoln for the first time in the spring of 1861 when Frederick Seward, the son of the Secretary of State, took the reporter to the White House. In his diary Russell recalls his first glimpse of the Lincoln features:

"The impression produced by the size of his extremities, and by his flapping and wide projecting ears, may be removed by the appearance of kindliness, sagacity, and the awkward *bonhomie* of his face; the mouth is absolutely prodigious; the lips, straggling and extending almost from one line of black beard to the other, are only kept in order by two deep furrows from the nostril to the chin; the nose itself—a prominent organ—stands out from the face with an inquiring, anxious air, as though it were sniffing for some good thing in the wind; the eyes dark, full, and deeply set, are penetrating, but full of an expression which almost amounts to tenderness; and above them projects the shaggy brow, running into the small hard frontal space, the development of which can scarcely be estimated accurately owing to the irregular flocks of thick hair carelessly brushed across it. One would say that, although the mouth was made to enjoy a joke, it could also utter the severest sentence which the head could dictate, but that Mr. Lincoln would be ever more willing to temper justice with mercy and to enjoy what he considers the amenities of life than to take a harsh view of men's nature and of the world... ."

As we come to sense the character of the world and the significance of life, we gain a greater understanding of Lincoln as a world character and of his part in the great drama of civilization. For the face of Lincoln is as great as the world itself. He is the symbol of those universal principles which are the aspiration of all mankind. To gaze upon his face is like beholding the grandeur of a rugged mountain.

There are no photographs or other representations from life which show Lincoln as a young man. But we know something of the type of life he lived and the surroundings in which he had his development and training. From this knowledge a sculptor or painter can assemble data to help him mold the forms of Lincoln's face and body in that period. In his youth he lived on a frontier and moved with its expansions. He had close associations with nature and with people who led rugged lives. In addition to his meager formal education, he was taught by the woods and life itself. Broad riverbanks were the school benches he sat upon as the streams whispered their stories and laughed at his delight in fishing in them. He knew the solitude of the glades. He listened to the music of the birds.

Lincoln grew to meet the responsibilities of manhood. He experienced the toils of life. He suffered the loss of his natural mother and, later, of his sister. Each experience had a part in molding the expressions of his face. His bony frame and his muscles developed with having to provide for living itself. His world demanded tremendous energy to till the land and build the fences. He learned to live with people. In the little Illinois village of New Salem he associated with varied personalities and learned that one must prove himself by his wits as well as by physical strength. Stories and humor became part of his ability to gain recognition. And the quiet laughter is apparent in the Lincoln face. He was confronted with a new approach to freedom and liberty, different from what he had learned in his youth. In this atmosphere Lincoln found a place for himself as a man among men. Unusual experiences gave him a better understanding of his fellow beings and this, too, is seen in the Lincoln face.

Lincoln was a man of many faces, and the great portraits and works of sculpture reveal this versatility. His partner, William H. Herndon, who had seen the Lincoln face for more than 20 years, in varied moods and under happy and difficult circumstances, said:

Pencil Sketch

"…he was not a pretty man… nor was he an ugly one; he was a homely man, careless of his looks, plain looking and plain acting; he had… that inner quality which distinguishes one person from another, as much as to say 'I am myself and not you.' … Mr. Lincoln was sad and… humorous by turns… . You will find the plains, mountains, and outlines of Lincoln's head and face hard to catch: they are so subtle."

The great Lincoln scholar, James O. Randall, summed it all up by saying:

"This aspect of singular attractiveness in Lincoln's countenance in moments of animation, something of the inner man shining through the weather-beaten countenance, was so clearly noted by various observers that it comes down to us with as much authenticity as the photographs themselves."

Fortunately, the Lincoln face has been preserved for us through the work of a Chicago sculptor, Leonard Wells Volk, who, in the spring of 1860, made a life mask* of the future President's face. This event has been hailed by a great art critic as one of the two most important accomplishments in American portraiture—the other being the making of a life mask of George Washington by the great French sculptor, Houdon, in 1785.

Every sculptor and artist has used the Volk mask. I have committed its lines to memory; it is the most reliable document of the Lincoln face. It is far more valuable than photographs, for it is actual form. All the world is indebted to Leonard Volk for his contribution. An eminent sculptor once described the Lincoln face as viewed from an examination of the life mask in these words:

"… a projecting face with unusual vigor and contrasts of planes; long, large, protruding ears, strong, angular lower jaw, and high chin; all lines of face muscular or bony, strongly, firmly, and delicately marked; the forehead wrinkled to the roots of the hair; the fullness above and immediately back of the temples very rich and firm, giving not only an important contrast to the line of the face below, but finishing that part of the head with a commanding form and outline. The profile is also unusual, in the character of the lines and in their construction: first, the full line of the forehead, carried from the top of the nose upward; second, the projecting nose, practically straight, and the distance from its end back to the upper lip, which is rather more than an eighth of an inch greater than with ordinary noses. The nose is thick in its body and wide on the top when looked at in front, and thus helps to make a harmonious face, because it catches so much light.

"The distance from the top of the nose, when seen in profile, to the inner core of the eye, is again unusual. The end of the nose appears almost blunt, but its outline, when carefully examined, is very delicate. The skin accords with Herndon's statement that it had a smooth and leathery surface. It is this kind of skin that gives such incisive directness and decision to all the lines of the face. The mask is especially living in that it strongly suggests Lincoln's undemonstrative self-consciousness as well as a knightly readiness. It bears the marks of both youth and age. Lincoln was in his fifty-second year. The mask is in short a perfect reproduction of Lincoln's face, and greatly beautiful in its human style and gravity."

Only America could have produced an Abraham Lincoln. He portrays the American ideal for all people to behold and respect. He represents this great nation as no other could because he is so much a part of it and so close to 'the people'—in his time, in our time, and forever. To behold the Lincoln features in sculpture, portrait, or photograph creates emotions to which all mankind responds. When the artist or sculptor portrays the character of Lincoln we come close to him, face to face, as did the artist, sculptor, and photographer of his own time.

As we respond to him with our inner consciousness, we know that he is our friend. His implied approval of our efforts to better humanity gives us strength and courage. Though separated from Abraham Lincoln in time and physical being, we the living can feel close to him, his ideals, and the life which he gave to a noble cause.

"The Face of Abraham Lincoln," by Avard T. Fairbanks is reprinted by courtesy of Broadcast Music, Inc., from a book edited by Ralph G. Newman, *Lincoln For The Ages, 76 Distinguished Americans Tell His Story,* Garden City, New York: Doubleday & Company 1960, p. 160-165.

* See section on Resources for Sculptors.

Lincoln The Frontiersman. Erected at Ewa Plantation School at Ewa, Hawaii, in fulfillment of a bequest of Katherine Burke, a former Principal.

Abraham Lincoln and Ann Rutledge

For many years a beautiful painting of Abraham Lincoln and Ann Rutledge hung in the living room of the Fairbanks home. It had been purchased from Dean Cornwall during a visit by Avard Fairbanks to the illustrious painter's studio a few years after the completion of the monument *Lincoln The Frontiersman*. The painting is an artist's concept of a friendly conversation between Abraham Lincoln and Ann Rutledge, two young people in New Salem Village, on a sunny Autumn afternoon.

Historians differ in accounts of the friendship between young Lincoln, age 25, and Ann Rutledge, the 20-year-old beauty. He was a postmaster, surveyor, grocer partner, and an aspiring politician, but deeply in debt and barely able to support himself. Ann was the third child in a family of nine. Her father, James Rutledge, co-founder of the town, operated a mill and tavern. Lincoln lived at the Rutledge Tavern, a boarding house, and was well acquainted with her, since they saw each other frequently. Ann was betrothed to another man, John McNeil, who had left New Salem for business pur-

poses. He had written her very few letters, and two years had gone by without communication. She may have wondered if he would ever return.

No letters between Abraham and Ann were known to have been written or kept, yet it appears that there may have been a fond friendship. No plans for a marriage have been demonstrated, and actual details their conversations remain a mystery. Writers have embellished on a few opinions, and attempts were made to create a beautiful but tragic love story.

Unfortunately Ann developed a respiratory disorder, became very ill, and was feverish. Lincoln returned in haste from the legislature and spent an hour privately in her sick room. She died two days later. He was reported to have become despondent after her death. The loss was surely reminiscent of his mother's and sister's untimely passing, and doubtless it was another very sad period in the life of a young man who had endured many hardships, disappointments, and grief.

Lincoln The Friendly Neighbor. A heroic bronze monument erected at The Lincoln Federal Savings and Loan Association in Lincoln Circle, Berwyn, Illinois. Later there was a change of the bank ownership. In 1997 the statue was donated and moved to the Lincoln School at Sixteenth and Elmwood Streets in Berwyn and was re-dedicated.

Bronze reliefs placed at the entrance of Old Main building commemorating the Centennial of the Lincoln-Douglas debates. Here at Knox College is the only remaining building where the historic debates were held. Photo courtesy of Special Collections and Archives, Knox College Library, Galesburg, Illinois.

To The Last Man. A heroic bronze monument erected in Ziegler's Grove in Gettysburg, Pennsylvania, honoring the Grand Army of the Republic and its last survivor, Albert Woolsen, age 106. A copy was also placed in his home town, Duluth, Minnesota.

The Chicago Lincoln. Erected at Ravenwood's Lincoln Square at the confluence of Lincoln, Lawrence, and Western Avenues in North Side Chicago. The inscription is quoted from one of Lincoln's speeches in Chicago, "A Free Society is not and shall not be a failure."

The Four Ages of Lincoln

Lincoln The Youth
A heroic portrait carved in Carrara marble, one of a series of four ages of Lincoln for Broadcast Music, Inc., at the Lincoln Sesquicentennial. It was presented to the Department of the Interior of the national government by the company and placed in the Ford Theater Museum, Washington, DC.

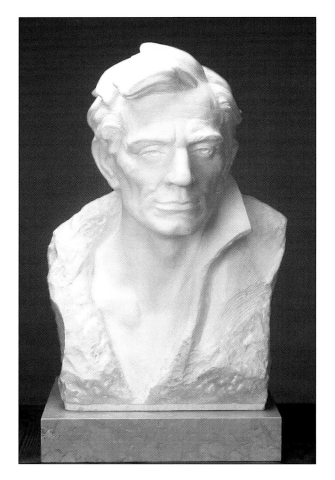

Lincoln The Frontiersman
The second of a series of four heroic portraits carved in Carrara marble for Broadcast Music, Inc. It was presented by the company to the Department of the Interior of the national government, and is placed in the Ford Theater Museum.

The Four Ages of Lincoln

Lincoln The Lawyer

The third in a series of four heroic portraits carved in Carrara marble for Broadcast Music, Inc., to commemorate the Lincoln Sesquicentennial. It was presented to the Interior Department of the national government and placed in the Supreme Court Building, The Temple of Justice, in Washington, DC.

Lincoln The President

The fourth in a series of four heroic portraits of Lincoln carved in Carrara marble for Broadcast Music, Inc., for the Lincoln Sesquicentennial. It was donated by the company to the Interior Department of the National Government and placed in the Ford Theater Museum, Washington, DC.

The Carl Sandburg Portrait. Modeled during a convocation honoring the newspaper columnist, poet, and illustrious Lincoln historian, called Sandburg Day at Knox College. It was at the conclusion of the Centennial Celebration of the Lincoln-Douglas debates. Copies of the portrait are at the Chicago Historical Museum and at Knox College, Galesburg, Illinois.

Fig. 1. Avard Fairbanks finish carving the colossal portrait of *Lincoln The Legislator* in Portuguese rose marble.

LINCOLN THE LEGISLATOR
A Colossal Portrait in Marble

Abraham Lincoln served one term as a Representative in the United States Congress during the Mexican War, in which most battles were won by the United States military forces. Lincoln became an influential legislator by using his persuasive speaking ability. The Polk administration wanted to secure from the Whigs a recognition that the war was just and right. As a Whig in a narrow Whig majority, Lincoln and others were opposed to the war and voted for a resolution that it had been "unnecessarily and unconstitutionally" begun and on that basis that it was unjustified. He made his debut in the House of Representatives with his "Spot Resolution," outlining the specific events preced-

Fig. 2. *Lincoln The Legislator* carved in Portuguese rose marble placed in the foyer of the House Committee Chamber in a prominent location.

ing the war. However, even though he opposed the justification of war, he did vote for support and supplies to the military. His position was not popular, and he was severely criticized in Illinois. When his term was over, he chose not to run again and did not return to Congress.

Avard Fairbanks had a plan to create impressive portraits of prominent historical persons, and had gone to Italy, where he ordered many marble carvings of his statuary. Among these was a portrait of Abraham Lincoln when he was an influential lawyer in Illinois, and about the time he was elected to the United States House of Representatives. Several of Fairbanks' statues had been carved in Portuguese rose marble, and he became very fond of that medium.

On a return to the United States, he stopped in Washington, DC, and visited his son David in Bethesda, Maryland. He told David that a colossal portrait of Lincoln was in process of carving and that it would be finished on his next trip to Italy.

They both thought it should be placed in Washington, DC. David contacted Florian Thayn, secretary of Frederick Schwengel, a former Representative from Iowa and the President of the United States Capitol Historical Society.

Although the District of Columbia has many statues, and there is an administrative restriction on additional placements, the Capitol Architect was consulted. A review of Fairbanks sculpture photographs and of Fairbanks' other sculptures in Washington, DC, rendered a positive consideration. A site was chosen in the foyer of the ground-level entrance to the chamber of the House of Representatives.

When the colossal, three times life size, portrait bust in Portuguese rose marble of Abraham Lincoln was complete, it was transported by ship from Italy and placed at the designated site at the entrance to the House committee chambers in a very prominent place.

George M. White, architect of the Capitol, presided over the dedication ceremonies in November, 1985. The invocation was given by Reverend James D. Ford, the Chaplain of the House. Fred Schwengel, President of the U.S. Capitol Historical Society, introduced Avard Fairbanks. Featured dignitaries included Senators Jake Garn and Orrin Hatch, both Republicans from Utah, Senator Paul Simon, Democrat of Illinois, Representative Frank Annuzio, Democrat from Illinois and Chairman of the House Administration Committee. A former Representative, Paul Findley, Republican from Illinois, was also featured. Senator Simon, who has written a book on Lincoln, said it was fitting that a bust of Lincoln should be on the House side of the Capitol, since Lincoln served his only term in Congress as a House member, 1847-49.

The statue was unveiled by Senator Hatch from Utah, who said, "When I look closely at this work of art, I see represented not only the life of our beloved president, Abraham Lincoln, but I also see imprinted in this marble the soul of its creator, the artist Dr. Avard Fairbanks."

As in all dedications, the sculptor was complimented and honored, then asked to say a few words. Among many people attending the ceremonies were Florian Thayn, David and Sylvia Fairbanks, other members of David's family, and Jonathan and Louise Fairbanks.

Fig. 1. *Lincoln of the Gettysburg Address*. Sculptor Fairbanks has modeled Lincoln with a sense of inspiration, tempered by sorrow, as he condenses his thoughts on the Civil War struggle.

ABRAHAM LINCOLN OF THE GETTYSBURG ADDRESS

Erected at Lincoln Junior High School,
Salt Lake City, Utah

ABRAHAM LINCOLN
OF THE GETTYSBURG ADDRESS

Erected at Lincoln Junior High School,
Salt Lake City, Utah

As Gettysburg was the turning point of the Civil War, so was President Lincoln's address at the dedication of the National Cemetery a milestone in American literature. Ornate and flowery expressions were to bow to concise and direct presentation, as the poetic beauty and the profound thoughts of this address gained the appreciation of the American people.

The sculptor has recreated a moment in which the President studies the wording and meditates while writing, editing, or rewriting the manuscript. The portrait reveals an interval of reflection, deeply conscious and saddened by the enormity of the battle casualties, yet desirous to honor and give full credit to the valiant men who fought and fell in battle. He gazes out as if with an inspired thought as to how best express his feelings and future hopes for the nation (Fig. 1).

Lincoln had accepted an invitation to attend the dedication, not a special invitation, but the routine circular sent to all government officials. The dedication committee was surprised and not necessarily pleased at his acceptance, as this might alter their plans. As an afterthought, they asked Lincoln to give a brief address. He agreed to give a "few appropriate remarks."

It is not definitely known why he wished so very much to attend. Some historians have suggested that he wanted to see with his own eyes the terrain and the battlefield to satisfy his own mind that he was right in urging General Meade to attack and prevent the retreat of the bulk of General Lee's army across the flooding Potomac river. Had this been done, the Civil War might have been appreciably shortened and many lives saved.

Dr. Edward Everett had been chosen to deliver the oration at the National Cemetery dedication. He was considered to be the foremost orator in the United States at that time. This eminent scholar was at one time a clergyman, then received an appointment as a professor of Greek literature. He had served in Congress ten years and was subsequently elected governor of Massachusetts three times. He was elected to the Senate, then served as a Secretary of State, and later served as a minister to Great Britain. At one time he served as president of Harvard University. He was an editor and author of renown, noteworthy for his biography of General George Washington, and for his successful efforts to preserve Mt. Vernon as a National Shrine. The committee had indeed chosen a man well qualified to honor the battle, the grounds, and the cemetery.

A chief executive of less humility might have felt slighted to sit on a platform for two hours, listening to another speaker's discourse, followed by a composition sung by the Baltimore Glee Club, only to render a "few appropriate remarks." Abraham Lincoln may have sensed that his position was even more humble, being aware that his efforts of self-education would be in contrast to the polish of the leading intellectual of the day.

The Gettysburg Address may have been written partly in Washington, DC, since the first page of the original manuscript was on Executive Mansion stationery. A second page was probably composed at Colonel Will's home in the evening before the dedication. It was written in pencil on blue-lined white paper. The next morning he restudied and copied it in ink on two sheets of white paper that he carried to the dedication. The first and second autographed copies are presently safeguarded in the Library of Congress.

In this portraiture, a quill is poised in the right hand while the manuscript is held in the left hand. At that period quills were still in common use as writing instruments. Photographs of the President on February 23, 1861, by Matthew Brady in Washington, DC, reveal a quill by the inkwell. Another photograph taken November 15, 1863, by A. Gardner also reveals a quill. Steel pens were manufactured in England after 1830, but not until 1860 in the United States. The sculptor has sought to portray with accuracy the historical event as well as the spirit of a great national character.

President Lincoln's presentation of the Gettysburg Address surprised most who heard it by its brevity, including the photographer who failed to capture the event on film. The audience had been attentive to the excellent two-hour presentation of Dr. Everett. Lincoln may not have been satisfied with his own address, for he told a friend that "it wouldn't come off cleanly," that "it was a flat failure," and he felt sure some people were disappointed in it. The widespread appreciation of ten sentences required time. However, there were some who recognized the literary masterpiece on the day of the dedication. Prominent among those were Dr. Everett, who wrote to the president:

"I should be glad if I could flatter myself that I came as near the central idea of the occasion in two hours as you did in two minutes."

Lincoln's reply in returning the compliment expresses both tact and sincerity in a beautiful manner:

"Your kind note of today is received. In our respective parts yesterday, you could not have been excused for a short address, nor I a long one. I am pleased to know that, in your judgment, the little I did say was not entirely a failure."

The little that Lincoln did say was so far from a failure that its oft quoted phrases are enshrined in the hearts and minds of the people, serving as principles to be followed.

This portrait was placed at Lincoln Junior High School, in Salt Lake City, Utah, but the school was later decommissioned for obsolescence and demographic changes in the city.

The family has cast a limited edition of this portrait in bronze.

Fig. 1. Avard Fairbanks reviewing his colossal portrait of Abraham Lincoln.

ABRAHAM LINCOLN
A Colossal Portrait In Bronze
Erected at Lincoln High School, Seattle, Washington

Margaret Fairbanks Garred, a teacher and girls counselor at Lincoln High School in Seattle, Washington, sensed a need for historical appreciation. She conceived and organized a Traditions Day that coincided with the anniversary of Abraham Lincoln's birthday, and it became an annual event. After teaching at this school for five years, Margaret resigned to be married and moved to California. Nevertheless, the Traditions Day she established continued. However, fate was unkind to Margaret, for a few years later she developed a incurable illness and after a brief period passed away.

In her honor, her two sisters, Lulu and Esther Fairbanks, distant relatives of the sculptor, chose to

Fig. 2. Avard Fairbanks with a Lincoln portrait (modeled in a demonstration lecture for the High School assembly), Mary Koss, and Roger Moffit, portraying Mary Lincoln and Abraham Lincoln in the pagent.

have a fitting memorial placed in Lincoln High School. They asked their cousin, Avard, for a statuette or portrait of President Lincoln. He had a better idea; A colossal portrait of the Young Abraham Lincoln had already been made for a sesquicentennial celebration. It remained only to be cast in bronze. This portrait would be more impressive and more appropriate, since the High School was dedicated in its efforts toward the guidance and development of youth. When Lulu and Esther saw this portrait, they were thrilled.

Each year for the pageant of Traditions Day, a senior boy and girl were selected who would best typify the great American president and his wife. Appropriate costumes of the period added to the atmosphere of a dramatic presentation. The announcement of the gift of the colossal portrait was made during the Traditions Day assembly of February 8, 1963. During the next year, the colossal portrait was cast in bronze at Pietrasanta, Italy. It was shipped by boat to Seattle, Washington, in time for a 1964 dedication.

One year after the announcement, the anniversary program of Traditions Day included the dedication of the colossal portrait of Abraham Lincoln. The 42-inch tall portrait was placed on a four-foot pedestal of marble, and was unveiled by Lulu and

Esther Fairbanks, assisted by the sculptor.

During the dedication assembly, an address was made by Ernest Campbell, superintendent of Seattle City Schools. He remarked that the history of the school is marked by the success of its graduates, due in part to the qualities exemplified by the illustrious man for whom the school is named. He accepted the portrait on behalf of the Seattle schools and termed it a magnificent work, saying, "It affords all the more opportunity for future generations of young people to draw inspiration from the life of Abraham Lincoln."

Homer Davis, the principal, thanked Lulu and Esther on behalf of the students and faculty. He spoke of admirable traits of Abraham Lincoln. Tim Rolf, the student body president, expressed the students' appreciation for the gift. Roger Moffit and Mary Koss, seniors who best exemplified school traditions, were presented in costume representing Mr. and Mrs. Lincoln.

The assembly was then honored by a demonstration lecture by Dr. Avard Fairbanks showing how a portrait of Lincoln was modeled. He included, while modeling, some of the thoughts and motivations of the artist and suggested how to portray the feeling for the ideals that the great president strove to achieve. At the conclusion he urged the students and guests to take inspiration from Lincoln's Gettysburg address, and said, "Let us renew our faith in the development of the tasks remaining before us as Lincoln did many years ago."

Some time later the principal of the school remarked to the sculptor that since the establishment of the Traditions Day there had been a reduction in some of the annoying problems of youth. The fine sculptured portrait had served as a continuous inspiration and incentive to pride and honor. This further served to reduce problems prevalent in other schools of the area.

A great masterpiece of art exerts a positive influence and inspiration in the lives, the motivations, and conduct of youth. It may well influence all others who may pass, pause, and appreciate.

A Few Notes About Family Ties

Lulu and Esther Fairbanks had been very close to their sister Margaret, and they had all trained as teachers at the University of Michigan. Lulu first came to Seattle from Saline, Michigan, in about 1915. On her way West, the train had a layover in Salt Lake City. Knowing nobody in the city and wondering what to see or do, she thumbed through the phone book to see if there were any Fairbanks in the city. The name of John B. Fairbanks (father of the sculptor) came to her attention. She called and John B. was happy to meet her, driving the family buggy to the station and spending the day showing her about Salt Lake City.

A strong kinship developed between the Michigan and the Salt Lake branch of the family. Lulu established herself in Seattle and, after teaching sev-

eral years, accepted a more challenging opportunity as secretary to Sam Hill, President of the Northern Pacific Railroad. Later she became associate editor of the *Alaska Weekly,* published in Seattle. This journal contributed substantially to the promotion and development of Alaska. Lulu was one of Seattle's outstanding business women, very active in efforts of civic improvement. She was also interested in history and art. Even after her retirement she busied herself promoting a home for disadvantaged boys. Girl Scouts also received considerable attention. She was a friend to people in need, especially old sourdoughs from Alaska, whom she frequently visited in hospitals or convalescent homes.

Esther came to Seattle on encouragement of Lulu and, after teaching a few years, accepted a position as secretary to William Boeing, founder and president of the Boeing Aircraft Company. She was also active in civic affairs.

Margaret came later and directed her efforts more in the field of education, teaching first at other schools in Seattle, then at Lincoln High School from 1945 to 1950, where she organized Traditions Day. She was highly regarded by students and faculty alike, and her untimely death was deeply felt by the family, friends, and members of the faculty.

[Author's Note: At the time of publishing this book, Lincoln High School is no longer being used for instruction. It is committed to office space. The address is 4400 Interlake Avenue North in Seattle, Washington. Another casting of the colossal portrait of Abraham Lincoln was placed at Utah State University campus at Logan, Utah, as a companion piece to a colossal bronze portrait of General George Washington.]

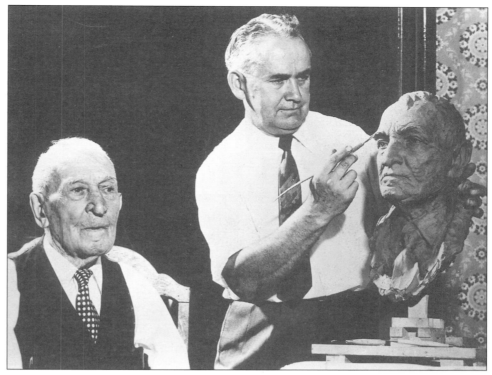

Fig. 1. Avard Fairbanks modeling a portrait of 106-year-old Albert Woolson, 1953.

TO THE LAST MAN

The Last Survivor of the Grand Army of the Republic, Albert Woolson

Portrait and Heroic Monument in Bronze
Erected at Gettysburg, Pennsylvania, September 12, 1956
and later in Duluth, Minnesota

A Portrait of Albert Woolson

Avard Fairbanks was commissioned in 1953 to model a portrait bust of Albert Woolson, age 106, the sole survivor of the Union Army, by the Auxiliary of the Sons of the Union Veterans of the Civil War. Fairbanks traveled to Duluth, Minnesota, with his clay and armature and modeled the portrait in the residence of the veterans and his daughter. The portrait likeness was later used to create a monument.

A descendant once told how the city of Duluth was so proud to have Woolson as a citizen that they arranged a small office in the city hall for him to meet his many visitors and tell of his Civil War experiences. Dr. Fairbanks had some fine impressions

during the week-long sitting of Mr. Woolson; although he was an old and bent man, he was alert and likable; he was one of the nation's great characters. Part of his longevity was due to the fine care and good attention paid him by his three daughters. He lived with one of them, Mrs. John Kobus.

Mr. Woolson liked to talk, and during the sittings talked in a very loud voice not anticipated from someone his age. He was often singing, and his favorite song seemed to be "Sweet Alice Ben Bolt." His mind was clear, and he talked well. His favorite subject was the greatness of Lincoln, and he was impressed by the military ability of General Grant. He asked many questions about Dr. Fairbanks and his family. Since Mr. Woolson was

Fig. 2. The portrait of Albert Woolson.

saying, "Thank you for this splendid assembly. I hope you enjoy your stay in this fair city of Duluth." Greetings were sent by General Douglas McArthur and Vice President Nixon. The portrait was accepted by the mayor and was to be placed in the rotunda of the Duluth City Hall.

The portrait was later used to create the heroic monument portraying Albert Woolson in the memorial to The Grand Army of the Republic placed at the Gettysburg Battlefield site.

More recently, in 2002, another portrait copy was placed in the national headquarters of the Grand Army of the Republic Civil War Museum and Library at Philadelphia, Pennsylvania.

Albert Woolson, Last Survivor of the Grand Army of the Republic

The monument to the last survivor of the Grand Army of the Republic, Albert Woolson, was erected in Ziegler's Grove on the Battlefield of Gettysburg, Pennsylvania. The heroic bronze figure was mounted on a massive pedestal of polished rainbow granite appropriately quarried in Minnesota, his home state. The dedication ceremonies were held September 12, 1956, during an encampment of the Sons of the Union Veterans.

Albert Woolson was 106 years old when he posed for the portrait in 1953. He joined the Union Army during the final years of the Civil War. At that time he was seventeen years old, and served in heavy artillery.... .

Although Albert Woolson enlisted after the Battle of Gettysburg, it is appropriate that a monument to a veteran from Minnesota be placed at that battle-site. The First Minnesota Volunteers Regiment fought in every campaign from Bull Run to Gettysburg, except Fredericksburg. When the frontal assault by General George Pickett's division of 15,000 on Cemetery Ridge became apparent, the 1st Minnesota Regiment was hurriedly sent in to oppose them. They suffered 700 killed out of a regiment of 1000 men, one of the highest casualty rates in the Civil War. The remaining 300 were later paraded in Washington as heroes and mustered out of the army.

Dr. Avard Fairbanks was commissioned by the Women's Auxiliary to the Sons of Union Veterans of the Civil War to make a heroic-size statue of the

deaf, Dr. Fairbanks had to use a heavy grease pencil and a large tablet to answer. The family kept the record as a souvenir. Appreciation of the personality of a person is very important for an artist to model character into a portrait.

Returning to Salt Lake City, Avard Fairbanks completed the portrait bust and had it first cast in plaster and then in bronze. By August of the next year, the bronze cast was ready for an encampment of the Sons of Union Veterans of the Civil War. The assembly was attended by over 600 people, including General U.S. Grant III, the national commander, the mayor, George B. Johnson, and Governor C. Elmer Anderson. The portrait was unveiled by Frances Ann Kobus, a five-year-old granddaughter of Woolson, at ceremonies in the Hotel Duluth. Woolson looked at the portrait and said, "It is a good likeness; the Sculptor cannot be too highly commended for his work." He continued in a loud firm voice, "We are all here for a good purpose." He thanked members of the Sons of Union Veterans for holding their encampment at Duluth in his honor, last survivor of the Grand Army of the Republic, as a monument in Gettysburg National Park.

Mr. Woolson was a good subject and an excellent choice for the Gettysburg memorial because he was a typical American citizen who volunteered for the army, served well, and adjusted to a normal life after the war, never trying to bring additional fame to himself.

The motto on the banner of the State of Minnesota carried in the Civil War reads: "TO THE LAST MAN." Albert Woolson, who volunteered from Minnesota, fulfills this statement. It is entirely fitting that a tribute be made To The Last Man.

Adapted from the feature article by Verne Larsen, "To the Last Man, Union Statue Under Construction," *The Daily Utah Chronicle,* Vol. 64, No. 85, February 17, 1955.

A Significant Memorial "To The Last Man"

A new monument has been added to the countless war memorials on the Gettysburg battlefield. It sits in Ziegler's Grove, shadowed by gentle trees. It bears only this inscription: "Memorial to the Grand Army of the Republic." But it is not alone symbolic of the vast army of Union soldiers who returned from the battlefields of the Civil War to form a veterans' organization, disbanded only when the last member died, August 2, 1956, at the age of 109.

The statue portrays the last survivor, Albert Woolson, of Duluth, Minnesota. The aged veteran proudly posed for the sculptor, Dr. Avard Fairbanks, and he witnessed his likeness slowly take form from the clay in the artist's hands. He was privileged to see the model of the finished masterpiece before his recent death.

Strong and sturdy, the old man appears in a reclining position with a heavy walking-stick in his right hand and his left resting on the brim of his G.A.R. hat by his side. He has firm, rugged features, determined chin, with face and mien of strength, determination, and character. The artist has epitomized the valor and devotion of all the comrades of the Grand Army of the Republic in this faithful portrait of "the last man." The sculptor could not have had a more appropriate subject.

The statue was unveiled at Gettysburg with impressive ceremonies on September 12, 1956, dur-

Fig. 3. Portrait details of the statue *To the Last Man.*

ing the annual encampment of the Sons of Union Veterans held in Harrisburg, Pennsylvania. Colonel Frederick Gilbert Bauer, national commander-in-chief, said in part:

"This statue is in many ways unique. Usually statues are dedicated to great and noble men, great military leaders, or men who have given their lives for their country.

"Here we have a statue of a man who was none of these things. He was a simple, humble youth who, when his country needed men, went into the army. He never rose to high rank, nor did he have the opportunity to do any outstanding deed. When he had completed his service, he returned to his home seeking no great position; he worked hard all of his life in humble posts and rounded out a great span of years as a simple, humble, good citizen of the United States.

"We note that the front of the statue does not bear his name. It bears the wording, 'In memory of the Grand Army of the Republic.'

"Comrade Albert Woolson symbolizes all the great virtues of the common, ordinary citizen, the citizen who becomes a soldier and then returns to ordinary life."

Mrs. Lenore B. Glass, of San Jose, California, National President of the Auxiliary of the Sons of Union Veterans, made the formal dedication of the statue and presented it to the U. S. Department of the Interior. The Auxiliary had sponsored the memorial.

Miss Celeste D. Gentieu of Wilmington, Delaware, was appointed by the National Auxiliary several years ago as the chairman of a committee to have a memorial made to the Grand Army of the Republic. It was at the national encampment held in Duluth in 1954 that a decision was reached to create a memorial in which Albert Woolson, the remaining survivor of the G.A.R., would be a central figure. At the encampment, Doctor Fairbanks had completed a portrait bust of Mr. Woolson which was presented to the City of Duluth as a part of the program of the convention. Doctor Fairbanks conferred with Mrs. Gentieu and her committee and submitted a model for the memorial. This was accepted by the members of the National Auxiliary at that meeting, and Doctor Fairbanks was authorized to proceed with the statue.

The annual encampment in 1954 was held in Duluth primarily to do honor to Mr. Woolson, who had outlived 2,675,000 of the "men who wore the blue." He had been a member of the Grand Army of the Republic for many years, and after his last comrade had died in 1953, he remained as the sole representative of the G.A.R., which technically existed until his death on August 2, 1956.

Woolson became a volunteer private in Company C of the First Minnesota Heavy Artillery Regiment when Lincoln was making one of his calls for more troops. Detailed to the regular drum corps, he did occupational duty in the South for slightly less than a year. After his discharge from the Army, he worked in a furniture factory, in a traveling minstrel band, and in mills and logging camps in Minnesota. He retired from active work 24 years prior to his death.

His birthday on February 11 in recent years drew widespread attention, with thousands of greeting cards pouring in from across the country. On his last birthday, he received greetings from President Eisenhower. He was well and vigorous until a few months before his death. He spent countless hours reading in an old high-backed chair in the dining room of his comfortable brick home on one of Duluth's hills.

Only three veterans of the Civil War, all members of the Confederate forces, survived in 1956. They are W. W. Williams, 113, Franklin, Texas; John Salling, 110, Slant, Virginia; and William A. Lundy, 108, Laurel Hill, Florida.

Lincoln Herald, Fall, 1956, Vol. 58, No. 3, p. 11. Reprinted by permission of the *Lincoln Herald.*

Heroes of Equal Greatness

An Editorial by Robert L. Kincaid

Two years ago, I had an interesting experience in Duluth, Minnesota. At the invitation of General U.S. Grant III, then Commander-in-Chief of the Sons of Union Veterans, I was a guest at the annual encampment of that organization. A feature of the program was the unveiling of a bust of Albert Woolson, the last survivor of the Union Army of 1861-65.

The encampment was held in Duluth so that the aged veteran, then 107, could be present. Mr. Woolson was the honor guest at the opening public session, and the Governor of Minnesota, Mayor of Duluth, and representatives of many patriotic organizations were on hand to join with the Sons of Union Veterans and the Auxiliary in a tribute to the one who was the last living member of the Grand Army of the Republic. The bust of Mr. Woolson, which was presented to the City of Duluth, was created by the noted sculptor, Dr. Avard Fairbanks.

It was a special privilege for me to join in the accolade, to shake his hand, to hear him respond to the greetings, and to see him pose for the photographers and television cameras. Here was history with significant meaning—I was joining hands with "the last man" who had been a member of "Mr. Lincoln's Army." Never again was I to have the opportunity, because last August Mr. Woolson joined his comrades in their final bivouac.

But my emotions on that occasion must have been a little different from those of the thousands of others who were showering their affections on this hero of the blue because he had lived so long. I was doing homage to one who had been my grandfather's enemy! I was proud of my Southern heritage, and I had heroes in abundance among

Fig. 4. The heroic statue of Albert Woolson, last survivor of The Grand Army of the Republic.

those who wore the gray. But I did not feel disloyal in this display of affection and appreciation for what Albert Woolson symbolized.

Rather I had a warm feeling that Albert Woolson and my grandfather had much in common in heart and spirit. Both had been equally sincere and devoted; both had been motivated by loyalties to ideals of home and country. It was the circumstances of birth and residence which had been responsible for placing them on opposite sides in a tragic conflict.

To me, the last man to wear the blue and the last to wear the gray represent heroes of equal valor and devotion in a nation which was bound together in the mingling of their offerings on the altar of liberty.

Lincoln Herald, Fall, 1956. Vol. 58, No. 3, p. 1.
Reprinted by permission of the *Lincoln Herald.*

This statuette was created for the Parts and Accessories Campaign award of the Chevrolet Automobile Company, 1963.

THE CHARGER

"Symbolic of courage and determination in the face of insurmountable obstacles," this small statuette was requested and specially created for the Parts and Accessories Campaign award of the Chevrolet Automobile Company.

"The Charger with saber drawn, leaning far forward in the saddle, vaults forward against the roar of the cannon, powder, and ball. The history of the United States abounds in tales of our cavalry, which was vital to both North and South in the Civil War, and in subsequent fights to win the West.

"In the din of battle, ever onward he rides until he accomplishes his goal of victory. Under hoof and foot, already one cannon lies crumbled… for the mind of man is stronger than the steel he forges. In the deep recesses of the heart and mind of the individual lie the seeds of which such courage and determination are born.

"Following an order to 'charge!' with unswerving loyalty to the team… but still persevering the carrying out each assignment… exercising individual initiative and drive… the Charger valiantly surges onward."

The above description was adapted from the company's explanatory folder.

This composition was selected in 1963 portraying a cavalryman charging over a hill on which a cannon had already been disabled by gunfire. The charge to pursue a retreating enemy was not particularly intended to portray any specific event of the Civil War, but it was modeled on a cavalry rider in the uniform of that time.

Fig. 1. A portrait bust of a young woman of the frontier simulating Nancy Hanks Lincoln.

NANCY HANKS LINCOLN

The inclusion of the portrait representing Nancy Hanks Lincoln was made by the author only after some serious hesitation. The forbearance of strict historians is implored for this conscientious exercise of artistic license. Nevertheless, it is hoped that the reader may appreciate the masterpiece for its expression of the earnestness, integrity, patience and devotion of a frontier mother.

Artists are often expected to portray persons about whom little is known or recalled regarding physical features or personality. By the time Abraham Lincoln was well on the path to fame, his beloved mother had been dead many years. Very little accurate information was recorded about her.

It was only after Dr. Fairbanks had made extensive studies of Abraham Lincoln and his life story that he felt inspired to model a figure representing Nancy Hanks Lincoln. He sought to honor a heroine of the American frontier who accepted a life of pioneer sacrifices and monotonous everyday chores, yet courageously faced the future. A bond of sympathy was strongly felt by the sculptor, for his mother also died when he was a child. He also experienced the loss and bereavement in the home when the family was left without the guiding influence of their own mother.

Although remarkable effort has been expended by scholars and historians to obtain details of Nancy

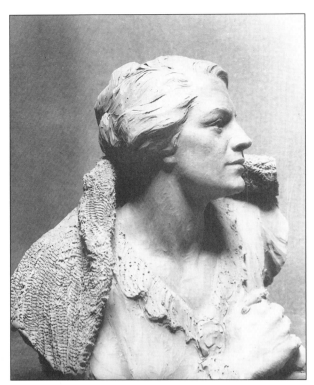

Fig. 2. A right lateral view of the same portrait bust.

Hanks, the search has resulted in very little data that is free of doubt or conflicting opinions. Dennis Hanks, a cousin and companion of Abraham Lincoln, when interviewed in his ninetieth year, described her in the following manner: "She was purty as a picture an' smart as you'd find 'em anywhere. She could read an' write. Tom thought a heap o' Nancy, an' was as good to her as he knowed how."

Other acquaintances indicated that she was a beautiful woman of medium height and slender proportions. She weighed about 130 pounds. John Hanks, a cousin of Nancy Hanks, described her in an interview with William Herndon: "I knew Mrs. Nancy Lincoln... She was a tall and slender woman, dark-skinned, black hair and eyes, her face was sharp and angular, forehead big. She was beyond all doubts an intellectual woman, rather extraordinary if anything... Her nature was kindness, mildness, tenderness, and obedience to Thomas, her husband. Abraham was like his mother very much."

Other biographers indicate that her eyes were gray or hazel. Her dark hair may often have been braided and coiled in a bun. She may have also secured it with a horn comb, as was customary in those times. One author wrote that she was a sweet-tempered and pleasant person. Her face sometimes gave an expression of melancholy. Another describes her as having beautiful eyes and a sweet, sensitive mouth. She was a kind, affectionate, and friendly person, and was deeply religious.

She took great pains to teach her children what she knew, reading Bible lore to them in the evening. "My earliest recollection of my mother is sitting at her feet with my sister, drinking in the tales and legends that were read and related to us," recalled Abraham Lincoln. As the children grew older, she encouraged their efforts to learn reading and writing.

Nancy was naturally talented and adept at the homemaker's crafts. In flax-spinning contests, her spools generally yielded the longest and finest thread. She was also skilled at weaving. Thomas, a wheelwright as well as a carpenter, had fashioned a spinning wheel and a loom for the household. Besides woolen blankets, Nancy wove other cloth on the loom. Linsey-woolsey, composed of linen and wool made of the fleece of sheep or buffalo, was woven, cut, and sewn into garments for Thomas, herself, and the children. The skins of animals were also tailored into clothing. Nancy's dresses of linen or linsey-woolsey could be put on and taken off without enlarging the neck opening, and one or two pins at the throat may have represented a luxury, according to one writer.

The first home of Tom and Nancy was a log cabin with one large room and a loft overhead, reached by a rough ladder. There was an outside shed for a storeroom and a summer kitchen. The cabin had a huge fireplace with a big hearthstone and a long stone mantel. It served both for warmth and cooking. It had some iron hooks and a long crane used to support iron pots or a Dutch oven. Baking was done in a clay oven. The furniture was handmade of rude construction. There were chairs, benches, tables, and a bedstead.

Besides the work in the cabin, the pioneer homemakers rendered lard, made soap, and prepared candles. During the summer, Nancy gathered berries and dried them. In the fall, apples and pumpkins were cut and dried in the sun. It was also customary for the housewife to milk the cow, churn butter, and prepare cheese.

Thomas and Nancy Lincoln, though poor by other standards, enjoyed a relative frontier prosperity in Kentucky. At one time they owned 586 acres of land. However, difficulty in the land titles arose, and Thomas became discouraged. He decided to start out on new land. They moved to Indiana in October 1816 and chopped down enough trees to make a small clearing for the crops. Game was abundant, and Thomas hunted to provide meat and skins. Nancy fashioned the hides into clothing for the children. The first winter they lived in a half-faced camp, a lean-to shack made of poles. Later he built a log cabin, but many months passed before he could put in a puncheoned or whipsawed plank floor. Living was found to be less rewarding in Indiana than it had been in Kentucky. The game available consisted of bear, deer, ducks, and grouse. Fish from the streams added to their fare. Potatoes and corn were staples. However, wheat flour was a scarce luxury. Corn dodger was the usual bread. Lye hominy was also frequently prepared and cooked. Dennis Hanks said: "We wasn't much better off'n Indians, except we tuk an interest in religion an' polyticks."

Soon after the cabin was built, an epidemic of milk sickness occurred in southern Indiana, which affected both humans and cattle. Nancy's relatives, the Sparrows, died of this malady. Not long afterwards, Nancy was afflicted. On her deathbed a few days later she said to her son: "I am going away from you, Abraham, and I shall not return. I know you will be a good boy, that you will be kind to Sarah and your father. I want you to live as I have taught you and to love your heavenly father." Her passing was a sorrow deeply felt by the family.

It has now been shown that there is a poison present in a plant called White Snakeroot, or *Eupatorium urticaefolium*. This plant is present in wooded areas of Indiana, Ohio, Illinois, and Michigan. When eaten by cattle grazing in the woods, it causes a disease called 'Trembles.' The toxin is present in the flesh and milk of these animals. The illness in humans occurs after ingestion of milk or flesh of affected cattle. The usual symptoms are a gradual onset of weakness, loss of appetite, vomiting, and abdominal distress. Later a marked thirst develops as vomiting increases. In the fatal cases, the illness progresses for seven to nine days until the victim becomes comatose. Then death may occur after several hours. The mortality rate is about 25 percent.

The severity of the illness depends on the amount of toxin ingested. Fortunately it is a rare disease today, since most cattle are pastured on plowed or cleared land.

The sculptor has modeled a pleasant face expressing sincerity and compassion, with an effort to include some of the features of Abraham Lincoln, however modified by feminization. Abe was much like his mother's family. Caroline Hanks Hitchcock has illustrated in a book about Nancy Hanks Lincoln how the resemblance between Abraham Lincoln and certain male members of the Hanks family was remarkable. Nevertheless, a photograph of Thomas Lincoln demonstrates a few features that Abraham inherited from his father. These include a prominent nose, a wide mouth, and the same lip contours. In other respects, however, Thomas was stocky and robust, height five feet ten inches, and broad-shouldered. Abraham Lincoln's tall, lanky build and angular features probably had been inherited from his mother. The face modeled by Dr. Fairbanks representing Nancy Hanks Lincoln is more an artistic expression than an attempt to restore information of facial features already lost to history. The clothing is similar to that which women of that period are reported to have worn. Her dress was probably of homespun linen or linsey-woolsey, a product of the hand loom. A fringe on the neckline adds a feminine touch to an otherwise plain garment. The mood is one of sincerity, deeply moved as though relating Bible lore to her children, or while attending a frontier church gathering, listening to the sermon of an itinerant minister. It could be a moment of reflection after reading passages from one of the few books they possessed. It might be a pensive moment of wondering about the future of her children, considering how she could educate them under such unfavorable circumstances. Dennis Hanks said: "But Nancy kep' urging Abe. 'Abe,' she'd say, 'you l'arn all you kin, an' be some account,' an' she'd tell him stories about George Washington, an' say that Abe had jist as good Virginny blood in him as Washington." She was dedicated to her children's future. Her sincere efforts were not forgotten, for Abraham Lincoln later said: "All that I am or hope to be I owe to my Angel Mother. Blessings on her Memory."

RESOURCES FOR SCULPTORS

In an autobiography, Abraham Lincoln gave a brief description of himself:

"If any personal description of me is thought desirable, it may be said, I am in height six feet four inches, nearly; lean in flesh, weighing on an average one hundred and eighty pounds; dark complexion with coarse black hair, and gray eyes-no other marks or brands recollected.
Yours very truly, A. Lincoln "

Other information regarding Abraham Lincoln may be considered in several categories. Verbal descriptions by acquaintances will give an insight into the character, the motivations, and the feelings of this great statesman. It can materially assist a sculptor to work animation into clay.

One of the finest verbal descriptions of Abraham Lincoln was by his capable and dedicated private secretary, John G. Nicolay, who set forth the well-known peculiarities of Lincoln's form and features:

"Large head, with high crown of skull; thick, bushy hair; large and deep eye-caverns; heavy eyebrows; a large nose; large ears; large mouth, thin upper and somewhat thick under lip; very high and prominent cheekbones; cheeks thin and sunken; strongly developed jawbones; chin slightly upturned; a thin but sinewy neck, rather long; long arms; large hands; chest thin and narrow as compared with his great height; legs of more than proportionate length and large feet."

Mr. Nicolay has also given an interesting description of Lincoln's face:

"The large framework of his features was greatly modified by the emotions which controlled them. The most delicate touch of the painter often wholly changes the expression of a portrait; his inability to find that one needed master touch causes the ever-recurring wreck of an artist's fondest hopes. In a countenance of strong lines and rugged masses like Lincoln's, the lift of an eyebrow, the curve of a lip, the flash of an eye, the movements of prominent muscles created a much wider facial play than in rounded immobile countenances. Lincoln's features were

the despair of every artist who undertook his portrait. The writer saw nearly a dozen (artists), one after another, soon after the first nomination to the presidency, attempt the task. They put into their pictures the large rugged features, and strong prominent lines; they made measurements to obtain exact proportions; they 'petrified' some single look, but the picture remained hard and cold. Even before these paintings were finished it was plain to see that they were unsatisfactory to the artists themselves, and much more so to the intimate friends of the man; this was not he who smiled, spoke, laughed, charmed. The picture was to the man as the grain of sand to the mountain, as the dead to the living. Graphic art was powerless before a face that moved through a thousand delicate gradations of line and contour, light and shade, sparkle of the eye and curve of the lip, in the long gamut of expression from grave to gay, and back again from the rollicking jollity of laughter to that serious, faraway look that with prophetic intuitions beheld the awful panorama of war and heard the cry of oppression and suffering. There are many pictures of Lincoln; there is no portrait of him."
~ *John G. Nicolay*

A description was also written by William Herndon, the law partner of Lincoln:

"Mr. Lincoln's head was long and tall from the base of the brain and from the eyebrows. His head ran backwards, his forehead rising as it ran back at a low angle, like Clay's, and unlike Webster's, which was almost perpendicular…. His forehead was narrow but high; his hair was dark, almost black, and lay floating where his fingers or the winds left it, piled up at random. His cheekbones were high, sharp, and prominent; his jaws were long and up-curved; his nose was large, long, blunt, and a little awry towards the right eye; his chin was sharp and up-curved; his eyebrows cropped out like a huge rock on the brow of a hill; his long, sallow face was wrinkled and dry, with a hair here and there on the surface; his cheeks were leathery; his ears were large

Fig. 1. An anterior view of the life mask of Abraham Lincoln, cast by Leonard Volk in Chicago, 1860.

and ran out almost at right angles from his head, caused partly by heavy hats and partly by nature.... there was the lone mole on the right cheek.... He was not a pretty man by any means, nor was he an ugly one; he was a homely man, careless of his looks, plain-looking and plain-acting. He had no pomp, display, or dignity, so-called. He appeared simple in his carriage and bearing. He was a sad-looking man; his melancholy dripped from him as he walked."

~ William H. Herndon, *Life of Lincoln*

Other resources are the oil paintings; Mr. Nicolay states that on 12 different occasions portrait painters had created a likeness of Mr. Lincoln. One notable portrait was painted in 1864 by William Cogswell, a young Chicago artist, who visited the White House and made sketches of the President. The finished portrait was entered in a contest authorized by Congress for a portrait of President Lincoln. It was chosen over twelve other entries. Later it was placed in the White House, where it has hung since then.

Photographs of Abraham Lincoln have also received much attention and are from several sources. Some of the finest were made at the studios of Matthew B. Brady. Historians are also indebted to the persistence of Frederick Hill Meserve who, during many years, acquired a collection of more than 100 photographs, some of which were excellent portraits. These have been of considerable assistance to sculptors and painters who seek to portray the sixteenth president. Meserve's interest in the collection was generated by reading Civil War experiences in his own father's diary.

William Neal Meserve, the father of Frederick H. Meserve, volunteered in Roxbury, Massachusetts, in 1862 for a three-year enlistment in the Union Army. He served four years, advancing through the ranks to a major. He saw action at Antietam, Fredericksburg, Vicksburg, the siege of Knoxville, the Wilderness, Cold Harbor, and Petersburg. During his service he kept a diary, from which he later wrote a manuscript entitled, "A Personal Record."

Frederick Hill Meserve was fascinated by his father's manuscript and sought photographs to accompany the text. Once he made a ridiculously low bid on a sealed packet of 50 photographs at a book auction. When he unwrapped the packet, he was happily surprised by pictures of subjects more interesting than he had anticipated. These further stirred his desire to acquire photographs of the Civil War period. It was already more than a hobby. He then became a serious collector of Abraham Lincoln photographs. He sought more auctions and avidly followed catalogues of sales.

A few years later he visited the New York offices of E. & H. T. Anthony Company, inquiring about photographs and negatives they had in storage. He was directed to the Hoboken warehouse in New Jersey to look over negative photographic plates. Many of these were the collection of Matthew B. Brady. A young company representative urged him to buy the negatives because they were in the way. There were thousands of plates stored in two-foot stacks. Some were broken and some spilled onto the floor. One negative Meserve picked up was a profile portrait of Abraham Lincoln. He did not need any more encouragement. He bought the negatives, which were so numerous that they filled two large vans.

Matthew B. Brady was the leading daguerrotypist and early portrait photographer of the nation when photography was in its infancy. With portrait parlors in New York and Washington, DC, he had been eminently successful, and had acquired a substantial fortune. His clientele included many of the leading persons of the times.

Lincoln's first visit to Brady's salon was February 27, 1860, the day of Lincoln's Cooper Union Speech in New York. The portrait made at that time was considered the best of all known likenesses made before he became president. Many thousand copies of this were made later that year and distributed during the campaign. It helped him immeasurably to be elected president.

During the Civil War, Matthew B. Brady conceived a plan of documenting momentous events with photographs. At his own expense, with a corps of assistants, he undertook photographing the men, weapons, battlefields, military officers, political leaders, and persons or events of importance. The courage and tenacity of this illustrious man has been aptly described by Carl Sandburg:

> "This pioneer photographer had an obsession to serve history and his country and for photo recording of the Civil War. In spite of mounting debts he went on… . The tribute to him as an artist and the true measure of his contribution to Civil War history and the American Culture was to come from later generations."

A truly fascinating book has been written about the life and accomplishments of this intrepid photographer by James D. Horan, an author of ten historical books. The book, *Mathew Brady: Historian With A Camera* is profusely illustrated with more than 500 pictures. These are a small part of the thou-

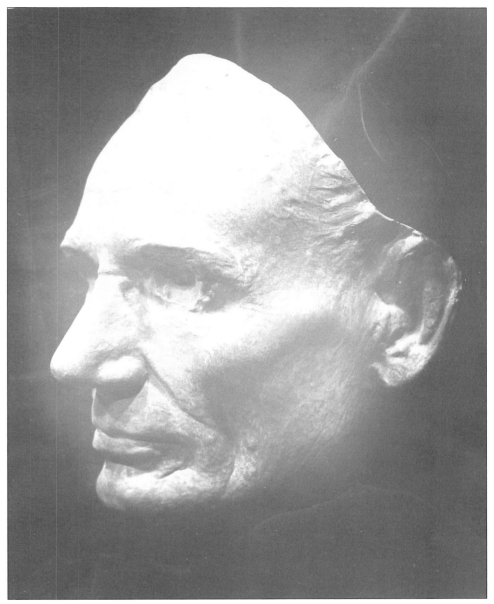

Fig. 2. Left lateral view of the life mask of Abraham Lincoln, cast by Leonard Volk in Chicago.

sands of plates in the Library of Congress and other collections of Brady and associates' photographs portraying notable persons and the history of the nation. One section records Civil War history and another depicts westward migration.

Brady bought most of his photographic and chemical supplies from the E.& H.T. Anthony Company. The federal government refused to appropriate money to subsidize his efforts, but it did later pay $25,000 for part of his prints and negatives. After the Civil War, he continued his portrait studios, but the expense of the war photographs still kept him in debt. Reluctantly in 1871 Brady conceded that his only recourse was bankruptcy. The E.& H.T. Anthony Company received the negatives as a partial satisfaction of the debt. In 1874 a great number of the plates were placed for auction to pay storage fees. The Secretary of War put up the money, and they were transferred to a government warehouse, where many of them later suffered damage through indifference and neglect. About 1887, John C. Taylor purchased 7000 plates from the Anthony Company. By the turn of the century, however, the company appears to have lost interest in the plates and was willing to sell the remaining collection to Mr. Meserve.

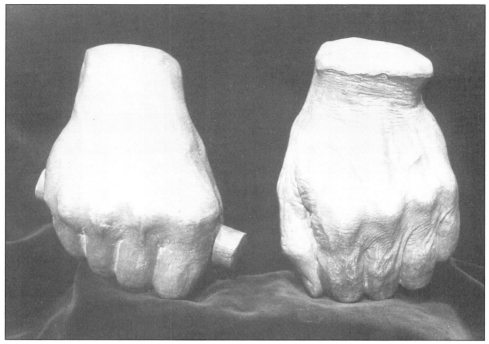

Fig. 3. Casts of Abraham Lincoln's hands by Leonard Volk in Springfield, Illinois, 1860.

Of special interest to Meserve were the portraits of Abraham Lincoln. By the early 1900s, he had collected 50 photographs. By seven more years, 100 had been assembled. In another seven years, eight additional Lincoln photographs were acquired. It took another 20 years to find the next eight photographs.

In 1911, F. H. Meserve published a limited edition of 100 copies of his first book, titled *The Photographs of Abraham Lincoln*. Intermittently newly found photographs were forwarded to him, and he became the unofficial registrar of Lincoln photography.

In 1944, an updated publication of F. H. Meserve's collection with an introduction by Carl Sandburg was published. A later book, using photographs collected by Meserve as well as other accumulated information and illustrations, was written by Stefan Lorant, *Lincoln–His Life in Photographs*. It serves as an excellent reference to artists as well as historians. Sculptor Fairbanks found this source of information very helpful.

THE LIFE MASK AND HANDS OF ABRAHAM LINCOLN

By Avard Fairbanks

When I was commissioned to make the Lincoln Statue I knew that I could develop a fine likeness of him, for I recalled seeing a life mask of him in the New York National History Museum. I also recall that Gutson Borglum used a life mask of Lincoln at the time that he was creating the colossal head now in the National Capitol in Washington, DC. I also remember that the Klaber Company in New York had a bronze cast of the Lincoln mask and hands. I had also seen masks in several sculptors studios. All of these made me realize that there were copies available somewhere of the original mask that I might use to perfect the statue. It could make it accurate and true to the Lincoln head in its features and proportions.

I inquired at various sources in New York where I thought castings might be available. The company mentioned was out of business and Gutzon Borglum was dead. I tried other sources without success. Then I recall talking to men in the Lincoln National Life Insurance Company of Fort Wayne, Indiana, and asked if they would have information as to where a mask might be obtained. They have a Lincoln museum in connection with their company which collects valuable documents. They were very interested in my inquiry and immediately sent me life mask and casts of Lincoln's hands in plaster, but colored like bronze. These gave a fair indication as to Lincoln's face and hands, but being a sculptor and having to deal with castings, I recognized that these were far removed in duplication from the originals and were not as detailed as I had hoped to obtain. The size and general form were sufficient to use when beginning the large, heroic study.

While modeling the Lincoln statue, people from various places became extremely interested in the work I was doing. Mr. Thomas Starr of Detroit, president of the Michigan Lincoln Club visited my studio and told me of a mask and hands that he had, saying that they were from the original molds, now in the National Museum in Washington, DC (Fig. 1).

He said that they were so perfect that the minute wrinkles and furrows of the skin of the face and hands were in evidence. He further offered to allow me to use them.

The opportunity to obtain a casting from the original molds seemed like a real find, and the next day I went to Detroit, and was amazed to find such fine castings from the molds that had been used many times to make masks for museums and people who were anxious to have original materials on Lincoln (Fig. 2).

These castings I gratefully used for modeling the head and hands for the heroic, nine foot statue planned to be placed in Hawaii. The opportunity to obtain such good material was exceedingly valuable in creating the fine characterization of our great Lincoln (Fig. 3).

All sculptors and artists are indebted to the man who had foresight enough to make the mold of Lincoln's face and hands while he was alive. He was a young sculptor, Leonard Volk living in Chicago. He was a friend of Stephen A. Douglas and was making a portrait of the Senator.

Fig. 4. Leonard Volk, famous Chicago Sculptor, photo courtesy of the Abraham Lincoln Bookshop in Chicago.

Leonard Volk

Leonard Volk of Chicago (Fig. 4) made a portrait, a life mask, and casts of Abraham Lincoln's hands prior to his election to the Presidency. A portrait bust was later made by Leonard Volk (Fig. 8). Another life mask during the Presidency was made by Clark Mills (Fig. 7). Both masks have been well preserved, and many copies have been made. In 1860, Thomas D. Jones, a Cincinnati sculptor, traveled to Washington and modeled a portrait bust. Vinnie Ream, encouraged by Clark Mills, also modeled a portrait of Lincoln during his Presidency, completing it a few days before the assassination.

Historians and artists of this nation are deeply indebted to the foresight of the capable pioneer sculptor, Leonard Volk. It is interesting to note that these artistic efforts were encouraged by Stephen A. Douglas and were partly an outcome of the famous debates of Lincoln and Douglas.

Leonard Volk was born in Wellstown, New York. He spent his boyhood in Rochester and Avon, New York. In his youth he spent considerable time in the marble quarries of Massachusetts. There he learned marble cutting, carving, and lettering. His ability

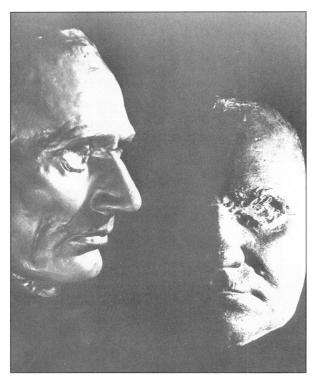

Fig. 5. Life masks of Abraham Lincoln and Stephen A. Douglas, cast by Leonard Volk, photo courtesy of the Abraham Lincoln Bookshop, Chicago.

as a sculptor was recognized and was brought to the attention of his wife's first cousin, Stephen A. Douglas. By the aid and influence of Senator Douglas, Volk was able to prepare himself for a professional career in sculpture. In 1848 he engaged in a marble business in St. Louis. There he did some modeling and carved a copy of a marble bust of Senator Henry Clay. This was the first marble carving made west of the Mississippi River.

In 1855, with the assistance of Stephen Douglas, Volk was able to study art for two years at Rome and Florence, Italy. He returned to Chicago, where he opened his sculpture studio. His first work was a sculptured bust of Stephen A. Douglas, and a life mask of Senator Douglas was also made (Figs. 5, 6). During the Lincoln-Douglas debates of 1858 he carved a life-size statue of the "Little Giant" in marble.

In April 1860, Leonard Volk, acting on the recommendations of Douglas, and his own recognition of Abraham Lincoln as a man of destiny, invited Lincoln to his studio to pose for a portrait. The following newspaper excerpt may demonstrate the difficulty of completing a portrait of a popular politician:

Lincoln was in Chicago to argue the famous 'Sand Bar' case. He traveled one day to Waukegan to address a Republican rally and received an invitation from his friend Julius White of Evanston to come to that town with a population of 200 for a reception.

On Thursday Lincoln was approached in court by the Chicago sculptor Volk, who wanted Abe to sit for preliminary sketches and work on a bust Volk was proposing to make of the leading Republican.

When Lincoln went to Volk's studio, he told the sculptor he could not sit very long since he had an appointment with White in Evanston. White was a personal friend of Lincoln's, a member of the Chicago Board of Trade, and harbor master of Chicago.

Volk went to White's office in Chicago and suggested that White might release Lincoln from the engagement so that the sculpturing session might continue. White refused, "because I've invited so many people to meet Lincoln in my home."

Abraham Lincoln rode through Uptown, Edgewater, Ravenwood, and Rogers Park on the afternoon of Thursday, April 5, 1860, but it is doubtful that he noticed much of the North Side.

Old Abe stationed himself on a seat in his coach on the Chicago & Northwestern Railway and told stories on his way to visit Evanston. Attorney Harvey B. Hurd of Evanston, Lincoln's escort, said that the lanky lawyer-politician planted his feet on the stove of the car as he rode.

Evanston still boasts of that day as the only occasion on which the future president visited the community. In fact, Evanston was rather lucky that Lincoln came at all.

From *Lerner North Side Newspaper,*
October 14, 1956, Chicago, Illinois.

The life mask was made within a few days, and the portrait was completed after many sittings. Some artistic license is in evidence, as the shoulders were draped in a classic Roman toga. A short time after the nomination, Lincoln is reported to have humorously remarked, "In two or three days after Volk commenced my bust, there was the animal himself." The sculptor once related that Old Abe

Fig. 6. A life mask of Stephen Douglas and tools of Leonard Volk, photo courtesy of the Abraham Lincoln Bookshop, Chicago.

Fig. 7. A life mask of Abraham Lincoln cast by Clark Mills at Washington, D.C. in 1865 during the presidency.

once told him he "didn't like to hear cut and dried sermons. When I hear a man preach, I like to see him as if he were fighting bees."

Casts of Lincoln's hands were made by Leonard Volk in Springfield on May 20, 1860, the Sunday following Lincoln's nomination to the Presidency. The right hand grasps a short rod, reported to be a section of broomstick which Abe whittled off the end of a broom. The pocketknife blade marks are evident on the cast. The left hand is lightly closed. They are large, powerful hands. The phalanges or segments of fingers measure about one and one-half the length of a similar segment of an average man's hand.

A description of the creation of the life mask and the casting of Lincoln's hands was written by Leonard Volk. *The Century Magazine* published this in an article in 1881, and excerpts add a very human dimension to these moments of history:

"My first meeting with Abraham Lincoln was in 1858, when the celebrated senatorial contest opened in Chicago between him and Stephen A. Douglas. I was invited by the latter to accompany him to Springfield. At Bloomington we stopped overnight at the only hotel. While we

were sitting in the hotel office after supper, Mr. Lincoln entered carrying an old carpet bag and wearing a weather-beaten silk hat.

"The next day I was formally presented to him. He saluted me with his natural cordiality, grasping my hand in both his large hands with a viselike grip, and said, 'I have read that you are making a statue of Judge Douglas.'

"'Yes, sir,' I answered, 'and sometime when you are in Chicago and can spare the time, I would like to have you sit for me for your bust.' 'Yes, I will, Mr. Volk, I shall be glad to, the first opportunity I have.'

"I did not see him again for nearly two years. I was considering whose bust I should begin when I noticed in the morning paper that Abraham Lincoln was in town—retained as one of the counsel in a 'sandbar' trial. I decided to remind him of his promise to sit for me. I found him in the United States District Courtroom. He instantly arose and met me outside the rail, recognizing me at once with his usual grip of both hands. He remembered his promises and said in answer to my question, 'I shall be glad to give you the sitting. When shall I come?' I answered that I would be ready for him the next morning.

"'Very well, Mr. Volk, I will be there, and I'll go to a barber and have my hair cut before I come.'

"I requested him not to let the barber cut it too short and said I would rather he would leave it as it was, but to this he would not consent.

"He was there promptly—indeed he never failed to be on time. Before commencing the cast, and knowing Mr. Lincoln's fondness for a story, I told him one in order to remove what I thought an apprehensive expression—as though he feared the operation might be dangerous. Upon hearing the story, tears actually trickled down Mr. Lincoln's bronzed cheeks, and he was at once in the best of humors.

"I put the plaster on without interference with his eyesight or his free breathing. It was about an hour before the mold was ready to be removed, and being all in one piece, with both ears perfectly taken, it clung pretty hard, as the cheekbones were higher than the jaws at the lobe of the ear. He bent his head low and took hold of the mold and gradually worked it off without breaking or injury; it hurt a little as a few hairs of the tender temples pulled out with the plaster and made his eyes water.

"The sittings were continued daily and during their continuance he would talk almost unceasingly, telling some of the funniest and most laughable of stories.

"On Thursday following, May 18, Mr. Lincoln received the nomination for President of the United States. As it happened, I was in Springfield. I went straight to Mr. Lincoln's house. I exclaimed, 'I am the first man from Chicago, I believe, who has the honor of congratulating you on your nomination for President.' Then those two great hands took both of mine with a grasp never to be forgotten. I thought my hands were in a fair way of being crushed.

"I was to cast Mr. Lincoln's hands on the Sunday following this memorable Saturday. I found him ready. I wished him to hold something in his right hand. Thereupon he went to the wood-shed and soon returned whittling off the end of a piece of broom handle. When I had successfully cast the mold of the right hand and begun the left, Mr. Lincoln told me about a scar on the thumb.

"'You have heard them call me a rail-splitter. One day, while I was sharpening a wedge on a log, the ax glanced and nearly took my thumb off, and there is the scar, you see.'

"The right hand appeared swollen as compared with the left on account of the excessive handshaking the evening before; this difference is distinctly shown in the cast.

"The last time I saw Mr. Lincoln was in January, 1861. He had lost 40 pounds in weight; the lines of his jaws were sharply defined through the short beard which he was allowing to grow. He announced to the gathered company that I had made a bust of him before the nominations and that he was then giving sittings to another sculptor, but could not see the likeness, though he might yet bring it out.

"'But,' continued Mr. Lincoln, 'in two or three days, after Mr. Volk commenced my bust, there was the animal himself.'

"And this was about the last, if not the last remark, I ever heard him utter, except the good-bye and his good wishes for my success."

This condensation of Volk's article is reprinted by courtesy of Lincoln Mutual Savings Bank of Spokane, Washington.

The portrait bust was later carved in marble by Leonard Volk and was on display in the historical building, but unfortunately it was destroyed in the Chicago fire of 1871. However, copies of the plaster cast had been made (Fig. 8). These portrait copies have also been a valuable reference for sculptors.

Leonard Volk continued in his endeavors to create fine statuary. He designed and erected a monument to Stephen A. Douglas in Chicago. He also erected the Soldiers' and Sailors' monument in Rochester, New York, surmounted by a bronze statue of Abraham Lincoln. He created bronze life-size statues of Stephen A. Douglas and Abraham Lincoln that were placed in the State House in Springfield, Illinois. He organized the first art exhibit in Chicago and promoted the Academy of Design. His son Stephan Arnold Douglas Volk also

Fig. 8. Leonard Volk in his studio carving the portrait of Abraham Lincoln, photo courtesy of the Abraham Lincoln bookshop, Chicago.

chose art as a vocation, studying to become a landscape and portrait painter. He was appointed as an instructor at the Cooper Institute and the Art Students' League in New York City, and would later receive many honors and awards for his excellent work.

A life mask was also made of Abraham Lincoln in 1865 by the famous American sculptor, Clark Mills of Washington, DC (Fig. 7). It was cast only a short time before the assassination of the President. There is a contrast between this and the Volk mask made only five years earlier. One cannot help noticing how much the demands of office and the concern for the war have furrowed his forehead and aged his countenance to a degree greater than

should be expected. This mask gives the sculptor additional details of the head; although the hair is covered as is also the beard, and chin details are less adequately demonstrated. However, it is an excellent mask of the President.

Sculptor Clark Mills already had a well-established reputation when he made the life mask of Abraham Lincoln. Like Leonard Volk, he was born in upstate New York. As a young man he had learned the trades of cabinetmaker and millwright, and he became a stucco worker in Charleston, South Carolina. In 1835, he became interested in modeling portraits in clay, and developed a technique of making life masks. He studied marble carving as well. In 1845, he carved a portrait bust of John C.

Calhoun. The sale of this piece to the city of Charleston encouraged him to devote his creative ability to sculpture.

In Washington, DC, he received a commission for an equestrian statue of Andrew Jackson. When the full scale plaster model was nearly completed, he found it necessary to learn about bronze casting, since there was no foundry prepared to accept such a project. He erected this statue (the first American bronze equestrian monument) in Lafayette Square across from the White House, and replicas were placed in Nashville and New Orleans. He also received a commission from Congress for an equestrian statue of George Washington that was unveiled in Washington, DC, in 1863.

Congress ordered him to cast in bronze the colossal statue by Thomas Crawford representing Freedom or Armed Liberty. This was later placed surmounting the dome of the capitol in 1863. Many portraits of illustrious persons were modeled by sculptor Mills. His last and greatest project was a design for an elaborate Lincoln memorial that was to contain 36 heroic statues. Like a prophet, Mills was ahead of his time. His plans did not materialize, but they served to demonstrate the need for memorializing of the greatness of the sixteenth President.

The Lincoln Memorial was destined to be completed many years later. The building was designed by Henry Bacon, an architect. The colossal marble statue of Abraham Lincoln, seated and in an attitude of contemplation, was created by Daniel Chester French. The memorial was dedicated in 1922.

Vinnie Ream

Besides the life masks of Lincoln and the portrait by Leonard Volk, there was a portrait modeled in sculpture by a 17-year-old young lady, who had requested special permission of the President.

Vinnie Ream's childhood dream was to become a sculptress. Senator Trumbull, a family friend, introduced her to Clark Mills, then one of the leading sculptors of the nation. A life mask of Lincoln during the Presidency had already been made by sculptor Mills. He recognized that Vinnie had talent and was highly motivated, and agreed to give her constructive criticism. Receiving instruction along with considerable encouragement, she spent time at Mills' studio when not involved in a busy work schedule of her job in the post office. She had started working at the age of 14 because of labor shortage during the Civil War. Much of her modeling was done at home with parental approval.

As her skill improved, Vinnie began to desire making a portrait of President Lincoln, and was supported in this effort by both Senator Trumbull and Clark Mills. She made this request at one of the President's receptions, and Lincoln cordially arranged a time when it would not interfere with his schedule. Miss Ream spent many hours at the White House, and a fond acquaintance developed with the President's family. The portrait was almost finished when the President was assassinated. This was a personal loss to the young sculptress of a cherished friendship. Nevertheless, the modeling was a very fine reproduction of the President's features and expression. Soon afterwards, the modeling was complete, and it was cast in plaster.

When Senator Trumbull saw the portrait and showed friends, they were very impressed. Later, they passed a bill in Congress commissioning Vinnie Ream to create a life-size figure and have it carved in marble. The figure was modeled in Washington, DC, and cast in plaster. The cast was then shipped to marble carvers in Rome. She later traveled there to complete the carving. On completion, the unveiling was a grand affair, and since that time the statue has been displayed in the rotunda of the national capitol. The portrait masterpiece represents not only the man, but also an intimate reflection on his personality. It serves as an excellent model for an artist to study.[*]

---

* Hubbard, Freeman H., *Vinnie Ream And Mr. Lincoln,* Whittlesey House, McGraw-Hill Book Company, Inc., New York; London; Toronto. 1949.

Additional Material Resources of Lincolniana

In Dr. Fairbanks' efforts to portray Abraham Lincoln with historical accuracy and yet give animation to the sculpture, considerable assistance was received from many sources. For the first study, *Lincoln The Frontiersman*, Thomas I. Starr, president of the Lincoln Club of Detroit, Michigan, made his personal extensive library and collection of Lincolniana available. Mr. Starr took a very personal interest in the progress of the statue and was of inestimable assistance in locating factual material.

Convenient to the studio on the University of Michigan campus was the William L. Clements Library, which has a special interest in American history, and this was a rich source of information. The Greenfield Village Museum at Dearborn, Michigan, was visited. Artifacts of the Lincoln era were reviewed, and the information was of considerable help.

The Lincoln Library and Museum of the Lincoln National Life Foundation has one of the largest collections of Lincolniana. The library contains nearly 10,000 volumes, more than 75,000 magazine articles, and more than 100,000 clippings. Here 120 Lincoln photographs from original negatives or contemporary prints are on exhibit. There are 235 sculptured busts and over 1000 Lincoln medals. There are also 28 original oil paintings by some of America's most famous artists. The director, Dr. Louis A. Warren, was most cooperative and demonstrated a personal interest in the progress of the sculpture.

Ralph G. Newman, proprietor of the Abraham Lincoln Book Shop of Chicago, served as an excellent consultant. His book shop has an abundance of material for historians and Lincoln scholars.

The Chicago Historical Society, begun in 1856, now maintains a library and museum. It is a treasure house of local and national artifacts and documents. Lincoln Hall contains many personal articles of the martyred president. It is one of the valuable and productive sources of Lincoln lore, with important manuscripts and books.

In Springfield, the Illinois State Historical Society and Historical Library, located in the Centennial Building, is another important source. It has a great collection of manuscripts and books.

The Library of Congress contains a remarkable collection of material on Abraham Lincoln. However, it is available mainly to governmental officials and to Lincoln scholars on invitation. It is the largest collection of manuscripts and books on Lincoln and the Civil War period. The National Archives in Washington, DC, has a collection of official government documents, also available only by special permission through the State Department.

The Huntington Library and Art Gallery at San Marino, California, has an important collection of manuscripts and books.

Noteworthy manuscript collections along with significant book collections are maintained by a bank, the Lincoln Federal Savings and Loan, of Los Angeles, California.

Additional significant collections of books and manuscripts include:

Cornell University Library, Ithaca, N.Y.

New York State Library, Albany, New York.

Brown University Library, Providence, Rhode Island.

University of Chicago Library, Chicago, Illinois.

Indiana University Library, Bloomington, Indiana.

Lincoln Memorial University Library, Harrogate, Tennessee.

The *Lincoln Herald* published by the Lincoln Memorial University at Harrogate, Tennessee, is a source of currently discovered artifacts, documents, and information of the Civil War period.

A list of the important collections of Lincolniana has been compiled by Ralph G. Newman, of the Lincoln Book Shop in Chicago. It is listed alphabetically by state, and some additions have been included.

California

Huntington Library and Art Gallery, San Marino

Lincoln Savings and Loan Association, Los Angeles

Mills College Library, Oakland

University of California at Santa Barbara, Library

University of Redlands, Redlands
Lincoln Memorial Shrine of the Redlands in Redlands
Department of Special Collections, Green Library, Stanford University

Colorado
Denver Public Library, Denver

Connecticut
Watertown Library Association, Watertown
Yale University, Beinecke Rare Book Library, New Haven

Delaware
Historical Society of Delaware, Wilmington
Wilmington Institute Free Library, Wilmington
Wilmington Public Library, Wilmington
University of Delaware Library, Newark

District of Columbia
Mr. Lincoln's Virtual Library, Library of Congress
Masonic Library
National Archives and Records Administration
Ford Theater National Historic Site
The American Presidency Exhibit, National Museum of American History
The Smithsonian Institute

Illinois
The Benedictine University Library, Lisle
Blackburn College Library, Carlinville
Bradley University Library, Peoria
Chicago Historical Society, Chicago
Chicago Public Library, Chicago
Decatur Public Library, Decatur
Eastern Illinois University Library
Illinois Freeport Public Library, Freeport
Illinois College Library, Jacksonville
Illinois State Archives, Springfield
Illinois State Historical Library, Springfield
James Millikin University Library, Decatur
Knox College, Lincoln Study Center, Galesburg
Lincoln College Library, Lincoln
Lincoln Public Library, Sangamon Valley Collection, Springfield
McLean County Historical Society, Bloomington
McMurray College Library, Jacksonville
Southern Illinois University Library, Carbondale
University of Chicago Library, Chicago
University of Illinois Library, Urbana
Watseka Public Library, Watseka

Indiana
Indiana Historical Society, Indianapolis
Indiana State Library, Indianapolis
The Lincoln Room, Lilly Library, Indiana University Library, Bloomington
Lincoln National Life Foundation and Museum, Fort Wayne

Iowa
Iowa State Department of History and Archives, Des Moines
State University of Iowa Library, Iowa City

Kansas
Kansas State Historical Society, Topeka

Kentucky
Berea College Library, Berea
University of Kentucky Library, Lexington

Louisiana
Louisiana State University Library, Baton Rouge

Maine
Colby College Library, Waterville

Massachusetts
Bridgewater State College, Clement C Maxwell Library, Chestnut Hill
Boston University Special Collections, Boston
Boston Public Library, Boston
Captain Forbes House Museum, Milton
Free Public Library, Concord
Harvard University Library, Cambridge
Massachusetts Historical Society, Boston
Winchester Public Library, Winchester

Michigan
Detroit Public Library, Detroit
University of Michigan, Clements Library, Ann Arbor
Western Michigan University Library, Kalamazoo
Plymouth Historical Society Museum, Plymouth

Minnesota
Minnesota Historical Society, Saint Paul

Mississippi
Evans Memorial Library, Aberdeen

Missouri
Missouri Historical Society, Saint Louis
Northeast Missouri State Teachers College Library, Kirksville
State Historical Society of Missouri, Columbia

New Jersey
Drew University Library, Madison
Princeton University Library, Princeton
Upsala College Library, East Orange

New York
Buffalo Historical Society, Buffalo
Cornell University Library, Ithaca
The Morgan Library, New York City
New York Historical Society, New York City
Public Library, New York City
State Library, Albany
Pierpont Morgan Library, New York City
Syracuse University Library, Syracuse
United States Military Academy Library, West Point
University of Rochester Library, Rochester
Wellsville Public Library, Wellsville

Ohio
Columbus Public Library, Columbus
Hayes Memorial Library, Fremont
The Lincoln Highway National Museum and Archives, Galion
Ohio Historical Society, Columbus
Western Reserve Historical Society, Cleveland
Wooster College Library, Wooster

Oregon
Portland University Library, Portland

Pennsylvania
Allegheny College Library, Meadville
Free Library of Philadelphia, Philadelphia
Historical Society of Pennsylvania, Philadelphia
W.W. Griest Collection of Lincolniana, Franklin and Marshall College, Lancaster

Rhode Island
John Hay Library, Brown University Library, Providence

Tennessee
Lincoln Memorial University, Harrogate

Washington
Washington State University Library, Pullman

Wisconsin
Beloit Historical Society, Beloit
Marquette University Library, Milwaukee
Rock County Historical Society, Janesville
State Historical Society of Wisconsin, Madison

Included are some listings compiled by the Lincoln Mutual Savings Bank, of Spokane, Washington (it sold its Lincolniana collection after merging with another financial institution).

Many university and city libraries have significant acquisitions, and in many states, inter-library loans facilitate research in a person's own community. There are important private collections, accumulated by the biographers of Abraham Lincoln and by other Lincoln scholars. Both Ida Tarbell and Carl Sandburg accumulated extensive collections (now contributed to institutional libraries) as they were engaged in writing their splendid books on Abraham Lincoln. There may be other noteworthy collections, and the inadvertent omission from this acknowledgment by no means depreciates their value to those who may aspire to create future portraits of the honored president, Abraham Lincoln.

Besides books and library resources, collectible items are available. Copies of early sculptured portraits, life masks and casts of Lincoln's hands can be bought from Stone Post Corp. in East Dummerston, VT. Information about other suppliers may be obtained from libraries, book dealers or journal listings.

Lincoln Related Bookstores and Book Dealers

Abraham Lincoln Book Shop, 357 West Chicago Avenue, Chicago, IL

Abraham Lincoln Memorial Bookstore, 23rd St. & Lincoln Circle, NW, Washington DC.

Antietam National Battlefield Bookstore, Sharpsburg, MD

The Lincoln Museum Bookstore, P.O. Box 7838, Fort Wayne, IN

Visitors Center Bookstore, Lincoln Home National Historic Site, Springfield, IL

Main Street Fine Books and Manuscripts, Galena, IL

McGowan Book Co., Chapel Hill, NC

Prairie Archives, Antiquarian Booksellers, Springfield, IL

Lincoln Book Titles from Museum Store, Chicago Historical Society, Chicago, IL

Chuck Hand; Books and Lincolniana, Paris, IL

Ford's Theater Bookstore, Washington, D.C.

The Presidents Box Bookshop, Association of American Presidents, Washington DC.

Books about Lincoln may be obtained through other book dealers and by browsing in used, old, and rare bookstores and in community or library book sales. Lincoln association officers, listed in the internet, may also be helpful in directing an artist to useful information sources

An artist who is interested in portraying President Lincoln, or one who has been commissioned to create a masterpiece, would be well advised to tour the Lincoln Heritage Trail. This is a circuit on modern highways with several side trips. Points of special interest include the log cabin birthplace at Sinking Springs Farm near Hodgenville in Hardin (now La Rue) County, Kentucky, and Knob Creek, his boyhood home. Traveling to Indiana, one may visit the farm, now a national historic site, with its reconstructed cabin and buildings on Little Pigeon Creek near Gentryville in Spencer County, where Abe spent his youth. A fine information and heritage center has been created for this national monument. The trail continues west across the Wabash River at Vincennes to Illinois. It proceeds to Macon County, to Decatur where he journeyed with his family to a new home in the Sangamon Valley.

At New Salem Village, now a state park, there is an impressive restoration of the town-site where he struck out on his own, lived, worked, and entered into politics. This is not merely an empty village with deteriorating cabins and roped-off exhibits. It has live people and animals using functional implements and livable buildings, with reconstruction as accurate as records allow. It is a dynamic portrayal of life as it existed in the decade of 1830. At the Information Center there is a well-stocked bookstore with some of the most interesting and informative books about Lincoln.

Springfield, the city where he entered law practice, is rich with Lincoln lore. One should visit the Lincoln home and law office, both preserved as historic sites. The former Capitol building, where he served as a legislator, has been restored and renamed the Centennial building. It is a public museum, and the Illinois State Historical Association is located there, with staff helpful towards any research. At Oak Ridge Cemetery the Lincoln tomb has a very impressive memorial, with fine statuary.

Continuing the tour, one could visit cities in which Lincoln attended courts, and cities where he debated with Senator Stephen A. Douglas. More detailed information about local points of interest may be available at museums and historical societies.

Other cities with prominent and active historical associations may have dedicated groups interested in the search and preservation of history and artifacts of the Civil War period. Members and officers of Lincoln clubs may be able to offer considerable expertise and encouragement. Librarians and museum curators may know persons to contact.

A study of existing portraits, both graphic and sculptured, may give one a greater sense of appreciation and inspiration. A sculptor is also well advised to avoid a gesture or stance similar to existing monuments, since it may appear like a copy or repetition. Three books may be helpful to review: *Lincoln In Marble And Stone* by F. Lauritson Bullard, *He Belongs to the Ages*; *The Statues of Abraham Lincoln* by Donald Charles Durman, and *Abraham Lincoln, Unforgettable American* by Mable Kunkel. Another recommended book is *Lincoln, a Picture Story of His Life,* by Stefan Lorant, a collection of his known photographs. The internet now has remarkable resources and references easily available to most artists. One should search Abraham Lincoln Online. The Abraham Lincoln Association is another valuable source.

Even though many statues have already been created, additional ones will be sought and can be of benefit to our society in order to convey a sense of reality of the principles for which Lincoln stood and the ideals he sought. While searching the literature, the author was pleasantly surprised to encounter a description of Abraham Lincoln by the eminent American sculptor, Augustus Saint-Gaudens. It seemed very appropriate to include in this book. Dr. Fairbanks frequently expressed his admiration of the magnificent creations of Augustus Saint-Gaudens, and was very disappointed that he never had the opportunity to meet this illustrious sculptor. Saint-Gaudens had passed away shortly before Avard Fairbanks, as a boy of 13, started studying sculpture in New York City. However, Avard felt honored that he was able to purchase some of the great sculptor's Plastilina from his widow. It was used by the aspiring young artist in the creation of his first bison statue. Years later, whenever traveling through Chicago, he would take his sons to Lincoln Park and admiringly show them the impressive statue of Abraham Lincoln by Saint-Gaudens. This heroic monument and its message served as a great inspiration to Avard Fairbanks.

The famous sculptor August Saint-Gaudens, as he stood modeling the Lincoln statue later erected in Lincoln Park, Chicago, said to William Agnew Patton, a New York journalist:

"When I began this work, I despaired of making a worthy or satisfactory statue. So many, almost all, of the likenesses of Lincoln represent him as ungainly, uncouth, homely, unpicturesque; but when I had made a study of his life, had learned more and more of his character, of his natural nobility and lovableness, his deep and true human sympathy, had read of him, talked of him with men who knew him and loved him, I became more and more convinced that his face must have been the most truly beautiful of all I have tried to model."

Rufus Rockwell Wilson,
Lincoln Among His Friends.
Caldwell, Idaho: The Caxton Printers, 1942, p. 327.

Bibliography

"Abe Lincoln Sculpture Presented to School," *Seattle Post-Intelligencer*, February 8, 1964.

Barton, William Eleazar. *The Lineage of Lincoln.* Indianapolis: The Bobbs-Merrill Company, 1929.

Berwyn Life and Berwyn Beacon (Berwyn, Illinois), June 28, July 1, and July 8, 1959.

Bowers, Claud G., Address at Lincoln Centennial Association, Springfield, Illinois, February 12, 1929, and presented posthumously at Knox College, Galesburg, Illinois, October, 1958. *Lincoln-Douglas Debate Centennial Program Brochure, 59th Annual Meeting Illinois Historical Society Conference of the Civil War Round Table,* p. 13.

Bullard, F. Lauritson. *Lincoln In Marble And Bronze.* New Brunswick, Rutgers University Press. 1946.

Catton, Bruce. *Convocation Address* , Knox College, October 7, 1958, at Centennial Celebration of Lincoln-Douglas Debates, Galesburg, Illinois.

Crawford, Frank (Executor Katherine Burke Estate). "She Was a Teacher," *Hawaii Educational Review,* XXXII:6 (February, 1944), p. 168.

Douglas, Paul H. "Stephen A. Douglas." An address at Quincy, Illinois, October 13, 1958, celebrating commemoration of 100th anniversary of Lincoln-Douglas Debates. Courtesy Chicago Historical Society.

"Dr. Fairbanks' Statue of Lincoln, Latest Creation by University Man Will be Exhibited Here Next Week," *Ann Arbor Daily News*, (Ann Arbor, Michigan), July 4, 1941.

Draper, Andrew S., *Selections from Abraham Lincoln.* New York: American Book Company, 1911.

Durman, Domnald Charles. *He Belongs to the Ages: The Statues of Abraham Lincoln.* Ann Arbor: Edwards Brothers, 1961.

Fairbanks, Avard T., "Engineering in Sculpture," *The Michigan Technic,* University of Michigan (February, 1942), p. 9.

Fairbanks, Avard T., "Lincoln the Friendly Neighbor," *Lincoln Herald* (Harrogate, Tennessee), 62:3 (Fall, 1960), p. 97.

Fairbanks, Avard T., "Making the Statue for New Salem," *Journal of the Illinois State Historical Society,* Springfield, Illinois (Summer, 1954).

Fairbanks, Avard T., "The Chicago Lincoln—A Chance to Portray Liberty," *Lerner Chicago North Side Newspapers, Souvenir and Historical Issue,* Sec. 2, Week of October 14, 1956, p. 8.

Fairbanks, Avard T., "The Face of Abraham Lincoln," *Lincoln for the Ages,* ed. Ralph G. Newman. Garden City, New York: Doubleday and Company, 1960.

Fairbanks, Avard T., "The Making of Lincoln," *Liberty,* 53:1 (January-March, 1958), p. 19.

Hitchcock, Caroline Hanks. *Nancy Hanks, The Story of Abraham Lincoln's Mother.* New York: Doubleday & McClure Co., 1899.

Horan, James D., *Mathew Brady, Historian with a Camera.* New York: Bonanza Books, 1955.

Horgan, Paul. *Citizen of New Salem.* Bronx, New York: H.W. Wilson Company.

Jennison, Keith W., *The Humorous Mr. Lincoln.* New York: Bonanza Books, 1965.

Kincaid, Robert L., "Heroes of Equal Greatness," *Lincoln Herald* (Harrogate, Tennessee), 58:3 (Fall 1956), p. 1.

Kunkel, Mable. *Abraham Lincoln, Unforgettable American.* Charlotte, North Carolina, The Delmar Company. 1976.

Larsen, Verne. "To the Last Man," *The Daily Utah Chronicle* (Salt Lake City, Utah), 64:85 (February 17, 1955), p. 1.

Lerner, Robert. "Lincoln Memorial, Once a Dream. How a Statue Became a Reality," *Lerner Chicago North Side Newspapers, Souvenir and Historical Issue,* Sec. 2, October 14, 1956, p. 3.

"Lincoln Statue, Congratulations from Governor William Stratton." *Berwyn Life and Berwyn Beacon,* July 1, 1959.

Long, Oren E., "Lincoln—A Heritage of Youth," *Hawaii Educational Review*, XXXII, 6 (February, 1944), p. 169.

Lorant, Stefan. *Lincoln, His Life in Photographs.* New York: Duell, Sloan and Pearce, 1941.

Meserve, Frederick Hill. *The Photographs of Abraham Lincoln.* New York: Harcourt, Brace and Company, 1944.

Nevins, Alan. *Lincoln, A Contemporary Portrait*. Garden City, New York: Doubleday and Company, Inc., 1962.

Newman, Ralph G., *Lincoln for the Ages*. Garden City, New York: Doubleday and Company, Inc., 1960.

Nicolay, John George and John Hay. *Abraham Lincoln*. New York: The Century Co., 1890, 1914.

"Only Lincoln Statue in Chicago Suburban Area." *Berwyn Life and Berwyn Beacon*, (Berwyn, IL) July 8, 1959.

Quinlan, O.D., "The Works of a Western Master," *Utah magazine* 13:5 (Winter, 1954), p. 5.

Rice, Allen Thorndike. *Reminiscences of Abraham Lincoln by Distinguished Men of his Time*. New York: North American Review, 1888.

Sandburg, Carl. *Abraham Lincoln: The Prairie Years*. 2 vols. New York: Harcourt, Brace and Company, 1926.

"Sculptor of Woolson Statue Honored for Lincoln Works," *The Gettysburg Times* (Gettysburg, Pennsylvania), 54:214 (September 7, 1956).

"Significant Memorial to 'The Last Man,'" *Lincoln Herald* (Harrogate, Tennessee), 58:3 (Fall 1956).

Stainback, Ingram M., (Governor, Territory of Hawaii). "Abraham Lincoln," *Hawaii Educational Review*, XXXII, 6 (February, 1944), p. 167.

Starr, Thomas I., (President Detroit Lincoln Group). "At the Crossroads of Decision," *Michigan Christian Advocate* (Adrian, Michigan), February 11, 1954.

Starr, Thomas I., "The Will of Katherine Burke has been Probated," *Lincoln Herald* (Harrogate, Tennessee), XLVI:2 (June, 1944).

Tarbell, Ida M., *The Life of Abraham Lincoln*. 2 vols. New York: Doubleday & McClure Co., 1900; and *The Life of Abraham Lincoln*. 2 vols. New York: The Macmillan Company, 1917.

"The Great Debates," *Program Brochure, Lincoln-Douglas Debate Centennial 1858-1958*, 59th Annual Meeting of Illinois Historical Conference of the Civil War Round Table, published by State of Illinois, 1958, p. 4.

Thomas, Benjamin Platt. *Abraham Lincoln, A Biography*. New York: Alfred A. Knopf, 1952.

Thomas, Benjamin P., *Portrait for Posterity: Lincoln and his Biographers*. New Brunswick, New Jersey: Rutgers University Press, 1947.

"Unveil Chicago Lincoln," *Edgewater Uptown News* (Chicago, Illinois), 54:44 (October 23, 1956), p. 1.

"Unveil Lincoln Statue." *Berwyn Life and Berwyn Beacon*. July 4, 1959.

Warren, Louis Austin. *Lincoln's Parentage and Childhood*. New York: The Century Co., 1926.

Warren, Louis Austin. "The Lincoln Statue at New Salem." *Lincoln Lore*, June, 1954: No. 1316, Fort Wayne, IN.

Wilson, Rufus Rockwell. *Lincoln Among his Friends: A Sheaf of Intimate Memoirs*. Caldwell, Idaho: The Caxton Printers, Ltd., 1942.

Wilson, Rufus Rockwell. *Lincoln in Portrature*. New York: Press of the Pioneers.

Volk, Leonard W., "The Lincoln Life Mask and How It Was Made," *The Century Magazine,* December 1881.

The Life and Work of Avard T. Fairbanks, Sculptor

By Eugene Fairbanks, his son

Avard Tennyson Fairbanks was born in Provo, Utah, on March 2, 1897, the tenth son of a family of eleven. His father, John B. Fairbanks, once a farm boy in a frontier village, had become one of the pioneer artists of Utah. He was an instructor in art at the Brigham Young Academy (now Brigham Young University). To supplement the low income of teaching, he operated a photographic studio with son J. Leo. The mother of this large family, Lilly Annetta Huish Fairbanks, had intended to see that her children were well educated, but an unfortunate accident prevented her from seeing her hopes fulfilled. She fell, injuring her neck, in August 1897, and remained bedfast until she died eight months later. She left an infant son and several young children to be reared by the father, assisted by the teenage children of the family.

Avard first showed interest in sculpture at the age of 12, when he modeled a pet rabbit under the direction of his brother, J. Leo, by this time an accomplished artist, who had studied in colleges and in Paris art schools and was supervisor of art in Salt Lake City Public Schools. This clay rabbit was entered in the State Fair and won a first prize. However, when the judge, a university professor, learned that it was the work of a boy, he refused to award the medal. This thoughtless act made young Avard resentful and determined to do even better work. He resolved to become an accomplished artist so that the professor would in time recognize him as a professional sculptor. "I'll show him some day!" he said.

Avard's father went to New York City to make copies for private sale of masterpieces at the Metropolitan Museum. (In an era before quality four color prints could be made, copies of masterpieces allowed a larger audience to enjoy them. This practice, early in the 1900s, was later discouraged and presently is not allowed.) Avard soon followed his father to New York. A permit, reluctantly granted because of his youth, was obtained for him to copy sculpture at this institution. When the curator saw how well he did, he apologized for his hesitation. A reporter one day observed his progress. Shortly, a story appeared in the New York Herald entitled,

"Young Michaelangelo of this modern day in knickerbockers working at the Metropolitan Museum." This article attracted considerable attention, which led to other opportunities. He showed such ability that in 1910 and 1911 he was awarded scholarships to study at the Art Students League at New York under James Earl Fraser. He also modeled animals at the Bronx Zoological Gardens. During this time, he became acquainted with several notable sculptors, from whom he often received advice and instruction. Among them were Herman A. McNeil, Cyrus E. Dallin, Adolph A. Weimer, Chester Beach, Gutzon Borglum, Solon Borglum, Paul Bartlett, A. Phimister Proctor, and Larado Taft. At the Bronx Zoo, he also received technical assistance and criticism from Anna Hyatt and Charles R. Knight. (Anna Hyatt later married Archer Huntington, a railroad executive. They established Brookgreen Gardens at Murrels Inlet in South Carolina, a premier sculpture garden. Charles R. Knight is famous for his restorations in sculpture of prehistoric animals at the New York Museum of Natural History).

Young Fairbanks displayed his sculpture in the National Academy of Design when he was only 14 years old. Payments for the copy work being done by his father were never regular and gradually dwindled. After a year and a half, it became necessary to return to Salt Lake City, following a period of physical impoverishment amidst intellectual wealth. Avard has said that he knew what it was to be very poor. He also knew what it was to go hungry.

The father, recognizing the son's artistic ability, promoted a plan for further study in Paris. During the next two years, they tried to obtain commissions for sculpture to finance the trip. All efforts ended in disappointment until Avard offered to model a lion in butter for a creamery exhibit at the State Fair. This attracted a large crowd, and the manager was well pleased. A change in fortunes occurred as several other sales were made, assuring finances for the study abroad.

In 1913, Avard went to Paris, accompanied by his father, to study at the École Nationale des Beaux Artes, under Injalbert. While in Paris, he studied at the École de la Grande Chaumière, at the Academy Colarossi, and at the École Moderne. His works were exhibited at the Grand Salon. Although he intended to continue in Paris, an adverse turn of events occurred—the outbreak of World War I interrupted his studies.

He and his father were sketching between school sessions in a small village near the Swiss border. News of the assassination of Archduke Ferdinand of Austria was soon followed by ominous rumors and reports and military mobilization in France. Each day several men of the village were called into military service and departed to join their units. In about three weeks, as mobilization progressed, it became imperative that Avard and his father return to the United States. Although the trip to the village by train had been only four hours from Paris, it took over two days to return. Civilian travel was sidetracked and diverted for troop transport to the border along the Rhine river. On their arrival, the once gay city of Paris was dismal. Shops of German merchants had been ransacked by angry mobs. The taxis were gone, pressed into service for troop movement. Only a few horse-drawn hacks were available. Hurried arrangements were made to leave the city, and they obtained reservations on a train to Calais.

On the morning of departure, they arose just after midnight and walked across Paris, carrying handbags, through the quiet, dimly lighted narrow streets to the railroad station. They felt relieved as the train moved toward the coast. However, the German army was advancing through Belgium, and the train was diverted to Boulogne. The bridges were blown up after the train passed. This was the last train northwest from Paris. They obtained passage across the English Channel to Folkestone. There, a considerate travel agent obtained two of the few remaining accommodations on a ship, the *Ausonia,* leaving Liverpool a few days later. He accepted as payment, without question, a check on a Salt Lake City bank. The voyage was stormy, in convoy, and out of the usual course. There was already concern for the submarine menace. (Several voyages later, the *Ausonia* was sunk by a German submarine.)

The view of the Statue of Liberty and New York

Avard T. Fairbanks, Sculptor

Harbor was a welcome sight indeed. On debarkation, they had only 15 cents. They obtained credit by telegraph from the family, which enabled them to return home by train.

They returned to Salt Lake City, where the young sculptor resumed his high school education. During this time he modeled several portraits that were exhibited in the Rotunda of the Fine Arts Palace of the Panama Pacific Exposition of 1915 in San Francisco. Soon his brother, J. Leo, and he received a commission to create four sculptured friezes for the Latter-Day Saints Temple in Laie, Hawaii. These were made of cast stone, a fine grade of concrete. Other sculpture included a bas relief honoring Hawaiian motherhood, and a heroic statue of Lehi blessing Joseph.

While in Hawaii, Avard sent for his sweetheart, Maude Fox of Taylorsville, Utah, and they were married in Honolulu. Their honeymoon was a trip by inter-island steamer to Hilo on the big island and a visit to the volcanoes of Mauna Loa and Kilauea. When the sculpture was complete in 1917, they sailed for home, but the spirit of *Aloha* and of the islands had etched a lasting memory in their hearts.

Returning from the Islands, Avard entered the

University of Utah. Since he already had advanced training in art, he chose other more academic college courses. Military experience was included in the Student Army Training Program.

World War I ended, bringing the boys back home, but the influenza epidemic closed colleges. He conceived an ambitious program of memorializing these veterans in heroic monuments, and modeled a figure he called *The Idaho Doughboy** for the State of Idaho, which was placed in two cities in that state. On a tour of the Northwest, he met Dean Ellis Lawrence of the School of Architecture at the University of Oregon. The dean was very impressed with his work and his training, and an appointment was offered in 1920 to teach sculpture at that institution in Eugene, Oregon. Avard accepted this challenging opportunity. Besides organizing sculpture courses on that campus, he also taught extension courses at Portland, Oregon.

His creative works while in Oregon included *The Awakening of Aphrodite,* an exquisite marble garden fountain, placed in the Washburn Gardens in Eugene. World War I memorials in bas relief were erected at Jefferson High School in Portland and at Oregon State University in Corvallis. Bronze doors were placed at the United States National Bank in Portland. A relief panel entitled *The Holy Sacrament* was placed at St. Mary's Chapel in Eugene, Oregon. A portrait of Ezra Meeker, founder of The Old Oregon Trail Association, was modeled, and bronze monuments marking the Old Oregon Trail were placed in Baker and Seaside.

During 1924, he took a leave of absence to study at Yale University, where he was granted a Bachelor of Fine Arts degree. Returning to Oregon, he continued as an assistant professor until 1927, when he was awarded a fellowship by the Guggenheim Foundation. This enabled him to go to Europe for further study and to do creative sculpture. By this time there were four boys in the family, the youngest of whom was six months old.

The family visited many museums of cities in England, France, and Italy; but he chose Florence, Italy, the cradle of the Renaissance, for most of the study. Sculpture in the great galleries and beautiful cathedrals inspired him. In Florence he studied under one of the great contemporary Italian sculptors, Dante Sodini. He also studied at Scuola Firentina de Pittura. Creative sculpture included a fantasy of springtime, *La Primavera,* and *Nursing Mother,* both carved life size in marble. A statuette honoring the *Archiconfraternite Della Miseracordia* was cast in bronze (this volunteer lay order in Florence, Italy, that has been dedicated for centuries to assisting the infirm or injured townspeople). He modeled the *Pioneer Mother Memorial* for Vancouver, Washington, and it was cast in bronze at a Florentine foundry.

Returning to the United States in 1928, Avard Fairbanks taught at the Seattle Institute of Art. He studied art courses at the University of Washington at Seattle, and in 1929 earned a Master of Fine Arts degree. He also completed one of his finest memorials, *The Ninety-first Division Monument,* a heroic bronze statue, erected at Fort Lewis, Washington.

Moving the family to Ann Arbor, Michigan, in 1929, he joined the faculty of the University of Michigan as an associate professor of sculpture in the newly established Institute of Fine Arts. There he organized a program of studies in sculpture. Annual sculpture exhibitions coincided with the May Festivals of Music. Within a few years, the hallways of University Hall were lined with the best works of students. He was called on frequently through the extension service to give demonstration lectures throughout the State of Michigan.

As a contribution to industry, he designed an original radiator ornament, *The Charging Ram,* for the Dodge Motor Company, which was modified each year over two decades. He created *A Winged Mermaid* for the radiator ornament of the Plymouth in 1930, symbolic of floating power. A *Griffin* of his design was chosen by the Hudson automobiles in 1933.

Commissions were scarce in the 1930s, because of the depression, and he turned his attention to studies in the field of anatomy in the Medical School. He was awarded a Master of Arts degree in 1933 and a Doctor of Philosophy degree in anatomy

---

* "Doughboy" was a term commonly used at that time to refer to United States Soldiers of World War I. Its equivalent a generation later was "GI."

in 1936. This led to an increased emphasis on anatomy in his teaching of sculpture. He was also able to give a greater expression to his sculptures, since he had done extensive dissection of facial musculature.

During the 18 years of residence at Ann Arbor, Michigan, Dr. Fairbanks was able to create many masterpieces. Prominent among these were *Winter Quarters Memorial* at Pioneer Mormon Cemetery at Florence, Nebraska, and a monument placed in Grand Detour, Illinois, to honor Leonard Andrus, who with John Deere developed the steel mold-board plow. *Lincoln The Frontiersman* was placed at Ewa, Hawaii, and *The Pioneer Family* was erected on the State Capitol grounds in Bismarck, North Dakota.

The North American Flower Show in Detroit, Michigan, commissioned him to create fantasy sculpture annually to grace floral exhibits. *Nebula,* a fantasy garden figure, was exhibited at the Flower Show in Detroit and again in 1939 at the New York World's Fair; *Rain,* a fantasy garden figure, also exhibited at the Northwest Flower Show, was selected along with works of America's greatest sculptors to be placed at Brookgreen Gardens at Murrels Inlet in South Carolina. Other statues included *Helle and Phryxus Riding the Golden Fleece Ram, Boy with the Shell, Flower Girl, Dawn and Morning Glories, Sunshine and Moonbeam,* and *Aquarius the Water Bearer.* He created *Young Pegasus* for the Wilson's Meadowbrook Gardens in Rochester, Michigan, that is now Oakland State University.

Sacred sculpture included intaglio reliefs of *The Madonna and Child* and *Christ Among the Doctors,* created for Mr. Frederick Zeder of Gross Pointe, Michigan. For the Latter-Day Saint display in the Hall of Religion at the Century of Progress World Fair at Chicago, 1933, he sculptured relief panels with a center piece titled *Eternal Progress.* He created a pioneer group titled *Youth and New Frontiers,* with a companion piece *A Tragedy of Winter Quarters* that was also exhibited in the Hall of Religion in the continuation of the World Fair in 1934.

Avard Fairbanks modeled many portraits during this period. Prominent among these were the Right Honorable William L. Mckenzie King, Prime Minister of Canada; Honorable Gerry McGreer, Mayor of Vancouver, British Columbia, and a mem-

ber of the Canadian House of Commons, and later a member of the Canadian Parliament; Dr. G. Carl Huber, one of the world's eminent neuroanatomists, Dean of the Graduate School, at the University of Michigan, and his anatomy professor. Other portraits included a portrait of Mrs. Alexander G. Ruthven, wife of the President of the University of Michigan; Mrs. Helen Gardner Phelan of Toronto, Canada; and Walter P. Chrysler, Chairman of the Chrysler Corporation.

During World War II, as university enrollment decreased, and wishing to be of service to the nation, he accepted a position at the Ford Willow Run Bomber Plant in the personnel department. Following the war, industries began retooling for civilian needs. The American Society of Automotive Engineers, to meet urgent needs, sought his services in collaboration with the College of Engineering at the University of Michigan. This was a new venture for industry, art, and education, but Michigan is noted for its initiative in these fields. The teaching of automotive body design and styling was decided upon and courses were established with the extension division of the University of Michigan in the Rackham Educational Building in Detroit. When the Automotive Golden Jubilee was celebrated in Detroit under the direction of General Knudsen and George Romney, Dr. Fairbanks was called on to create the award, entitled *The Genius of Man, His Mind, His Works.* It was awarded to the living pioneers of the automotive industry in honor of their great services.

The University of Utah was expanding in the post World War II period. Dr. Fairbanks was appointed dean and asked to organize a College of Fine Arts at this institution. He moved the family to Salt Lake City in 1947. He began an ambitious program with a new studio on the ground level, where he created more great statuary. Among these statues was the heroic bronze of *Dr. Marcus Whitman,* pioneer physician in the Pacific Northwest. This monument, placed in Statuary Hall in the nation's capitol to represent the State of Washington, has been heralded as one of the powerful and impressive studies of our day. Later, copies were placed at the state capitol in Olympia and at Walla Walla, Washington.

Other Fairbanks memorials in the Hall of Fame

include *Esther Morris* of Wyoming, active in securing equal rights for women of that state. North Dakota is represented by his heroic bronze statue of *John Burke,* three times Governor, for many years a state Supreme Court Justice, and Treasurer of the United States during the administration of Woodrow Wilson.

A monument by Fairbanks was erected honoring the distinguished mining engineer, *Daniel C. Jackling,* who developed the Utah Copper Company, predecessor of Kennecott Copper, the greatest mining project ever undertaken by man. The statue was placed in the Utah State Capitol by the Kennecott Copper Corporation under the sponsorship of the Sons of Utah Pioneers. Another statue by Fairbanks was erected at Colorado Springs, Colorado, honoring *Spencer Penrose,* an associate of Jackling.

Other great monuments to Lincoln were commissioned. Fairbanks created a heroic bronze statue, *Lincoln Statue for New Salem,* that was erected in the restored New Salem Village in Illinois, as a gift of the Sons of the Utah Pioneers. This portrays the young vigorous Abraham Lincoln in transition, at the crossroads of decision, resting his ax and picking up the law books. During Lincoln's years at New Salem, his living was earned by labor, but his developing interest was in public speaking, and his future lay in law and politics.

He erected another monument to Lincoln at Lincoln Square in Chicago, *The Chicago Lincoln.* Fairbanks' heroic bronze monument, *Lincoln The Friendly Neighbor,* was placed at nearby Berwyn, Illinois. This is a group portraying him as a friend to children of the neighborhood. Bas relief bronze panels commemorating the *Lincoln-Douglas Debates,* featuring Abraham Lincoln and Stephen A. Douglas, were erected at Knox College in Galesburg, Illinois, at the centennial celebration of the debates. His marble portrait busts of Abraham Lincoln representing four ages—*The Youth, The Rail-Splitter, The Lawyer,* and *The President*—were placed in the Ford's Theater Museum in Washington, DC. Later, *Lincoln the Lawyer* was placed in the Supreme Court Building.

The Commander of the Phalanx of Knights of Thermopylae, Mr. Harris J. Booras of Boston, Massachusetts, collaborated with officials of the city of Sparta, Greece, to commission Avard Fairbanks to create and place a memorial of heroic proportions to Lycurgus, the ancient lawgiver of that city. Nine centuries before Christ, this wise monarch established a constitutional government and created a senatorial system that granted a voice for the people, an intermediary between the king and his subjects. This was the first constitutional government in recorded history. The monument was erected in October 1955 near the site of the ancient senate forum. It stands at the present Temple of Justice, the choicest location in Sparta, Greece.

Other monuments include *Guidance of Youth,* erected in Bush Park, Salem, Oregon. One outstanding portrait study was a monumental bust of *Albert Woolson, the Last Survivor of the Grand Army of the Republic,* 107 years old. This work adorns the corridor of the City Hall of Duluth, Minnesota. Later, Dr. Fairbanks was commissioned to create a monument to this man, placed on the Gettysburg battlefield with a copy in Duluth, Minnesota. A bas relief panel honoring *Anthony W. Ivans,* active with youth and Boy Scout activities, and the University President, was placed at Utah State University in Logan. *Louis F. Moench,* founder of Weber State University, Ogden, Utah, was memorialized by a bronze statue at that campus. On the University of Utah campus he created a heroic statue in bronze that represents the *Ute Brave,* a crouching Indian preparing to put an arrow to his bow.

These many fine monuments did not interfere with modeling numerous portraits of persons of eminence and renown from various parts of the world. One significant study was an intimately felt portrayal he made of his brother, Professor J. Leo Fairbanks, at one time Supervisor of Art in Salt Lake City Schools. He organized the city's first planning commission and later was appointed Chairman of the Department of Fine Arts at Oregon State University. The portrait is exhibited at the Springville Art Museum in Springville, Utah.

The Pony Express has always been a topic of interest for historians, and it has also captured the imagination of artists. A sketch was modeled in demonstration lectures before various groups. During the Utah centennial, Fairbanks created a life-size model that was displayed in a parade in Salt Lake City. William Harrah of Reno, Nevada, who has taken a keen interest in history, particularly that which pertains to transportation, commissioned Dr. Fairbanks to create another heroic monument to *The Pony Express* and to its courageous young riders. This was erected and dedicated April 4, 1963, at Lake Tahoe. Mr. Harrah was so pleased that he ordered a duplicate to be placed in a museum to the Pony Express that he was developing at Reno, Nevada. The earlier *Pony Express* monument planned for Salt Lake City was delayed by lack of funding, but it was remodeled in heroic size, posthumously, by Avard Fairbanks' sons and erected July, 1998, in This is the Place State Park in Salt Lake City, Utah.

From among his small works of sculpture may be noted the creation of medals of distinction. These include the *Washington Roebling Medal,* given by the Mineralogical Society of America; *Appreciation Medal,* given each year to the First Citizen of Portland, Oregon; *Faith in Man and His Works* for the United States National Bank of Portland; *The Will to Achieve* for the Oregon Mutual Life Insurance Company (now the Standard Life Insurance Company) of Portland, Oregon; and the Utah Centennial emblem entitled *Vision and Our Heritage.*

Another of his medals with historic importance, *Courage,* was presented to Prime Minister Winston Churchill by the former Prime Minister W. L. Mackenzie King during the Second World War, at a conference of the Prime Ministers of the Commonwealth of Nations of Great Britain. The same study was also presented to President Eisenhower by the Sons of Utah Pioneers shortly after his election. Another study in numismatic art is a plaque, commissioned through the Medallic Art Company by the American Institute of Mining and Metallurgical Engineers, with a portrayal of *Colonel Daniel C. Jackling.*

Fairbanks bronze reliefs recognize outstanding doctors of medicine, among them: *Dr. Harley Haynes,* Director of the University Hospital, Ann Arbor, Michigan; *Dr. Fred Stauffer* of Salt Lake City in the Medical Arts Building; *Dr. Maxwell Wintrobe,* eminent hematologist at the University of Utah; *Drs. Willard Richards and Sons* at the Pioneer Medical Center, Salt Lake City, Utah: and *Dr. John E. Bordley,* Andelot Professor of Laryngology and Otology at Johns Hopkins University Medical School.

Regarding personal matters, the demands of teaching and creative sculpture did not exclude concern for family life. As the years went by, Avard Fairbanks' family increased to eight sons. The first was born in Utah, three more were born in Eugene, Oregon, and four in Ann Arbor, Michigan. Each son received instruction, personal attention, and practical experience in modeling and casting. Finish work such as retouching and coloring was included in the training. Preparation for exhibits or placement of monuments became a part of the family enterprise. The boys also learned photography, and had the opportunity to assist in photographic reproductions of sculpture.

As these boys matured, two chose careers in engineering, two continued in art, and four have studied to be doctors of medicine.

Lectures and commissions often called the sculptor out of town, but sometimes part and occasionally all of the family would travel with him. Visits to Museums, historic points of interest, and National Parks would be included on the way. In fact, the boys traveled more than most of their classmates. Boy Scout work, camping, and outdoor activities were an important part of family life.

Maude had always hoped for a daughter, but although she was disappointed, she remained undaunted. During a tour of Greece, following the dedication of the monument to *Lycurgus* at Sparta in 1955, she and Avard happened to visit an orphanage in that city. Maude's heart was moved when she saw many beautiful little girls. She wanted a daughter, and asked if she could adopt one or even two. The administrator said they would try to arrange adoption. It took several months to obtain the papers, but in time Avard and Maude received notice that a small girl would arrive at the Salt Lake City Airport. The seven-year old arrived unattended, probably bewildered, but happy and well cared-for by the airline hostess. Three weeks later, her 11-year old sister arrived. They adapted well to the family, and were readily accepted by their new brothers.

The girls were from a family of five children living in Yerkion, Greece. Their grandfather had been killed after World War II when the Communists tried to take over Greece by fostering a revolution. Their father had been killed later in an accident. The older children and mother survived on small jobs and by gleaning in the olive orchards, and the opportunity for adoption was a sad but welcome relief to the family. As years passed, occasional letters were exchanged. Maria entered college, soon married, and started rearing a family. Georgia studied music and taught singing in high schools. She was able to visit her mother and brothers in a joyful reunion, after they had emigrated to Australia. At another time during a trip to Greece, when accompanying her foster parents, she was able to visit her grandmother, who died soon afterwards at 105 years old, happy that her granddaughters had received fine care.

In 1965, Dr. Fairbanks was called to the University of North Dakota as Special Consultant in Fine Arts and Resident Sculptor for two years. He gave many demonstration lectures throughout that state and modeled several portraits. There he produced impressive sculptures entitled *An Invitation to Learning* and *Alma Mater*.

Avard Fairbanks last heroic monument was created to honor Woodbridge Nathan Ferris, who was an illustrious governor of the state of Michigan and continued service to the people of Michigan as an educator, an outstanding president of a State College (later named in his honor), and now Harris State University at Big Rapids, Michigan. It was erected and dedicated in 1983. The last significant public sculpture was a heroic portrait of George Eisenberg, a prominent Chicago philanthropist. This bronze portrait was commissioned by the Mayo Foundation and placed in the Eisenberg Building of the Methodist Hospital at the Mayo Medical School, Rochester, Minnesota.

During his professional career, Dr. Avard Fairbanks had many honors bestowed upon him. He was a fellow of the National Sculpture Society, a member of the Architectural League of New York, a member of the International Institute of Arts and Letters, and an honorary member of the Society of Oregon Artists. He was a member of *Circolo Degli Artisti di Firenze* (Florence, Italy). He was elected a member of the *Protetore Della Contrada Della Torre da Siena,* Italy. The National Sculpture Society granted Dr. Fairbanks the "Herbert Adams Memorial Medal" for distinguished service to American sculpture.

He was awarded a medal of the "Knights of Thermopylae" by King Paul of Greece at the an-

cient battle site where Leonidas and 300 Spartans fought to their death against King Xerxes and the army of 10,000 Persians. From Lincoln College at Lincoln, Illinois, he received an honorary degree of Doctor of Fine Arts. The Lincoln Memorial University in Harrogate, Tennessee, conferred upon Dr. Fairbanks their highest recognition, the Lincoln Diploma of Honor. Another very outstanding recognition was the Lincoln Medal of the Sesquicentennial Commission of the Congress of the United States.

In addition to these many recognitions, there was a constant desire to create additional great masterpieces of art. The great artists of past ages left lasting influences on their cultures. Dr. Fairbanks hoped to create and produce many more heroic and important works that would reflect the civilization and culture of our times.

During the eighth decade of his life, Avard T. Fairbanks continued with enthusiasm to create fine sculpture. In addition to his creative endeavors, he spent much of his life teaching, and it was not surprising that he invited grandchildren to his studio, that they might continue the artistic tradition of the family. He also made several trips to Pietrasanta, Italy, to the marble-carving studios of Pietrasanta de la Marina, not far from Pisa, to finish his portraits and fantasy sculpture. Sometimes his sons or grandsons would accompany him.

The marble carvers expressed admiration for his ability as an artist, and his energy and stamina, as an older man, through long days of work. They encouraged him to order more pieces to be finished. The letters he wrote home expressed a sense of satisfaction tempered with loneliness. He had come to love the Italian people and the countryside of the Carrara Mountains and the Italian Riviera; but during six-week marble-carving sessions, in which he worked long hours, he would miss his wife and family. A colossal portrait, *Lincoln The Legislator,* was carved in Italy in Portuguese Rose Marble. It was placed near the entrance where House Committee meetings are held at the Capitol Building in Washington, DC.

Some of his later significant bronze statues were cast in Italy, where he could arrange for the assistance of technicians and facilities for three-dimensional enlargement. At an age when other men were enjoying leisure pursuits, Avard Fairbanks continued to create great monuments and portraits. When not modeling with clay, he was drawing plans for other statuary.

His last planned statue would be of St. John the Revelator, receiving the vision that he recounted in the New Testament Book of Revelations. A few days before Christmas, 1986, he was rushed to the hospital with a heart attack. As he was improving, he renewed his optimism and continued to formulate plans for the monument. He even asked a friend to arrange for about a ton of modeling clay. On New Year's Day, another attack occurred, and his heart did not respond to treatments. He died just two months short of 90 years.

Dr. Fairbanks was survived by ten children, more than 50 grandchildren, and more than 40 great-grandchildren. Several family members have chosen art as a career. Justin, a professional sculptor, taught sculpture at Eastern Arizona College and created several monuments. Jonathan studied portrait painting and became a museum curator. A nephew, Ortho Fairbanks, is a professional sculptor and has taught Art at the LDS Church College of Hawaii, at Laie, and at Holbrook College in Holbrook, Arizona. Two granddaughters, Teressa and Hillary Ann, have studied art and museum science in Massachusetts. Another grandson, Daniel Fairbanks, a plant geneticist and professor on the faculty at Brigham Young University, has demonstrated a keen interest and talent in sculpture, and has been commissioned to create some fine statuary. Many grandchildren have chosen health science and other fields of endeavor, with art as an avocation. His son, Eugene, author of this book, modestly admits to creating a heroic bronze monument at Squalicum Harbor in Bellingham, Washington, honoring fishermen lost at sea. It is titled *A Safe Return,* the hope of all seafaring persons.

The influence and inspiration of the art of Avard Fairbanks have touched the lives of his many students, a number of whom have chosen to teach art or have succeeded at professional careers in sculpture.

Since many of Dr. Fairbanks' efforts were directed towards teaching sculpture in universities, a review is incomplete without a few quotations of his thoughts and philosophy of Art:

"The Arts are created for contemplation and edification, the expression of the highest ambitions and the spiritual hope of a people. These produce a culture that lives on to uplift subsequent generations. The influential cultural periods came about in times when men with understanding, with technical skills, and with high purpose were willing and ready to put their ideals into form. We are now on the verge of a great civilization. We may say we have opportunities for a new golden age of Art… .

"A sculptor must comprehend a significant civilization, one that is indicative of intellectual advancement of the times in which he lives. The hope of the world lies in our faith and in our spiritual ideals. Such ideals we express in material form. If we possess these and strive vigorously for the accomplishment of these, we will produce a great culture. Our civilization should not be contained in material welfare only. Nor should all sorts of frivolity and fanfare creep in and become our objective. For the great inspiration comes to souls whose thoughts turn in the direction of the eternal things of life… .

"To be sure, art must be intellectual and must therefore have a thoroughgoing terminology, technical—in accord with scientific terms—and philosophical as well. However, instead of being vague and occult, with the intent of mystification, art must clarify and be simple and direct in its purposes. It should be understandable to children and the untutored, as well as the most highly learned and technically trained.

"When our work is erected in public places for all to behold, we build an atmosphere and an environment. For this reason masterpieces of sculpture, because of their very nature of attracting attention, evoke admiration. Our products therefore become great factors in large-scale education and community uplift and pride… .

"Our kind of work is one dealing primarily with order. Thus, it is a process of organization and coordination. The adjustments and arranging of dissimilars into unity and unification, and the expression of the universals into material, have a way of giving soul to substance. All who see our works in the varying moods of weather see them thus standing solid and firm and undaunted. Observers are able to sense their meanings and know of those ideals of which they bespeak... .

"Through simple harmonies, art can bring understanding and uplift to the downtrodden. It can recognize the finer qualities of men of all stations of life and cause people to believe their own kind of living is worthwhile, particularly since art ennobles the struggles of life. We who are given the powers to express these must sense the problems of life in its many conditions and express them through our various media, thus enabling our deep soul-felt concepts and feelings to have real and tangible form... .

"Along with social and domestic and the varying personal things of life, art too must have deep concern in the industrial progress, religious inspirations, and political programs. Because art itself theoretically is striving to achieve a harmony in the total of a composition, the principles involved can be systematized in writing and in diagrammatic patterns. As scientific principles have become important formulae, so too our art principles of harmony can be utilized in formulae for social adjustments and international diplomacy... ."

~ Avard Fairbanks

About the Author

Eugene F. Fairbanks, the second son of Maude and Avard T. Fairbanks, was born in 1921 in Eugene, Oregon, while sculptor Fairbanks was teaching art at the University of Oregon. During an appointment to the faculty of the University of Michigan, 1930-48, his sons often helped at the studio, assisting with modeling and plaster casting. They also learned about photography for sculpture. There was a progressive expectation of skill and responsibility for both sculpture and photography. This continued from grade school through high school and into college. An older brother chose engineering as a vocation. Younger brothers studied engineering, art, and medicine. The family, in time, had eight sons and two adopted daughters.

Eugene chose to study medicine. He married Florence Sundwall in 1944 in his last year of the University of Michigan Medical School, graduating in 1945. He interned at Wayne County General Hospital near Detroit, Michigan, and started raising a family. After internship he served in the Army Medical Corps as a transport surgeon on a troop transport ship. Following military service, he practiced medicine as a family physician in Pasco and Kennewick, Washington.

After an anesthesiology residency in Seattle, in 1959, he moved the family to Bellingham, Washington, and practiced anesthesiology, then family practice. He became a diplomat of the American Board of Anesthesiology and the American Board of Family Physicians.

In time Florence and Eugene became the proud parents of five sons and five daughters. He practiced medicine in Bellingham until retirement in 1995.

With Dr. Charles J. Flora, he co-authored a marine biology species identification handbook in 1966 and 1977, *The Sound And The Sea*. His first book about Avard Fairbanks' sculpture, *A Sculptor's Testimony In Bronze And Stone* (1972 and 1994), featured sacred sculpture. In 1995 he was asked to create a monument honoring fishermen of Bellingham lost at sea. This figure was modeled in a web locker (a net warehouse), at Squalicum Harbor and dedicated on Memorial Day, 1999, in Zuanich Point Park.

During spare moments in the practice of medicine, Eugene has composed poetry to complement his father's fantasy sculpture. He has collected photographs and made many enlargements of Fairbanks' sculpture for this and other projected publications. In 2001 he published *A Sculpture Garden Of Fantasy,* featuring the fantasy sculpture of Avard Fairbanks.

Other planned publications about Avard Fairbanks' sculpture include the study of human proportions; Avard Fairbanks' technique of modeling statuettes and portraits; and an illustrated documentary book of many public monuments.

Documentary Books
About the Creative Sculpture
of Avard T. Fairbanks

Profusely illustrated books compiled and written by his son, Eugene F. Fairbanks.

Abraham Lincoln Sculpture, Created by Avard T. Fairbanks

A book with more than 160 photos, some in color, with background information about the process of creating public monuments. 176 pages, hard bound. $29.50

A Sculpture Garden of Fantasy

Imaginative, mythical, and with complimentary verse and descriptive information. 200 pages, approximately 100 illustrations, soft cover. $28.00

A Sculptor's Testimony in Bronze and Stone, The Sacred Sculpture of Avard T. Fairbanks

Creative sculpture of religious figures and personalities with descriptive text. 160 pages, approximately 100 photographs, hard bound. $21.95

Coming Soon

Human Proportions

A reference book for art students and serious amateurs about adult male and female form with illustrations and accompanying tabulation of measurements in many ratios from heroic size to one twelfth life size, including relative proportions of different body parts.

Modeling a Sculpture Portrait

A step by step instruction with photographs of modeling a portrait of George Washington with considerations of expression and facial proportions.

Fairbanks Art and Books
2607 Vining Street
Bellingham, WA 98226-4230
(360) 733-3852

Please Visit Our Websites

http://www.fairbanksartbooks.com/
This website lists the documentary books about Avard T. Fairbanks, with sample photographs from books, and ordering information for all books.

http://www.fairbanksart.com/
An online gallery featuring the artwork of Avard T. Fairbanks; includes selected major works and locations and selected museums, sites, and gardens. Features a slideshow gallery of fantasy sculpture, historical sculpture, sacred sculpture, and ordering information.

http://www.avardfairbanks.com/
A tribute to the sculptor Avard Fairbanks—his life and his art. This website is non-commercial in nature.

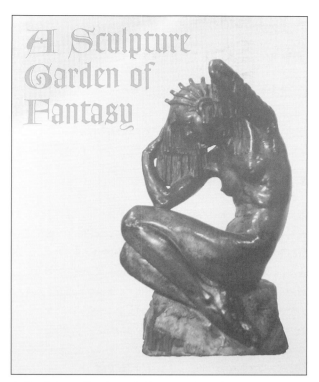

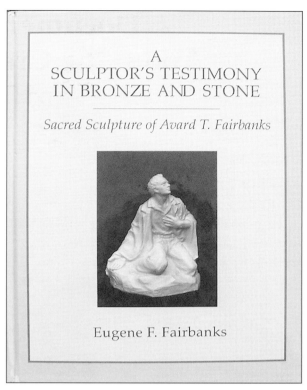

A Sculpture Garden of Fantasy: Imaginative, mythical sculpture with complimentary verse and descriptive information. 200 pages, approximately 100 illustrations, soft cover.

A Sculptor's Testimony in Bronze and Stone, Sacred Sculpture of Avard T. Fairbanks: Creative sculpture of religious figures and personalities with descriptive text. 160 pages, approximately 100 photographs, hard bound.

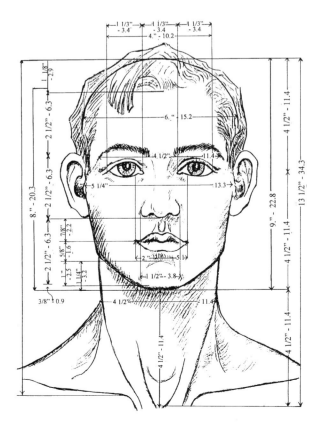

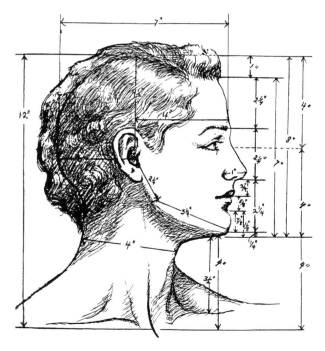

Human Proportions: A reference book for art students and serious amateurs about adult male and female form with illustrations (examples shown) and accompanying tabulation of measurements.

Published by:

Fairbanks Art and Books
2607 Vining Street
Bellingham, WA 98226-4230
(360) 733-3852